The Art of Ageing:
Textualising the Phases of Life

Compiled and edited by

Brian J. Worsfold

The Research Group:

GRUP DEDAL-LIT
Department of English and Linguistics
University of Lleida
Lleida, Catalunya, Spain.

Series Editor: Brian J. Worsfold

DEDAL-LIT 5
July 2005

Acknowledgements

This compilation of essays has been made possible thanks to work carried out by members of the research group *Grup Dedal-Lit* of the Department of English and Linguistics at the University of Lleida under the auspicies of the *Fondo Nacional para el Desarrollo de la Investigación Científica y Técnica* within the *Programa Nacional de la Promoción General del Conocimiento, Ministerio de Ciencia y Tecnología*. The editor gratefully acknowledges the financial support given by the Spanish Ministry of Science and Technology for the research project BFF2000-1076 "Percepciones de la vejez en la literatura contemporánea escrita en inglés" and for the grant BFF2002-1167-E that have made this publication possible.

First published 2005

© Héctor Blanco Uría, Tatjana Djurik Kuzmanovic, Carles Feixa Pàmpols, Edurne Garrido Anes, Pere Gifra Adroher, Eduardo de Gregorio Godeo, Rached Khalifa, John Kinsella, Tom Kirkwood, Noga Levine-Keini, Cynthia Port, David Rampton, Félix Rodríguez Rodríguez, Jeffrey Skoblow, Lourdes Torrelles Pont, Brian Worsfold and Tova Yedidia.

Grup Dedal-Lit members: Nela Bureu Ramos, Núria Casado Gual, Emma Domínguez Rué, Marta Miquel Baldellou, Maria O'Neill, Maricel Oró Piqueras, Isabel Santaulària Capdevila, Maria Vidal Grau, Brian Worsfold and Carmen Zamorano Llena.

Opinions expressed or implied by contributors to this publication are not necessarily shared by all members of the research group GRUP DEDAL-LIT.

Cover design: Francesc Català i Alòs
Cover backdrop: Judith Sol i Dyess (www.judithsol-dyess.com)

© Edicions i Publicacions de la Universitat de Lleida, 2005

ISBN: 84-8409-176-7
Imprès: INO Reproducciones, S.A.
Dipòsit legal: L-674-2005

Contents

Preface

The Art and Science of Ageing

Art and science can make uncomfortable bedfellows. Much preliminary and uncertain exploration may be required before meaningful intercourse can be established. The artist is unsure of the mysteries of science, while the scientist is nervous about the exhibitionism that characterises artistic display. The intellectual and emotional frisson, though, when the breakthrough happens, can be spectacular.

In the case of ageing, however, foreplay in the engagement between art and science might seem unnecessary. Consciousness of senescence, and of the intrinsic mortality it heralds, has left its imprint in every artistic medium since earliest times. And what scientist, grappling with the complex biological mechanisms that underlie the ageing process, can be unaware of the ground turned already by the many thousands of writers and painters who have struggled to portray what it means to know that we, and those we love, will quite soon age and die.

The fact that art and science have for so long grappled with ageing might suggest that we should by now be approaching some mature union of the two views of this most mysterious process. The facts suggest otherwise. Society today seems if anything more confused and anxious about ageing than it did when life expectancy was decades less than it is now and when old people were a great deal rarer. Each year a clutch of new books is published by those excited by the potential of the new science to make us all live even longer, if not for ever. Attaining great age, however, is no longer seen as a blessing. To be old is, in the eyes of many, to be a loser. Beauty, power, enjoyment, sexuality are all thought to be extinguished by those dread signs of ageing, despite the experience of many that actually life with wrinkles can be rather good fun. Curiously, in a recent study of eighty-five-year-olds in my own city of Newcastle upon Tyne, the great majority, when asked to assess their quality of life, thought they were doing better or very much better than the average for their age group. This pleasing statistical impossibility shows that most maintain an encouragingly positive attitude, even when nearly all of them suffer from longstanding disability or disease. On the other hand, scientists like myself who suggest that we might one day harness our growing knowledge of the mechanisms of ageing to delay the onset of some of the more distressing and disabling conditions of old age, tend to be referred to Swiftian Struldbrugs as some terrible proof that to fiddle with human longevity is bound to end in tears.

* * *

It is high time that we updated our ideas about ageing. Not only are we faced with a world in which, contrary to all the forecasts, life expectancy continues steadily to increase. We are also confronted by insights from science that tell us that most of what we have grown up assuming to be true about the ageing process is wrong.

It is widely believed that ageing is some fixed biological process, driven by some kind of programme written in our genes. When pressed to explain why we should be programmed to age and die, many of us still offer, as an almost self-evident truth, that it must be so or the world would be overrun by a catastrophic explosion in population numbers. It may indeed be true that the human population is growing alarmingly fast, but ageing has nothing to do with population control. For the vast majority of wild animals, as was the case for humans before the modern era, life expectancy is curtailed not by any intrinsic programme for ageing, but by accidental death from injury, infection, starvation or cold. There never was a need to evolve a programme for population control, and ageing was, in fact, rarely seen. In these circumstances the idea, that we age because some inner clock has evolved to tell us to, makes no biological sense at all.

We age and die because we fall apart. Every day of our lives, all kinds of little things go wrong in the molecules and cells of our bodies. Lots of these faults get fixed by our clever systems for maintenance and repair. But maintenance costs. It costs energy, and for most animals energy is a scarce resource. So, in the wild environment, where sudden death is an ever present danger, the priority is not to invest in a body that might last for ever but in one that grows up, reaches reproductive maturity and procreates as soon as it can. We age and die because our genes settled for a compromise that rendered the body, or 'soma,' disposable. We maintain the soma sufficiently well for it to serve out its expected lifetime in good enough shape, but not so well that it lasts forever.

* * *

If it appears a little gloomy to recognise that our genes did not even bother to programme our end but simply let us fall apart, we should take hope from what this tells us about the malleability of the ageing process. We are seeing people reach old age in better and better shape each decade. This is because of the kinder conditions of modern life. We are damaged less by infections, injury, cold, hard physical work and undernutrition than our ancestors. It is this malleability that has been responsible for the continuing increase in life expectancy, long after we reaped the first wave of increase by taming death from infectious disease, and it is to this malleability that we should look as we hope to extend the healthy years of life and postpone ill health and dependency for as long as possible.

The new scientific view of ageing also highlights something we have to some extent known all along but tend to forget. Ageing does not begin at forty or fifty or sixty, or whenever we begin to see its outward signs. The build-up of faults occurs throughout life, beginning in the womb. The continuum of ageing from youth to death is something that needs to be factored both into our scientific understanding of ageing and into our attitudes and images. When we look at a very old person, we need to remind ourselves to see the young boy or girl that still lives in that consciousness. It was no doubt this mischievous little girl that prompted longevity world-record holder Jeanne Calment to joke, near to the end of her 122-year life that "I have only ever had one wrinkle, and I'm sitting on it." Similarly, when we look at a baby, we should glimpse the old man or woman that child will hopefully become and recognise that there is nothing predetermined about the length and course of his or her bodily and spiritual journey along the road that is ageing.

To judge from the poetry of earlier centuries, the continuum between youth and age was better appreciated when the two ends of the average life were separated by fewer years than they are today. If art and science can succeed in bringing about a union that helps us better to appreciate the ageing process, in all its dimensions, let us also hope that they can rebuild bridges between the generations so that age is again less divisive an attribute than it has become today.

Tom Kirkwood
Professor of Medicine
School of Clinical Medical Sciences
Gerontology
University of Newcastle (England)

Introduction

18 I am he that liveth, and was dead; and, behold, I am alive for evermore, Ämen; and have the keys of hell and of death.

19 Write the things which thou hast seen, and the things which are, and the things which shall be hereafter;
Revelation 1: 18-19

The passage of time is something that physicists have rather set aside, and taken a view that, in a sense, it is not really physics. It is a subjective issue and subjective questions are not part of science.
Roger Penrose 1999 [1]

Ageing and the flow of time

Unlike any other major discourse, the topic of ageing is universal and total. Growing older is a process that affects everything, literally, and is the experience of all life. Seemingly obeying some natural law, ageing appears to be intrinsically linked to time and the passing of time. But, as with our understanding of those phenomena, our understanding of the nature of ageing is only partial.

Few people would dispute the contention that our perceptions of ageing are associated with our perceptions of the flow of time. Yet, if ageing is a derivative of the passing of time, then, for physicists, ageing does not occur. Adhering to theories of the world based on Albert Einstein's special relativity theory, physicists have mathematical evidence for a four-dimensional spacetime in which time is, but does not flow. According to relativity theory, all time, like all space, exists simultaneously; past, present and future time is equally existent, a state that enables time travel. In respect of ageing, special relativity theory means that, since time is frozen, everybody is equally alive and dead at the same time, something that can affect the way in which a bereaved person may think of someone who has died. Moreover, the relativity model of time states that all time occurs simultaneously, precluding the need for decision-making and choice, thereby denying free will.

A more recent mathematisation of time is modelled on quantum mechanics. With no certainties, only probablilities, the quantum model is incompatible with the special relativity model in that, while not supporting the

---

[1] Roger Penrose (physicist). *The Flow of Time* (Dir. David Malone. BBC TV documentary, 1999). [Spoken quotation]

possibility of the flow of time, it does allow for the indeterminacy and unpredictability of time. This means that the future is not prescribed and that free will is admitted.

However, both models discount the possibility that time flows. Consequently, for scientists, the perception that time flows is an illusion; it is simply the way in which the human brain reconciles the four-dimensionality of the world so that space and time are made to appear as at one with events that occur in everyday life. Vesslin Petkov has stated that, "the flow of time is a minddependent phenomenon" (Petkov 1988: 3).[2] In the event that this is true, then the process of ageing is a manifestation of the passing of time as perceived by human consciousness. H. Weyl relates consciousness with the flow of time when he observes:

> The objective world *is*, it does not *happen*. Only to the gaze of my consciousness, crawling upward along the life line of my body, does a certain section of this world come to life as a fleeting image in space which continuously changes in time. (Weyl 1963: 116)[3]

For physicists, then, the human body is a four-dimensional "world line," that is, "a three-dimensional body existing at all moments of its history" and the sense of ageing is, as H. Weyl has stated, "consciousness crawling upward along" our worldlines.[4]

* * *

To dispute this is to dispute Einstein's special theory of relativity. Yet many people will dispute it. Can it be merely a terrible irony of human existence that almost everything we do in this world is determined by our individual and collective understanding that time passes – something we *think* happens, but which, in fact, does not occur? Heedless of mathematical constructs, human beings have a strong feeling that time *does* flow, and the sense that the process of ageing is a temporal progression is located deep within human consciousness. The flow of time is perceived by the human brain as a linear sequence of events that emerges from the past and moves onwards into the future, quantified in years, months, weeks, days, hours, minutes and seconds. Perceptual evidence for this are memories,

---

[2] Petkov, Vesselin. "The Flow of Time – Objective or Minddependent." [Paper presented at the XVIII World Congress of Philosophy, Brighton, England. August 1988] <http://alcor.concordia.ca/~vpetkov/time.ht> 22 May 2005.
[3] Weyl, H. *Philosophy of Mathematics and Natural Sciences* (New York: Atheneum, 1963) 116. Quoted in "On the Ontological Status of Minkowski Space." <http://alcor.concordia.ca/~vpetkov/minkowski.ht> 22 May 2005.
[4] See Vesselin Petkov. "Relativity and Its Profound Implications for the Human Free Will." <http://alcor.concordia.ca/~vpetkov/freewill.html> 22 May 2005.

occurrences, expectations and predictions. Moreover, human beings also have a strong sense that, as time passes by, it is in their power to make choices and take decisions that will determine future events. But physicists will argue that it is our consciousnesses that divide these events into illusory, time-zoned categories – a trick of the human psyche.

It would appear, then, that the only way to achieve a better understanding of the perceived dynamics of time, and consequently of ageing, is through a deeper understanding of how human consciousness works. The description and analysis of our awareness of the flow of time might well form the groundwork for an "art of ageing." In broad terms, representations of the consciousness of the flow of time are the subject of *The Art of Ageing: Textualising the Phases of Life*. The contributions are necessarily eclectic; writers and literary commentators analyse textualisations of ageing in poetry, song, theatre and prose in an attempt to achieve a deeper understanding of the ageing process as an act of consciousness, while the effects and impact of ageing on individuals and societies is the focus of psychiatric, sociological and anthropological studies.

* * *

Ageing – a facet of consciousness

Music is the art form that most cogently gives the lie to the physicists' contention that time is, but does not flow. Musical form depends on the listener's ability to remember a note, hear a note in present time, and then anticipate the next note. In *The Flow of Time*, the composer Flaun Flynn observes:

> Music unfolds in time in such a way that we have a memory of what we heard and this memory conditions what we expect. Music is a distillation or a side-effect of that mental faculty we employ to perceive time and things changing in time.[5]

Yet, although a piece of music is made up of discrete notes individually perceived, it is also a whole – a symphony, a concerto, a song. Perhaps it is this ambiguity that underlies Jeffrey Skoblow's study of rock 'n' roll song, a genre, he says, that "has helped me grow up and kept me young for as long as I can remember." In "Summer Days are Gone: Age and the Poetics of (Rock 'n' Roll) Song," Jeffrey Skoblow's analysis of the songs on Bob Dylan's album *Love and Theft* (2001) exposes an ambiguity; Dylan, at sixty, underscores a sense of mortality in songs such as "Summer Days," but he also presents the theme of love in songs such as "Bye and Bye" and "Po' Boy." In "Moonlight," the ambiguity is crystalised; appearing to evoke the process of dying in naturalistic images, "moonlight" is a love song. Furthermore, he argues that, through the poetics of songs such as

---

[5] Faun Flynn (composer). *The Flow of Time* (Dir. David Malone. BBC TV documentary, 1999). [Spoken quotation]

"Floater (Too Much to Ask)," Dylan deconstructs the concept of ageing, denying its distinction from youth, and perceiving it as a continuation of the process of living and loving. In his rock 'n' roll music, Dylan is seen to seek a convergence of age and youth. Jeffrey Skoblow contends that it is the genre of song which provides the medium *par excellence* for expressing this vision and that it is the temporal beauty of performed song that fuses youth, age and identity into one, annulling the difference between dying and loving. In what may be interpreted as a relativistic perception of time, for Jeffrey Skoblow the deconstruction of the conscious constructs of youth and ageing represents freedom, the ethos of rock 'n' roll.

Music and time are also central in David Rampton's study of Philip Roth's novel *The Human Stain* (2000). In "Love's Knowledge? Growing Old Disgracefully in Philip Roth's *The Human Stain*," David Rampton looks beyond the sexual desires of Coleman Silk, a libidinous, retired university professor, towards the unknown areas of old-age sexuality, in which old people break the norms of respectability and decency. In what, again, conforms to a relativistic model of time, Philip Roth's mutually-consenting adults are predestined to 'know' one another, but never know much about each other. In this sense, the importance of love in erotic encounters is subverted; on the one hand, love is relegated to a simple distraction in the face of sexual desire while, on the other, we know love exists because we experience the suffering of rejection and loss. To this extent, sexual desire, love and suffering are all markers in the ageing process, all complex and interpenetrating, and all forms of confronting one's own mortality.

For Philip Roth, ageing is a series of markers – moments of enlightenment – in a long-term process characterised by routine. During one of these "anti-epiphanies" – a concert of music by Rachmaninoff, Rimsky-Korsakov and Prokofiev performed by the Boston Symphony Orchestra at Tanglewood – the timeless quality of the music lays bare the dualities inherent in the occasion – young America and old Europe, being here and being somewhere else, knowing someone and not knowing them. Yet, as David Rampton emphasises, by the end of the novel, Roth has minimalised everything down to "the only human marker in all of nature, like the X of an illiterate's signature." The solitary man sitting on an upturned bucket on an ice lake somewhere in North America is the ultimate, relativistic image linking human existence with spacetime. For David Rampton, Philip Roth's greatness lies in his attempt to grapple with this difficult aspect of the human predicament, namely, man's symbiosis with frozen time.

And it is frozen time, not the flow of time, that underlies the therapy used to help Holocaust survivors by Tova Yedidia and Noga Levine-Keini. In their "Making Use of a Family Collage as a Means for Processing Traumatic Experiences in Working with Holocaust Survivors," Tova Yedidia and Noga Levine-Keini show how the creation of a collage of selected images of past events can assist in bringing survivors to a greater degree of closure, an increasingly urgent requirement as they live on, well into old age.

Individual Holocaust survivors suffer from a complex of emotions, including fear, despair, guilt, loss, denial and loneliness. By getting survivors to select images from their past, arrange them in a personalised way and construct a collage, Tova Yedidia and Noga Levine-Keini help aged survivors to re-arrange their past experiences into an organised sequence, enabling individuals to regain control over their personal histories and, consequently, their present. Presenting the case of a sixty-seven-year-old Holocaust survivor, Tova Yedidia and Noga Levine-Keini describe how, after selecting a collection of images to construct a collage, Pinchas overcomes denial of his past and is able to restore his sense of identity, supporting their contention that collage-construction and subsequent interpretation is a valuable tool in psychotherapy, especially for old people who have been traumatised earlier in their lives. This psychiatric therapy enables Holocaust survivors, who are still trying to come to terms with horrific memories of the past, to overcome the trauma and achieve some relief. Significantly, the images used to construct the collage recall moments, frozen in time, of the survivor's past, and together they make up a collage *of the same images* frozen into the 'now.' In this sense, then, collage-construction is the visual representation of the relativity of time.

* * *

If time does not flow, then what are clocks for? This aspect of time, time passing and the process of ageing is the subject of anthropologist Carles Feixa's "The Hourglass of Time: Life Cycle in the Digital Era," in which time-keeping and ageing are shown to be cause and effect, interrelated and inseparable. An analogy is drawn between different types of clock and different youthful psychologies. The hourglass presents perceived natural temporality, analogous with an individual's social progress; the analogical clock measures time arithmetically, in linear sequence, allowing society to move relentlessly forward into the future and different generations to develop different perceptions of the past and different aspirations for the future; the digital watch quantifies time in binary format, enabling total control of the beginning, duration and suspension of periods of time that are random and produced on demand.

In terms of time flow, unlike the hourglass and the analogical clock, digitalisation is shown to relativise time-keeping, reducing time to the 'now' only, with no past and no future. Carles Feixa contends that the digital watch blurrs class and generational boundaries, and causes events and localities to lose their temporality. Focusing on the younger generation, he distinguishes three models of youth that derive from the natural, analogical and digital presentations of time respectively. Today's youth are subject to what he terms the virtual *Blade Runner syndrome* that invokes modulated separation from parental authority and that, through access to new technology formats, facilitates their escape to cyber-spatial worlds devoid of responsibilities prior to the unavoidable acceptance of adult consciousness. The potential of digitalised time can be exploited more fully on the Internet, for example, where surfers can select, adopt and exchange age-group roles and status. Today, in the spirit of temporal relativism, youthful dilettanti can play the game of life by logging into the time mode that best suits their purpose.

* * *

Youthful perceptions and creation is the topic of John Kinsella's "Grapholagia Poetica: Ageing as Confrontation with or Avoidance of Death," in which he demonstrates that poems written when one is young and immature can contain values and principles that are the same as those held when one is much older. For John Kinsella, with respect to the phases of life, poetry marks the point of transition from one awareness to a new one. Drawing on youthful memories, he recalls how, as a young man, his own writing showed signs of crossing over the borders of age. Claiming that inexperience is not a determining factor in the quality of poetry, John Kinsella takes Arthur Rimbaud's "*Le dormeur du val*" as a case in point, arguing that, at the age of sixteen, the French poet already knew how to cross generation boundaries.

In comparisons of early poems and adult poems by Tracy Ryan – "Letting go" and "Wungong Dam" – and himself – "A Call for 'Freedom'" and "Death Sentence in Ohio: epicedium," John Kinsella demonstrates how ageing equips the poet with more mature techniques and an ability to express grief more adequately. However, following a comparison of his "Death of a Brushtail Possum" with a poem by his twelve-year-old daughter Katherine – "Metaphor," both of which relate to a shared experience in the bush of Western Australia, he concludes that ageing is a process whereby gained experience inculcates responsibility that, while sophisticating expression, forfeits the directness and innocence of youthful representation.

John Kinsella's perspective on ageing reveals that the difference between the early and late works of a poet is one of form, not substance. Irrespective of age at the time of writing, a poet's textualisation of events, feelings and emotions is a defiance of mortality. This contention is borne out by the experience of W.B. Yeats. In "Willie's 'Monkey Gland' or the Bio-Aesthetics of Ageing in the Poetry of W.B. Yeats," Rached Khalifa notes that, from his earliest poems, W.B. Yeats developed a "poetics of ageing" – an aesthetical approach that combats the ageing process and death – and he reveals a conviction that the sexual and creative fervour of youth progressively fades with the onset of old age. When he was sixty-nine years old, Yeats underwent an operation to enhance his sexual prowess. Rached Khalifa maintains that the surgery *did* energise the poet's imagination and he sees the licentious language in poems such as "The Chambermaid's Second Song" (1936-1939) as evidence of Yeats's awareness of his sexual incapacity and his fear of death. From a reading of the poet's correspondence,[6] he argues that Yeats tried to deny consciousness of his own approaching death and that, in order to cope with his growing anxiety, he attempted to disempower death by aestheticising it, by making it poetically tragic and by immortalising it. With reference to poems such as "An Irish Airman Foresees his Death" (1919) and "Sailing to Byzantium" (1928), Rached Khalifa shows how Yeats considered the taking of one's own life as a strategy for undermining natural death. Further, in "To be Carved on a Stone at Thoor Ballylee" (1921) and "The Tower" (1928), Yeats proposed textualised memorials and self-mythologisation as alternative strategies for cheating death and achieving immortality. In his rebellion against ageing and death, Yeats took on the mantle of national hero and championed poetry, which he saw as being under threat of extinction from encroaching modernity. In this sense, Yeats equated the progressive ageing of his own body and consciousness with the dying process of his art.

Awareness of the transitory nature of one's own life and the finality of death is evident, too, in the poetry of Philip Larkin. In "The Topic of Ageing in Philip Larkin's Poetry," Héctor Blanco finds that the poet, anxious that he will not find love, sees the passing of time as a negative force. For Larkin, time is a great eroder, causing the body to wrinkle and crack. But wrinkles are ambiguous symbols – the signs of experience and of decay. Poetry reveals both the physicality and the psychology of ageing – the ways in which the individual is affected mentally by the process – and Larkin's poetry is filled with deep hurt – a regret for time past, gone forever, a past of unfulfilment and lost opportunity, something he finds entirely unsatisfactory. The poet's regret grows into envy of the younger generations and their freedom to be sexually promiscuous, a feeling made even more intense by the poet's growing fear of his own death. This fear leads eventually to outright panic as the poet rages against the incapacities and dependency of elderly people in "The Old Fools."

To escape death W.B. Yeats tried to freeze his achievement in time by mythologising his memory in poetry and, in "Failure to Listen to the Voice of the Ancestors: Ben Okri's Perception of Nigeria as an *Abiku* Country," Lourdes Torrelles shows how Ben Okri calls for the restitution of traditional Yoruba myths and traditions as a way of resolving present-day problems. Explaining that the Yoruba perception of history is an eternally cyclical process of regeneration, in which an individual's ancestors are as much a part of everyday life as any other living person, she contends that this perception translates into the situation whereby, because of their longevity, old people are the best-connected with their ancestors and the living source of knowledge and creativity. Ben Okri sees the lack

---

[6] See W.B. Yeats. *The Letters* (Ed. Allan Wade. London: Rupert Hart-Davis, 1954).

of socio-political progress in Nigeria as due in part to the fact that the authority of old people and all reference to ancestors have been sidelined.

In her analysis of Ben Okri's *Flowers and Shadows* (1980) and *Dangerous Love* (1996), Lourdes Torrelles reveals how Okri believes that, since Independence, Nigeria has moved towards "the precarious edge of total destruction"[7] because the Yoruba tradition of respect for the elders and their close affinity with the ancestors has been deconstructed and, with it, Nigeria's history and sense of nationhood. However, in her analysis of *The Famished Road* (1991), *Songs of Enchantment* (1993) and *Infinite Riches* (1998), Lourdes Torrelles detects a new development in Ben Okri's thinking. Using an *Abiku* – a mythological spirit-child capable of constant regeneration – as a conceit, the writer moves from an exclusive focus on Nigeria to a universalised vision. Just as the *Abiku* in *The Famished Road* transacts between the spirit world and the real world, so post-colonial Nigeria is caught between its traditional heritage and the new world order, resulting in political instability and social chaos. However, as Lourdes Torrelles points out, Ben Okri does not lose all hope; he believes that, like the *Abiku* who finds the strength to stay on in the real world, the people of Nigeria have within them spiritual resources in the form of their ancestors sufficient to regenerate their country and guarantee its longevity. In the final analysis, Ben Okri believes that the only hope for salvation lies in dialogue between the two worlds, a dialogue in which all coloniality is relegated to a footnote in Nigeria's ageing mythology.

* * *

The Impact of Ageing

If, as Faun Flynn says, "we only know about time by the things that happen in it; we are conscious of the occurrences of events; we are not conscious of time in any other way,"[8] then the ageing process is a sequence of events that exist only because we are conscious of them. Yet, the impact of this consciousness is felt at every level of human life and, in spite of the fact that Einstein's special relativity theory provides the basis for the most satisfactory description of the world in terms of physics and mathematics to date, as individual human beings living on this planet we feel we cannot afford to sit back in the knowledge that our futures are already 'out there' in spacetime and that any belief in recourse to free will is illusory. In our societies, the impact of increased longevity on national demographies, economies and psychologies is manifest, and individuals and societies are having to adopt strategies and plan contigencies to lessen the impact in their perceived

---

[7] Quoted from Wole Soyinka. *Myth, Literature and the African World* (1976. Cambridge: Cambridge UP, 1995) 30.

[8] Faun Flynn (composer). *The Flow of Time* (Dir. David Malone. BBC TV documentary, 1999). [Spoken quotation]

futures. Pension plans, retirement date adjustments, help for carers, dependency programmes, cosmetic surgery, life-enhancement drugs – all are evidence that ageing, while it may be only a creation of consciousness, is a sense so strong that societies the world over are having to make increasingly more complex provisions in order to cope with it. Those individuals and societies that rely on a relativistic model of the world to manage and provide for their old age open themselves to uncertainty and risk.

An awareness of the flow of time has permeated human consciousness from its conception. The perception of time passing governs all cultural, societal and individual activity, and has become deeply ingrained in the collective consciousness of all humanity. In medieval Europe, people conceptualised time in a different way from ourselves; they identified two distinct types of time, eternity and transience. For the medieval believer, God reigned in eternity, overlooking the transitory lives of earthly mortals. In her study of medieval medical texts "'Aware too late,' said Beauty as she passed.' The *Expiry Date* to be Liked and to Love: Some Medieval Views on Old Age and Sexuality," Edurne Garrido reveals how, in societies in which physical health and fitness were at a premium as one grew older, especially insofar as sexual competence was concerned, youth, beauty, wealth and status were the principal guarantees for successful relationships. On the other hand, for the elderly the only remaining virtue was wealth. She records that, in the Middle Ages, writers believed that sexual intercourse in old age would lead to premature death and that, furthermore, abstinence was recommended as a way of increasing longevity. From her survey of the opinions of several well-known writers of the period, among them Geoffrey Chaucer, Rodrigo de Cota, Isidore of Seville, Ambrose, Petrarch, Christine de Pisan, Philip of Novare, Andreas Capellanus, Averroes, Arnold of Vilanova, Peter of Spain, Albert the Great, Maimonides, Jean Froissart, Vincent of Beauvais and John Gower, it is clear that, in medieval times, sexual activity after a certain age was understood to be detrimental to general health and that, specifically, loss of sperm shortened a man's life.

Such myths and beliefs have permuted in time. In present-day society, the consciousness of ageing in terms of corporeality and sexuality has become transmuted. Yet certain features endure, especially in regard to the differentiated consciousness of ageing by diverse age-groups. In "Ripeness is Gall: Images of Ageing in the Theatre of Edward Bond," Pere Gifra analyses aspects of ageing, focusing on the humanist qualities in the playwright's drama, a humanism that reveals the mechanisms of power that oppress human beings throughout their lives. Specifically, he argues that elderly people are subjected to institutionalised injustice by their fellow human beings. Yet Bond's characters do not acquiesce; rather, they resist in an attempt to transmit their knowledge and experience to the younger generations. Pere Gifra goes on to show how, in his early plays, Bond focuses on the impact that relationships between the young and the elderly will have on the lives of the latter. The dilemma for elderly people is that they are simultaneously empowered by their personal histories and disempowered by their dependence. In an analysis of *Lear* (1973), Bond's nihilism becomes evident as he presents the ageing protagonist as a man tormented by cruel afflictions meted out by younger generations, and in *Bingo* (1973) he demonstrates how inaction against such injustice in one's youth leads to bitter regret in old age. In more recent plays, Edward Bond has shown how human society is condemned in that young people must fight with their elders in order to break free. However, Pere Gifra concludes that Bond's elderly protagonists reveal two sides of the ageing character – resolve and dependence, and in this Bond portrays humanism, not nihilism.

Pere Gifra shows how Edward Bond presents old men as victims of the collective consciousness of their generation. However, in "The 'Aging Fallacy': Older Scholars and Cultural Belatedness," Félix Rodríguez argues that such victimhood might be self-inflicted in a way, especially in ageing academics. Taking as his point of departure the German dictum *Methode ist Erlebnis*, he looks at what might be termed cultural ageing and contends that the way people age is determined by singular, cultural experiences during formative years. In the case of Leo Spitzer's defence of "the humanities,"[9] he sees such academic determinism as a means of rejecting new methodologies in his field. For comparable reasons, Félix Rodríguez sees E.H. Gombrich and René Wellek as perpetrators of similar neo-conservatism in respect of their disciplines. In general, he maintains that ageing academics share a tendency to belittle contemporary methodological constructs.

In an analysis of René Wellek's defence of his academic approach, Félix Rodríguez argues convincingly that Wellek, by praising his teachers, introduces an element of moral responsibility into the narration of his personal history. In this respect, Wellek presents his defence for his scientific method and intellectual standpoint as an act of ethics. But consciousness of this kind means that ageing academics become cultural misfits and are left with two options: either to adopt the new culture, or fight it. For elderly academics, to choose to accommodate the new order is to forfeit their entire cultural construct, while to resist means trying to prevent the deconstruction of their personal histories. For a resolution, Félix Rodríguez turns to the narrative of the Italian philosopher Norberto Bobbio who argues that the neo-conservatism of elderly academics has its roots in their growing intellectual incapacity, what Félix Rodríguez calls their "aging fallacy" which, intensified by nostalgia, can result in exclusion and self-destruction, an act of weakness or of heroism.

Yet for today's young men, an alternative consciousness pertains. In "Problem Columns and the Discourse of Masculine Ageing Anxieties in Britain,"

---

[9] See Leo Spitzer. *Linguistics and Literary History: Essays in Stylistics* (Princeton: Princeton UP, 1948).

Eduardo de Gregorio draws attention to the fact that nowadays men from as early as twenty-years-old become anxious about their deteriorating looks. He turns to lifestyle magazines for evidence that, in the United Kingdom, they are becoming increasingly concerned about the effects of their personal ageing. From problem columns, matters such as hair loss, diminishing sexual capacity and fear of long-term heterosexual relationships are identified as the worries uppermost in young male minds. Holding that the topic of ageing constitutes a discourse in British journals, Eduardo de Gregorio applies Norman Fairclough's model of Critical Discourse Analysis (CDA) to examine lexis, verbal processes, material processes, directive speech acts and cohesion resources in a text taken from *FHM* and argues that the discursive nature of such texts problematises and generalises anxiety expressed by men regarding the physical impact of the ageing process on their corporealities. Furthermore, Eduardo de Gregorio sees this male-driven discourse as reflecting changes in gendered power relations in the United Kingdom, and even as a threat to traditionally-patriarchal constructs.

The male and female consciousnesses of ageing share a preoccupation with transmuting corporealities, but for different reasons. It is sometimes argued that while men focus on retaining their sexual aptitude, women concern themselves with sustaining the quality of their attraction. In her study of economy and ageing in Doris Lessing's *The Diary of a Good Neighbor* (1983), Cynthia Port contends that the ageing experience can be understood using models of economic theory. She analyses the basis of the relationship between the protagonist Jane (Janna) Somers and Maudie Fowler, the over ninety-year-old woman she cares for, in transactional terms, conceiving the relationship as being founded on the economic principles of exchange and reciprocity. Cynthia Port observes that Maudie's acts of generosity and her sense of fair play are set against the backdrop of her relative poverty. With ageing, years accumulate memories and experience, but this profit is balanced against various losses, such as physical deterioration, degradation of social relationships and growing financial constraints. Cynthia Port argues that, although the value of goods augments over time, in the same capitalist economy the value of an old person who is a consumer but not a producer diminishes progressively. But she points out that, in her novel, Doris Lessing underscores the moral value of older people, not their material value. As Janna becomes increasingly involved with Maudie, her values are transformed; from being an insatiable consumer of goods destined for obsolescence, she learns that goods can be retained and recycled. Caring for Maudie has caused a change in Janna's economic logic. Cynthia Port argues that Janna's empathy with Maudie is mutually beneficial; Maudie is cared for and Janna is shown how to extract herself from her fashion magazine mindset and to believe that degradation and obsolescence are not the only options open to her as an elderly woman. Their relationship as carer and cared-for enables this mutual exchange of values.

What are things worth? What are people worth? This, for Cynthia Port, is the theme of Doris Lessing's novel. The way to eschew such questions is to opt for alternatives, for example, by entering into intergenerational exchanges based on mutual respect and reciprocity. Yet the ability of individuals to sustain their quality of life is conditioned largely by the societies in which they find themselves. In "Old Age in Serbia: Transition for all Ages," Tatjana Djuric Kuzmanovic informs that by 2050 there will be more people over sixty than under fifteen in the world. In Serbia, the over-sixty population – almost a fifth of the total – are the poorest, a situation brought about by low pension payments and the running down of the social services since the communist era when Serbia formed part of the former Yugoslavia. Their predicament is giving rise to widespread discontent and the situation is aggravated further by the large number of refugees and displaced persons, especially for elderly women who suffer generalised inequality.

In recent decades, the consequences of political change in Serbia have led to even greater economic straits, especially for old people. Today, large numbers of elderly displaced persons find themselves in truly desperate circumstances, with vaguely-defined citizenship and pension rights, and an inability to turn to traditional forms of subsistence. While, as Tatjana Djuric Kuzmanovic notes, in accordance with the recently-passed Law on Pensions and Disability women can retire at fifty-eight and maternity, not parenthood, is the criterion for crediting years worked for pension calculations, she decries the gender inequalities and ageism that persist in contemporary Serbian society. She argues that old people should be allowed to participate in the developmental and decision-making processes in modern Serbia, contending that various sectors of the national economies can benefit from the economic activities of the older generations. Tatjana Djuric Kuzmanovic believes that greater cross-national cooperation using statistics and population data-bases to establish indicators will help to eradicate gendered discrimination and to improve the lot of old people, especially the elderly poor, something she claims is a human right.

* * *

Conclusion

Who are we? Where do we come from? What are we here for? These are questions posed by philosophy that science is trying to answer. When we study ageing, however, we seek answers not to these questions, but rather to the question "what is conscious life?" But for scientists, as David Malone points out, there is a conundrum:

The tragedy of modern physics is that it explains so much of the objective universe, but at the cost of what we subjectively feel – about our conscious free will and our perception that time does flow. (1999)[10]

Einstein's special theory of relativity states that, while the speed of light is the only absolute constant, space and time are variable – spacetime is a fabric that can be stretched and distorted – and a correct interpretation means, therefore, that time does not flow. Given this reality, our perception of ageing as process is not objective, but only subjective – a figment of human consciousness. Consequently, growing older cannot be mathematised. According to relativists, what we perceive as ageing corporealities and the physical disabilities endured as we grow older are predetermined; they are already 'out there' in four-dimensional spacetime and nothing can alter that.

* * *

Ageing is a duality; mathematically it does not exist, yet science enables a better understanding of the biomedical, psychological and sociological facts of the process of growing older so that increasing longevity can be planned for and the quality of long life enhanced. To make adequate provision for old age and to age comfortably are aspects of the art of ageing, aspects rooted deep within human consciousness. For this reason, much textualisation of ageing is, consciously and unconsciously, relativist. Lines from John Keats's "Ode on a Grecian Urn," referred to by both Rached Khalifa and David Rampton, for example, are relativist:

> Thou still unravish'd bride of quietness,
> Thou foster-child of silence and slow time,
> [. . . .]
> Thou, silent form, dost tease us out of thought
> As doth eternity: Cold Pastoral!
> (John Keats "Ode on a Grecian Urn")

"Cold Pastoral!" – the urn records an event that is frozen in time, a concept that "dost tease us out of thought," and the ode ends with a riddle – "Beauty is truth, truth beauty, – that is all / Ye know on earth , and all ye need to know." Is not this equation between truth and beauty an expression of Keats's consciousness that, like "that heifer lowing at the skies" depicted on the urn, all life *is*, in time? Though written in 1819,[11] Keats's "Ode on a Grecian Urn" is a perfect, albeit unconscious, representation of the four-dimensionality of spacetime. That time is and does not flow is a mathematised concept of great beauty; it means that life does not start and

---

[10] Malone, David. *The Flow of Time* (Dir. David Malone. BBC TV documentary 1999). [Spoken quotation]
[11] John Keats, who had qualified in medicine (London) in 1816, died of tuberculosis in Rome in 1821, at the age of twenty-six.

end, and that birth and death simply *are* because we are conscious of them. The awareness of this "truth" *is* "beauty" and, as Keats contends, it is the most important realisation that we, as human beings, need to come to.

Yet there is also much textualisation of ageing that assumes that time *does* flow, that the future *is* 'out there,' and that free will *does* exist. The only way out of the anomaly seems to be the hope, as Roger Penrose has put it, that,

> when we understand more about how quantum mechanics and relativity fit together, we shall see a passage of time out there also, not just within ourselves. (Malone, dir. 1999)[12]

Until *that* moment in time, there appears to be no alternative to our perception that ageing and the passing of time are inseparable and, for as long as this quirk of the human condition endures, human beings will continue to make provision for old age, relying on consciousness to ease and understand better what for them, despite mathematical models, remains a life-long challenge.

Brian Worsfold
The editor

---

[12] Roger Penrose (physicist). *The Flow of Time* (Dir. David Malone. BBC TV documentary 1999). [Spoken quotation]

DEDAL essays

The Topic of Ageing in Philip Larkin's Poetry

Héctor Blanco Uría

The fear of ageing and death is a universal, human concern. The English author Philip Larkin (1922-1985), the most important poet of The Movement,[1] wrote on the topic of ageing over many years. As he himself experienced the process, the subject gained increasing presence in his poetry and became a growing concern in his own life. The most significant poems in respect of ageing are to be found in four books of his poetry that were published while Larkin was alive – *The North Ship* (1945), *The Less Deceived* (1955), *The Whitsun Weddings* (1964) and *High Windows* (1974). The poems present Larkin's ideas on growing older and his attitude towards the inevitability of the experience of old age, revealing the development from the sinister predictions of his youth to the harsh frankness and sad meditations of his last years. Yet ageing is more than a concern for Philip Larkin; it is closely related to his own poetics and, on the subject of Larkin's poetics, it is essential to mention two other poets, William Butler Yeats and Thomas Hardy, who were associated respectively with two different stages of his work.

The name of Yeats corresponds to a first stage. The contact with Yeats' poetry, owing to the figure of the poet Vernon Watkins, had a tremendous impact on Larkin, as the words in his "Introduction" to the reissue of his first collection *The North Ship* testify:

> The predominance of Yeats in this volume deserves some explanation. In 1943 the English Club was visited by Vernon Watkins, then stationed at an Air Force camp nearby; impassioned and imperative, he swamped us with Yeats until, despite the fact that he had not nearly come to the end of his typescript, the chairman had forcibly to apply the closure. As a final gesture Vernon distributed the volumes he had been quoting from among those of us who were nearest to him, and disappeared, exalted, into the blackout. I had been tremendously impressed by the evening and in the following weeks made it my business to collect his books up again – many of them were Cuala Press limited editions, and later Yeats was

---

[1] A group of writers – including Philip Larkin, Kingsley Amis, John Wain and Elizabeth Jennings – who, in the fifties, reacted against mystical and symbolic Modernism and produced an ironic, disaffected literature arising from a strictly empirical attitude to life.

> scarce at that time – and take them to him at Bradwell, where he was staying with some people called Blackburn who kept a goat. This time Vernon read me Lorca.
>
> As a result I spent the next three years trying to write like Yeats, not because I liked his personality or understood his ideas but out of infatuation with his music (to use the word I think Vernon used). In fairness to myself, it must be admitted that it is a particularly potent music, pervasive as garlic, and has ruined many a better talent. (Larkin 1983: 29)

But after those three years, the "Yeatsian fever" abated, and Thomas Hardy came to occupy the place of Yeats:

> When reaction came, it was undramatic, complete and permanent. In early 1946 I had some new digs in which the bedroom faced east, so that the sun woke me inconveniently early. I used to read. One book I had at my bedside was the little blue *Chosen Poems of Thomas Hardy*: Hardy I knew as a novelist, but as regards his verse I shared Lytton Strachey's verdict that 'the gloom is not even relieved by a little elegance of diction.' This opinion did not last long; if I were asked to date its disappearance, I should guess it was the morning I first read 'Thoughts of Phena At News of Her Death.' (Larkin 1983: 29-30)

Under Hardy's influence, Larkin settled into a poetic tradition very different from Yeats'. Larkin's poetic universe, the way in which he understood and valued poetry, was altered and moved to a second, and definitive, stage. Instead of the use of images which derived from French Symbolist sources, now there was realism; instead of grand music, there was the sound of a mind thinking aloud; instead of high rhetoric, there was colloquial tone; instead of transcendence, there were everyday things. By reading the works of Thomas Hardy, Larkin learned to use in his poems the language of ordinary speech to talk about the central issues of ordinary life: love and the fading of love, time and the passing of time.

And it is time seen from the point of view of a young man, rather than a specific concern about ageing, that underlies many of the poems contained in *The North Ship*. For example, in the four lines of "This is the first thing," Larkin employs a simple image to symbolize the beginning of the awareness of time and the effect of that consciousness on the poet himself:

> This is the first thing
> I have understood:
> Time is the echo of an axe
> Within a wood.
> (*Collected Poems* 295)

The concentric rings within the trunk of a tree mark the development of that tree, and anything which happens to the tree, like a fire or an attempt to cut it with an axe, will have its reflection in those rings, which will keep memory of it.

Particularly significant is the fact that Larkin makes an axe appear in the poem, symbolizing by means of this object the harmful nature of the passing of time.

But for the time being, Larkin – who was just twenty-three when *The North Ship* was published – was less interested in past time than in time to pass. Several of the poems contained within this volume can be described as sinister predictions about what time will bring rather than as nostalgic elegies about what now belongs to the past. Larkin's hopes for the future are concentrated on finding love, but his awful pessimism denies, again and again, this possibility of happiness. This pessimism is, to be more precise, fatalism, since it is based on a negative conception of the universe: it is nature itself which answers the question of this young man, anxious about his future, as in the neo-Yeatsian murmuring "I put my mouth":

> I put my mouth
> Close to running water:
> Flow north, flow south,
> It will not matter,
> It is not love you will find.
> (*Collected Poems* 276)

Such fatalism is also present in "Ugly Sister," the most narrative of all the, usually lyrical, poems included in *The North Ship*. In "Ugly Sister," Larkin resorts to the characterisation of an individual as a means of distancing himself from the topic he will deal with in the poem, a topic which could be too painful for him to talk about. By talking about this woman, Larkin is talking about himself, about his own fear: he himself may be this "ugly sister" whom nobody will ever love. The first stanza of the poem shows Larkin's mastery of compression in diction and imagery:

> I will climb thirty steps to my room,
> Lie on my bed;
> Let the music, the violin, cornet and drum
> Drowse from my head.
> (*Collected Poems* 292)

As Lolette Kuby perceptively observes about these lines, "two words, 'thirty steps,' poignantly convey the inner hurt of a misfit by suggesting repeated nights and days of withdrawals in which the number of steps to loneliness were routinely counted and learned by heart" (1974: 165). And in the second, final stanza of "Ugly Sister," Larkin's fatalism can be clearly appreciated: the woman's capacity of choice is, actually, illusory. She can decide whether she stays where music and company are or whether she goes back to loneliness, but deep inside she knows her choice would not mean much; her fate was fixed in adolescence:

> Since I was not bewitched in adolescence
> And brought to love,
> I will attend to the trees and their gracious silence,
> To winds that move.
> (*Collected Poems* 292)

If in *The North Ship* Larkin reflects the anxieties of a young man who thinks, without much hope, about what the future will bring him, when *The Less Deceived* was published, in 1955, Larkin, who was thirty-three by then, was a poet who had already experienced the effects of ageing, effects whose first and most obvious manifestation have to do with physical state and body appearance, rather than with mental, psychological aspects.

In the poem "Skin," from *The Less Deceived*, the poet speaks to his own skin as if it were an objective thing. The skin is seen as something qualitatively different from the "I," the mind which constitutes the true self of the poet. The skin is an "obedient daily dress" (*Collected Poems* 92), something different from the intrinsic subjectivity of the poet who must use this dress to cover his true, naked self and face daily life. In the poem, the poet warns his skin, symbol of external appearance, about the inevitable changes that the passage of time causes. This inevitability is reflected in the poem by means of the use of a verb like "must": "You must learn your lines – / [. . .] You must thicken, work loose" (*Collected Poems* 92). Time itself is presented, by means of a highly visual metaphor, as an eroding agent, a "Sand-laden wind" (*Collected Poems* 92) which, through a continuous action from the moment that we are born, keeps eroding the "young surface" (*Collected Poems* 92) of our skin until it ends up showing the effects of that process of erosion. These signs are the lines of life, the wrinkles that cause the different experiences which have left a trace on us: "You must learn your lines – / Anger, amusement, sleep" (*Collected Poems* 92). From this point of view, the lines caused by the wind which scratches the skin, the surface of our being, can be seen as something positive, as symbols of the wisdom accumulated through our different vital experiences – no matter whether they were good (amusement) or bad (anger).

But in the second stanza of the poem Larkin goes deep into the negative description of the changes that the young body undergoes as time passes by. By means of a careful and precise selection of vocabulary, the poet makes use of a series of terms, full of negative connotations – "soiled," "parch," "be roughened," "sag" – with the intention of prompting an unpleasant feeling in the reader. As the title of the collection suggests, Larkin does not want to be deceived; the lines on the skin are not a symbol of wisdom but of terrible physical decay. The poem finishes with a remembrance of youth, when the skin was clean and the body was beautiful and strong. Larkin's vision of the past is overwhelmingly negative; he considers his past wasted time and he feels remorse because he did not enjoy his skin in youth, when it was at its best, and now time has gone by and the dress is out of fashion.

It is interesting that this vision of youth, the past as a time of wasted chances, can be found in "Triple Time," another poem in the collection *The Less Deceived*. In this poem, Larkin accuses these wasted chances of being the cause of the bad perspectives for the future and the present state of decay:

> And on another day will be the past,
> A valley cropped by fat neglected chances
> That we insensately forbore to fleece.
> On this we blame our last
> Threadbare perspectives, seasonal decrease.
> (*Collected Poems* 73)

By this time in his life, when he was between thirty-five and forty years of age, Larkin's depressing vision of the past as a wasted time whose effects spread to a present and a future inevitably marked by decay begin to have an increasing presence in his thoughts, as can be seen in these two quotations from Larkin's letters. The first was written in April 1961 to his friend and lover Maeve Brennan:

> I think I've come to the time of life now when you really feel the passage of years. At first one wants to get older in order to be grown up; then there's no difference between 25 and 26, it's just like wearing a different tie; but once past 35 it's impossible not to feel that each year is taking one further from what is desired and pleasant and nearer to what is loathed and dreaded. (Motion 1994: 315)

The second was written one month later, in May 1961, to his friend Judy Egerton:

> The sense of approaching forty is strong upon me, and [of] having completely wasted the time of twenty to forty, when power should be greatest and relish keenest. Anything I do now will be a compromise with second or third best. I suddenly see myself as a freak and a failure, and my way of life as a farce. I suppose work normally shields one's eyes from home truths of this nature. (Motion 1994: 315)

Larkin's words in these letters show how, at this time in his life, the passage of time has begun to have effects not only on the body, but also in the mind. Maturity is a period of life given to vital reflections. When people reach this time, they usually tend to think about what their life has been up to that moment, what has taken them to where they are, and what the prospects for the future are. In the case of Larkin, these considerations are, as usual, apocalyptic.

* * *

A good example of this kind of reflection can be found in "Love Songs in Age," a poem included in *The Whitsun Weddings*, the volume published in 1964 when

Larkin was forty-two. Several things are known about the process of writing "Love Songs in Age." The opening and conclusion of this poem were composed over an extended period of time; a "first attempt [. . .] was made in July 1953, but it was then dropped and not taken up again until December 1956, being completed on 1 January 1957" (*Collected Poems* xvii), prompted by a Christmas visit the poet paid to his mother Eva in December 1956. Larkin described his feelings during this visit in a letter to Judy Egerton:

> Soon I shall be the only unmarried man in the western hemisphere. I feel like some ancient enemy of youth and spirit – how *can* they? What do they *gain* by it? (Motion 1994: 279)

It is not too speculative to suppose that these feelings of worry and frustration, together with Larkin's memory of the song-books that Eva used when she played the piano in her youth – one had even been "coloured" by Larkin's sister, Catherine, as a child – provided the basis for the writing of "Love Songs in Age."

In the poem Larkin resorts, once again, to speaking about another person as a means of distancing himself from the topic he is dealing with, but the observer is here the observed. He is really talking about himself when he talks about this widow who recovers the song-books of her youth. If originally the songs had inspired hope, now they seem to describe a world of delightful but impossible illusions. Between the time of the young, romantic dreams of her courting days and the time of her widowhood, when those dreams, now beyond even the illusion of possible fulfilment, reappear as sharp nostalgias, there were years of domestic life filled with the concerns suggested in the first stanza – tending a home, raising flowers, rearing a child:

> She kept her songs, they took so little space,
>   The covers pleased her:
> One bleached from lying in a sunny place,
> One marked in circles by a vase of water,
> One mended, when a tidy fit had seized her,
>   And coloured, by her daughter –
> (*Collected Poems* 113)

During this time of life, the dream was put aside, not cynically discarded, because "She kept her songs" (*Collected Poems* 113), and only in age, with the husband dead and the daughter grown up, is the old ideal revived as a memory. The "unfailing sense of being young" (*Collected Poems* 113) spreads like a perfume from the song-books and prompts in her the old hope of love: the extraordinary promise of a future of pleasure and order. But those were the romantic hopes of youth, and now time – age – has given perspective to this woman, who can recognize that love "had not done so then, and could not now" (*Collected Poems* 113). These are Larkin's thoughts as he grows older; he did not find in youth this ideal love which solves and satisfies and sets in order, and he knows he will never find it, probably because it does not exist. Love will not be able to redeem him from his unsatisfactory life.

* * *

As the years go by, a fear invades Larkin's mind in an increasingly pressing way, a fear of what he himself described in a poem as "the only end of age" (*Collected Poems* 153) – death. This fear was not alleviated by a belief in eternal life after death. Larkin was never a religious man; his only interest was in the externals of religion – the religious rituals as the embodiment of formal values and time-honoured tradition. In this respect, Larkin's answer, both witty and brutally sincere, to a question in an interview with *The Observer* in 1979, when the poet was fifty-seven, is revealing:

> *Do you think much about growing older? Is it something that worries you?*
>
> Yes, dreadfully. If you assume you're going to live to be seventy, seven decades, and think of each decade as a day of the week, starting with Sunday, then I'm on Friday afternoon now. Rather a shock, isn't it? If you ask why does it bother me, I can only say I dread endless extinction. (Larkin 1983: 55)

Together with this fear, Larkin also began to develop another kind of feeling in the last part of his life – a feeling of jealousy and envy of young people. This emotion appears in several of the poems that are included in *High Windows*, the last of Larkin's volumes of poetry, published in 1974, when he was fifty-two.

Larkin's envy is centred mainly on the new sexual freedom that young people enjoy, as opposed to the miserable repressions of the past. With the sexual revolution of the early 1960s, Victorian morality came to be superseded by new values concerning sexuality – pornography was legitimized and sexually-explicit scenes shown on public cinema screens. But Larkin felt he had been born too late to benefit from that freedom, and he expresses this feeling in his poetry. In "High Windows," he laments missed occasions of promiscuity:

> When I see a couple of kids
> And guess he's fucking her and she's
> Taking pills or wearing a diaphragm,
> I know this is paradise
> Everyone old has dreamed of all their lives –
> (*Collected Poems* 165)

and in "Annus Mirabilis," he suggests that with the introduction of the contraceptive pill, the act of sexual intercourse had been made as accessible to everyone as a paperback novel and a pop music record:

> Sexual intercourse began
> In nineteen sixty-three
> (Which was rather late for me) –
> Between the end of the *Chatterley* ban
> And the Beatles' first LP.
> (*Collected Poems* 167)

As can be appreciated, Larkin's usual clarity of tone and topic intensifies in this last collection, to the extent that some of the poems can be considered simple emotional outpourings rather than veritable poetry. This harshness is dominant in his poem "The Old Fools" which is a release of rage against something Larkin knows he cannot avoid becoming, a rage that hides a naked summary of all his fears as he confronts advanced age.

* * *

"The Old Fools" opens with direct questions, all of them showing Larkin's cruelty, the psychological means of defense for someone who feels overwhelmed by panic:

> What do they think has happened, the old fools,
> To make them like this? Do they somehow suppose
> It's more grown-up when your mouth hangs open and drools,
> And you keep on pissing yourself and can't remember
> Who called this morning?
> (*Collected Poems* 196)

To Larkin, the worst delusion of these people would be to suppose they could recover their happy youth, "if they only chose" (*Collected Poems* 196). Nearness to death has reduced them to a passive state in which their capacity to choose is lost.

At the beginning of the second stanza Larkin's voice changes and becomes more plainly descriptive – "At death, you break up: the bits that were you / Start speeding away from each other" (*Collected Poems* 196). But he cannot hold this tone for long. Explaining the difference between the oblivion of being in the mother's womb and that of being dead, he is reminded too painfully of the precious "million-petalled flower / Of being here" (*Collected Poems* 196). The first signs of death begin to press on him too heavily. These signs, which the poet describes with a fascinated horror, are both mental and physical:

> Not knowing how, not hearing who, the power
> Of choosing gone. Their looks show that they're for it:
> Ash hair, toad hands, prune face dried into lines –
> (*Collected Poems* 196)

In the third stanza, Larkin tries to imagine the condition of being old, which he describes as "having lighted rooms / Inside your head, and people in

10

them, acting" (*Collected Poems* 196). As Andrew Motion says in *Philip Larkin: A Writer's Life*: "In a different context this might be a paradigm of the imaginative life; it might be Larkin miming his own creative singleness. Here, though, it describes something so purely 'over' it seems asphyxiated" (1994: 427). Old people try to live in the past world of their memories, and yet they live in the present, and this inescapable duality leads Larkin to the final image of his poem "Extinction's alp" (*Collected Poems* 197):

> This must be what keeps them quiet:
> The peak that stays in view wherever we go
> For them is rising ground.
> (*Collected Poems* 197)

This mountain reminds Larkin that he is not yet as old as they are – the reader notes the careful use of "we" and "them" – but he knows too that sooner rather than later he will become one of them. The last verse of each stanza includes the third person plural pronoun "they," referring to "the old fools," but at the end of the poem Larkin includes himself in the category with his use of the first person plural pronoun – "We shall find out" (*Collected Poems* 197). He knows that old age is superficially similar to childhood, but profoundly different in essence; childhood leads into life, old age out of it, and he is terrified by this thought. The product of his terror and frustration is "The Old Fools." One reader wrote complaining that she found the poem hard-hearted, to which Larkin replied in a letter:

> It is indeed an angry poem, but the anger is ambivalent: there is an anger at the humiliation of age (which I am sure you would share), but there is also an anger at the old for reminding us of death, an anger I think is especially common today when most of us believe that death ends everything. This is of course a selfish and cruel anger, but is typical of the first generation to refuse to look after its aged. Here again you will have ample evidence of what I mean. (Motion 1994: 425-6)

* * *

The path which leads from "This is the first thing" to "The Old Fools" traces the treatment and evolution of the topic of ageing in Philip Larkin's poetry and reveals the increasing presence and intensity of the topic in Larkin's poetical work. The stylistic process of clarification, from early Yeatsian symbolism to the almost shameless harshness of the last collection, is linked to an emotional development which includes the beginning of an awareness of time, reflections prompted by the effects of the passage of time, first on the body and then on the mind, and finally a fear of death. The work of any artist must be valued taking into account original authorial intention. If Larkin's intention was to talk in his poems, with the language of ordinary speech, about such a central issue of ordinary life as time and the passing of time, he achieves his aim. And he does it memorably.

Works cited

Kuby, Lolette. *An Uncommon Poet for the Common Man: A Study of Philip Larkin's Poetry*. The Hague: Mouton, 1974.

Larkin, Philip. *The North Ship*. 1945. London: Faber and Faber, 1966.

—. *The Less Deceived*. 1955. Hessle: Marvell, 1966.

—. *The Whitsun Weddings*. 1964. London: Faber and Faber, 2001.

—. *High Windows*. 1974. London: Faber and Faber, 1979.

—. *Required Writing: Miscellaneous Pieces 1955-1982*. London: Faber and Faber, 1983.

—. *Collected Poems*. 1988. London: Faber and Faber, 1990.

Motion, Andrew. *Philip Larkin: A Writer's Life*. 1993. London: Faber and Faber, 1994.

Old Age in Serbia:

Transition for all Ages[1]

Tatjana Djuric Kuzmanovic

Defining old age

There is no general agreement on the age at which a person becomes old, even though it is generally accepted that a person's calendar age and biological age may not coincide. On many occasions the definition of old age is associated with the age at which one can begin to receive pension benefits. Thus, despite its arbitrary nature, the ages of sixty and sixty-five are often used as the default definition. Most developed countries, as well as international institutions, have accepted the age of sixty-five years old as the definition of an elderly person. At the moment, there is no United Nations standard numerical criterion, although sixty-plus years is the generally agreed cutoff age when referring to older people. Age classifications have varied between countries and over time. They often reflect the social class differences and functional abilities related to work, as well as the political and economic situation.[2] For my purposes here, I will use sixty-five years of age and older as the general definition of an elderly person.

* * *

Populations are ageing in almost every country in the world. While in 1950 there were 200 million old people in the world (Kinsella, *et al.*, 1993), now there are 550 million and by 2025 there will be 1.2 billion. Between now and 2050, the number of old people will rise from about 600 million to almost two billion; then, for the first time in history, the world will contain more people over sixty than under fifteen. The fastest growing group within the population of old people is that of the oldest elderly, meaning those who are eighty-years-old or older; they numbered 70 million in the year 2000 (United Nations. *Report on the Second World Assembly on Ageing*, 2002).

---

[1] I have benefited from comments and suggestions on earlier drafts by Dubravka Zarkov and from editing by Lee Nordgren.
[2] See Thane, P. "The muddled history of retiring at 60 and 65." *New Society* 45. 826 (1978): 234-6.

As elsewhere in the world, Serbia is an ageing society; by the end of the 1990s, the people aged sixty and over made up eighteen percent of the population. For example, the population of Vojvodina, the northern, most highly-developed Autonomous Province of Serbia, has one of the ten oldest populations in the world (Vesti B92, 24.05.2003). Furthermore, elderly people are among the poorest, regardless of whether they live in the north, south or east. Particular difficulties for older people in Eastern and Central Europe are connected with the falling value of pensions and the reduced or withdrawn services that used to be provided by governments. Elderly people in Serbia, like over fifty-year-olds in other Eastern and Central European countries, have become disenchanted, suffering from inadequate basic services, unsupportive social attitudes and worthless pensions (Hinchliff, and Hall 2002).

Ageing issues in Serbia are also poverty issues. Many elderly people in Serbia have difficulties paying for rent, heating and electricity. At the same time, older people tend to give high priority to settling their bills. Although healthcare is nominally free, many basic prescription medicines are unaffordable. Over half of the population of the elderly live in extended families, and many support family budgets with their pensions or take care of grandchildren while parents work. Furthermore, many old people in Serbia have suffered post-communist erosion of entitlements and savings, expulsion from homes in Bosnia-Herzegovina, Croatia or Kosovo, damaged infrastructure as a result of NATO bombing, and international sanctions. Across Serbia, there are 750,000 refugees and internally-displaced people, and 100,000 of them live in collective centers – a third of them aged sixty-five or over (Hinchliff, and Priestley 2001: 20). Without citizenship and contribution records, they cannot claim pensions in Serbia, and loss of pension and property rights in their native country means that most of them live in poverty, with an insufficiency of food, clothing and other basic facilities.

* * *

Gendered ageing

Societies discriminate on the grounds of old age, and this results in the exclusion of old women from social and developmental policies. Their contributions remain unrecognized, and they do not receive an equitable share of national or global resources (Clark 2002: 2). Most cultures tend to undervalue women's time compared to men's, which is a key reason for unequal treatment of men and women throughout their lives with respect to education, jobs, incomes, social benefits, healthcare, and so on. Women spend more time in household production and in caring activities, while men's traditional role is as the breadwinner. This unequal treatment of men and women remains with them into old age.

Worldwide, elderly women outnumber elderly men (United Nations. *Report on the Second World Assembly on Ageing*, 2002). Compared with men, women have a greater chance of being widowed and of having had inadequate education, nutrition, and access to services in earlier life. They make up a larger proportion of the 'old old' age group; older women make up two-thirds of the global population over eighty, and as life expectancy rises, this proportion will increase (Clark 2002: 2). For example, in the United States of America women aged sixty-five and over are more than twice as likely as men to be unmarried and to live alone; nearly 40 per cent of all older women live alone compared to 16 per cent of older men (Sunhwa, and Shaw 2003: iii).

Although there is a lack of gender- and age-sensitive data, it is clear that ageing in Serbia is, as elsewhere, a gendered phenomenon. Women in Serbia live an average of two to eight years longer than men and, as almost everywhere else, they have limited access to resources. In Serbian society, despite the fact that past communist ideology proclaimed gender equality a main goal, the patriarchal frame remained unchanged. Under communism, the concept of women's emancipation was part of official socialist theory. Communist ideology referred to the realization of equal rights and opportunities for women in a socialist society and to the entry of women into the sphere of social production.[3] Women shared equal legal rights with men in the spheres of education, employment and political participation, and they had the right to divorce and to abort. But the socialist state granted women legal equality while maintaining traditional gender relations and associated structures both within the family and society. The *de jure* equality, moreover, could not lead to *de facto* equality because the gendered social structures were either precluding women from assuming the rights they had been granted or were marginalizing and ghettoizing them when they took their rights.

Regarding marital status and living arrangements, there is a general tendency for women to marry men who are older than themselves and to live longer than their husbands. The majority of older men are married while women are more than twice as likely as men to be unmarried. These differences in marital status and living arrangements are closely associated with the economic well-being of older people. Elderly people who live alone are more likely than others to be

---

[3] The purpose of the women's emancipation project was not, however, the liberation of women. The concept of liberation would have meant the destruction of the highly patriarchal nature of society, and transformation at all levels, including sexuality, the family, the household and the personal, in addition to freeing women from all forms of oppression. The socialist women's emancipation project never went beyond the 'women's question' into the transformation of gender relations. Consequently, both the images of women and the position of women at various levels of society were highly ambiguous (See Zarkov, D. 1991).

poor. This also means that older women face a greater risk of poverty because it is they who more often live alone. This is also the situation of older women in Serbia.

* * *

One pilot study on social status and the needs of older women in Vojvodina and Novi Sad (Markov 2003) shows very poor conditions of life for older people, although the results are still not analyzed in detail. Older people are mainly satisfied with their social status, although women are more critical about it. There is evident reproduction of the patriarchal family frame, with women considered responsible for caring for family members. The research indicates that elderly men and women rely on a combination of income sources – their own labour, support from family and community and, in a few instances, support from the state. Over half the population of elderly people live in extended families and many support family budgets with their pensions or take care of grandchildren while parents are at work. Older women in Serbia are still expected to care for elderly and young relatives. Very few older women are eligible for pensions or social assistance and, at the same time, they face discrimination when trying to obtain credit and training. Older women are less likely to qualify for state support, as they mostly work outside the formal sector. Women are less likely to have assets, and if widowed, may not have access to their husband's property. Worldwide, many older women face particular constraints, as they do not have the same inheritance and property rights as men. They continue to work into very old age – they work by themselves to produce food or earn income, or they take on domestic responsibilities to enable other family members to produce income (Beales, Pages, Patel, and Wafer 2000). For example, among women aged sixty-five and above sixty-five in the United States of America, those who work full-time all year round earn only about two-thirds of what men earn in full-time work. Furthermore, during retirement, women's median annual benefits reach only seventy percent of men's benefits (Sunhwa, and Shaw 2003: 7-15).

* * *

The older generation in Serbia in state-directed non-development during the 1990s

During the times of socialism, elderly people were generally well provided for by state-run services, both medical and social. Inclusive retirement pensions and care systems were available to all elderly people due to the notion of full employment as one of the highest official ideals of the socialist state. Great emphasis was placed on employment as both a right and a duty for both men and women. Due to these facts, Serbia, like other socialist countries, presented high labour market participation for both men and women during socialism. At the same time, nothing changed regarding patriarchal gender relations in the family and society; labour segregation – that is, the tendency for women to be in lower paid sectors of the economy and relatively low paid occupations – was widespread. The breakup of the socialist system and of Yugoslavia itself went hand in hand with the strengthening of the new collectivist ideologies – nationalism and ethno-democracy.[4] The ex-socialist Serbian government rejected reforms that could have led to a market economy and to parliamentary democracy. It prevented development and thus induced many negative, even devastating, consequences – economic chaos (Lazić 2000: 10), the politics of war and nationalism, and international isolation.

During the 1990s, adjustment of employment to the decreasing level of economic activity in Serbia was not carried out by dismissing surplus workers, but rather by sharply decreasing real wages, by increasing the number of workers or paid and unpaid leave, by forcing workers into retirement, and by augmenting employment on the informal labour market. Due to these state measures, the standard of living was preserved from total collapse, but the result was a large decrease in labour productivity in the formal sector, a large increase of latent unemployment and expansion of the informal labour market. In 1992, under Resolution 757, the Security Council of the United Nations imposed economic sanctions on the Federal Republic of Yugoslavia, thereby excluding Serbia almost entirely from international market and legal economic relations.

Throughout the 1990s, the Serbian regime had unlimited political and economic power and used it to ensure its continuity and later to hold on to that power. This specific state economic policy and strategy of non-development (Djuric Kuzmanovic 1997) not only prevented transition to a market economy and parliamentary democracy, but also led to the paralysis of functioning social institutions as they were dominated increasingly by false state structures, corruption and crime. Under such circumstances, the former socialist government perpetuated its privileges while wide sections of the population were getting poorer and social inequalities were growing rapidly. The state economic policies threatened the position of women and men in the labour market, forcing them into unemployment or work on the black market and reducing their standard of living and social security such as health, pension, or maternity benefits. These circumstances made a strong impact on the older generation; this was the time when pensioners, many of them supporters of the nationalist regime of Slobodan Milosević,[5] lived on nothing.

* * *

---

[4] See Laslo Sekelj. "Realno samoupravljanje, realni nacionalizam i dezintegracija Jugoslavije." *Sociologija* 33. 4 (1991): 587-99.
[5] See Bora Kuzmanovic. "Drustveno – politicki stavovi, glava 9." Golubovic, Kuzmanovic, and Vasovic, eds. (1995) 262.

Older people in Serbia during transition

The extensive socio-economic transformation undertaken by the transition countries of East and Central Europe has affected the structure of these countries' economies, the living standards of their populations and gender relations as well. The dissolution of the socialist planning system and transition into the market-led economies across East and Central Europe brought, among other problems, financial instability, unemployment, crises in public funding and increases in unemployment and the informal economy. The role of the state declined with cuts in government budgets and reductions in pension and social welfare systems. At the same time, these countries experienced an increase in the proportion of older people as a percentage of total population.

These reforms that started in Serbia three years ago, as in other transition countries, have had serious consequences for older people and for gender relations (Djuric Kuzmanovic 2002). The older people in Serbia are affected by transition economically, socially, psychologically and physically. To what extent these processes affect older women and men in Serbia is still a relatively under-explored issue. After a turbulent nationalistic decade of state-directed non-development, the situation of older people is dire. Together with people with disabilities, refugees, the rural poor and uneducated people, the elderly and the children in Serbia are the most vulnerable groups in transition, and they make up 10.6 percent of the total population, that is, 800,000 poor people (*Strategija za smanjenje siromastva u Srbiji* 2003). Moreover, only a very small rise of the poverty-datum line will mean a two-fold increase in the number of poor people.

The experiences of other countries in transition show that it is the nation's elderly who are hardest hit by transition because of collapsed socialist-state safety nets. But already in the 1990s, during the Serbian nationalist, state-directed decades of non-development, Serbia's elderly constituted a significantly vulnerable group, a situation that has remained the same during the recent Serbian transition. Their specific needs and contributions are often barely recognized, undervalued and misunderstood. Research conducted by HelpAge International in Serbia during 2000/2001 found that the life of many older Serbs was very hard in terms of poor accommodation and little government support for rent and utility costs, badly fitting footwear and unsuitable clothing, poor stoves and little fuel to get through the winter months, and problems in paying for medicines and fresh foods (Priestley, Hinchliff, and Saim 2001: 8-10). Serbian pension payments are still inadequate and unreliable and savings have plummeted. After paying for rent, light and heating many older people have insufficient money left to buy adequate food. High unemployment has eroded the ability of younger people to help parents and grandparents and has placed new responsibilities on older people. Conflict and economic crisis have often disrupted traditional bonds between families and older people, with one-in-five elderly Serbs now living alone. Particularly vulnerable are the seven percent of the population who are refugees and internally-displaced people. Older people form a third of the 100,000 displaced people still housed in more than one hundred and fifty collective centres. Existing in legal limbo, with their citizenship rights and entitlement to pensions and lost property undefined, and unable to return to such traditional forms of self-reliance as animal husbandry and horticulture, many are driven to despair. They feel isolated and invisible and have few contacts with local people.

* * *

Older people and pensions

The risk of falling into poverty is greater for women than for men, particularly in old age where social security is based on the principle of continuously remunerated employment. Until recently, during the state directed non-development in the 1990s, pension payments were irregular or delayed for several months. At the moment, the average level of pension is low and fails to cover many basic needs of older people.

There are basically two kinds of pension system – funded and un-funded, with very different characteristics and different implications for old men and women. A funded system assumes that some percentage of the salaries of employees will be collected in special capital funds and invested in the financial market. The pension system in Serbia is still un-funded, or a 'pay-as-you-go' system. The basic characteristic of that system is intergenerational solidarity because every employee pays some percentage of their salary for the pensions of retired people. Thus, in an un-funded pension system there is immediate transfer of money to pensioners without any investment in the capital market. It is usually expected that the relation between employees and pensioners is 4-6:1. But, in Serbia that relation in 1952 was 5.2:1 while in 2001 it decreased to 1.2:1.[6]

In spite of democratic change in Serbia, universal age-related pensions based on intergeneration solidarity – the un-funded system – still remain the norm and a universal entitlement for all elderly citizens. However, a radical switch to a funded system is expected in the near future. There appears to be no strong public debate in Serbia about the future kind of pension system; some take the demographic situation, that is, the increased ageing of the population, as the basic argument against the un-funded system, while others emphasize the point that increasing production and employment could permit adequate support for the existing un-funded system.

---

[6] See "U susret reformi penzijskog sistema." *Ekonomski ravnopravne* (2002) 13.

Some lessons from other transition countries as well as from the other regions in the world could be useful. The Tanzanian study *Strengthening Village and Neighbourhood Organisations: Safety Networks for the Vulnerable* (2000) suggests that minimal but guaranteed and regular income in old age will have important intergenerational and anti-poverty effects. Also, research in poor rural and urban communities with high unemployment rates in Southern Africa – Mauritius, Namibia and Botswana – found older people's pension incomes supporting several household members (Willmore 2001).[7] Spending priorities were school fees and household food. However, pension income alone may not guarantee that basic needs of older people are met. The same study found that older people face severe problems accessing healthcare services, particularly highlighting poor treatment by health staff. Relatively rapid population ageing in poorer countries implies that, unless policies and social protection schemes specifically address issues of old age poverty, targets for poverty reduction will not be achieved. The studies also suggest that un-funded pensions encourage household economic activity by strengthening the contributions of older people.

Due to the new Serbian Law on Pensions and Disability (2001), retirement now begins for women at fifty-eight and for men at sixty-three. Also, pension credit for full-time work status for women requires thirty-five years of full-time work and for men forty years. The minimum requirement for retirement is fifteen years of full-time work. Pension benefits are calculated on the basis of fifty percent of average living expenses and fifty percent of wages. A decrease in pensions is not allowed by this Law. The key change in the new law is that the level of an individual's pension will depend on the level of that person's wages during all working years. Also, there is a possibility for people who have never worked or have worked in part-time jobs to pay for their pension by themselves. In practice, this means that housewives can now become pensioners. In general terms, current Serbian law reflects the principal of maternity, not parenthood, and at the same time discriminates positively in favour of the child-bearer. For example, a woman who gives birth to a third child will earn the right to add two years in the computation of her working years (Zakon o osnovama penzijsko invalidskog osiguranja Republike Srbije 2002: cl 51).

* * *

The potential of the elderly for development

All societies discriminate against people on the grounds of age. Ageism and stereotyping influence attitudes which, in turn, affect the way decisions are made and resources are allocated at household, community, and national levels. Age factors and stereotypes about age, rather than capacity, deny older people

---

[7] See I. Willmore. "Universal Pensions in Low-income Countries." 2001.

opportunities for participating in development. Moreover, the different roles men and women have played in their lives affect their individual ageing experience.

Old people remain a neglected social group and largely invisible to the Serbian government in respect of economic development, healthcare, education and poverty reduction. Despite the fact that older people are being disproportionately affected by the decline in social welfare, they are not consulted or involved in programmes dealing with the side effects of transition. The HelpAge International report *Building a better future: older people in Serbia* (Priestley, Hinchliff, and Saim 2001) and my own research show that, when matters concerning older people in Serbia are under discussion, their needs and contributions in the economic development of Serbia are poorly understood. Among other surveys, another HelpAge International report *Equal treatment, equal rights: ten actions to end age discrimination* (HelpAge International 2001), which was produced in preparation for the Second World Assembly on Ageing held in Madrid in 2002, disproves stereotypes and emphasizes the evidence that the elderly are good credit risks and do not make disproportionate use of healthcare provisions. With adequate resources, older people can successfully run home-based preventive and primary healthcare programmes and, as the experience from South Africa has shown, the engagement of older people in policing forums can contribute to the fight against crime.

It is becoming common knowledge that populations in developing as well as developed countries are ageing rapidly. But little is known and less action is being taken on the possibility of including older people in development processes. There are economic, social and human reasons to assume that ageing issues could become welfare issues with the full economic and social participation of older people in the development process. Involving older people in decision-making is a particularly effective way of tackling the economic and social exclusion often linked with ageing. Such an approach considers that poverty is inter-generational and argues that the older poor are net contributors to family and community and are not necessarily dependent. Half the world's older people support themselves through informal labour such as child care, trading, or small-scale agriculture, all invisible in official statistics. Ageing increases the level of home services for the person older than fifty-five to seventy percent (Cvijic 2002). Furthermore, there is strong evidence that ageing actually supports some economic branches of the economy such as tourism, banking and insurance as well as some pharmaceutical products necessary for health.

* * *

Affirmative action

Governmental policy should take into account the productive capacities of older men and women and should support their contributions to poverty reduction (Beales 2001). Age- and gender-sensitive research on ageing, including age and gender-sensitive data collection and analysis, provides an essential base for effective policies. There is still need for more knowledge about gender and ageing and better research into the different impacts of ageing on men and women in Serbia. This knowledge could be derived from sustainable research projects and maintained data regarding elderly women and men in Serbia. In meeting this challenge, several issues will be raised. For example, there is the question of key indicators with which to inform policy makers about the situation of older Serbs; what are the indicators and how should they be defined, stored and disseminated? There is also the question of currently available data and how various international data sources can be integrated. A minimum data set should include a list of data collection and indicators adjusted for age, sex, educational level and household, and should relate to the demographic, social and economic situation of older people, their health, mental and functional status, care access and service utilization, old people's homes, family and home care, healthcare and social services financing (Kowal, Wolfson, and Dowd 2000).

It is obvious that a better future for older people should be assured not only as a development imperative, but also as a human right. There are a lot of recommendations for action both by older people themselves and by governmental and non-governmental organizations. Participation of older people and especially of older women in development is defined as one of the five core principles in United Nations resolution 46/91 to ensure that their rights are delivered. At the United Nations Second World Assembly on Ageing in Madrid, 2002, "The International Plan of Action on Ageing" was adopted to promote the development of a society for all ages in three priority directions: older persons and development, advancing health and well-being into old age, and ensuring enabling and supportive environments.[8] Furthermore, the Plan recognizes the need to mainstream a gender perspective into all policies and programmes to take account of the needs and experiences of older people. Finally, gender-sensitive policies for older people need to address the particular vulnerabilities to long-term poverty in old age that result from women's life-long disadvantages in health and nutrition, limited labour force participation and discrimination in property and inheritance *(The Ageing and Development Report: Poverty, Independence and The World's Older People,*

---

[8] "The International Plan of Action on Ageing" was adopted at the first World Assembly on Ageing in Vienna, 26 July-6 August 1982 (United Nations Publication, Sales No. E. 82. I. 16, chap. VI, sect. A). Issues of human rights for older people were taken up in 1991 in the formulation of the United Nations "The Principles for Older Persons" (General Assembly resolution 46/91).

1999). There are also many declarations about the full participation of older people in the social, cultural, political and economic life of their communities. They all ask that older people's empowerment should be promoted through organizing at the community level, inclusion in mainstream development processes, capacity building and networking. But gender inequalities between older men and women persist.

Works cited

Beales, Sylvia. *The mark of a noble society: human rights and older people*. London: HelpAge International, 2001.

Beales, Sylvia, Samantha Pages, Sagneeta Patel, and Paul Wafer. *Gender and ageing, a position paper*. London: HelpAge International, 2000.

Clark, Fiona. *Gender and Ageing Briefs*. London: HelpAge International, 2002.

Cvijic, Zoran. "Sve vise starih lica menja kompletnu sliku evropskih drustava." *Danas* (8-9 Jun. 2002). <http://www.danas.co,yu/> 10 June 2002.

Djuric Kuzmanovic, Tatjana. *Dirigovani nerazvoj i feministicka perspektiva*. Novi Sad: Expopres, 1997.

—. *Gender and Development, from Directed non-Development to Transition*. Novi Sad: Buducnost i Zenske studije i istrazivanja, 2002.

Golubovic, Zagorka, Bora Kuzmanovic, and Mirjana Vasovic, eds. *Drustveni karakter i drustvene promene u svetlu nacionalnih sukoba*. Beograd: Institut za filozofiju i drustvenu teoriju "Filip Višnjić," 1995.

HelpAge International. *The Ageing and Development Report: A Summary. Poverty, Independence and the World's Older People*. London: HelpAge International, 1999.

—. *Strengthening Village and Neighborhood Organizations: Safety Networks for the Vulnerable*. Dar es Salaam: HelpAge International, 2000.

—. *Equal treatment, equal rights: ten actions to end age discrimination*. London: HelpAge International, Nov. 2001.

—. *The State of the world's older people – Executive Summary*. London: HelpAge International, 2002. <www.helpage.org>

Hinchliff, Paul, and Bo Priestley. *Making our voices heard: Older people and decision-making in East and Central Europe*. London: HelpAge International, 2001.

Hinchliff, Paul, and Céline Hall. *A generation in transition: older people's situation and civil society's response in East and Central Europe*. London HelpAge International, 2002. <http://www.id21.org/society/s8aph1g2.html>

Internet Coverage of the United Nations Second World Assembly on Ageing. Madrid, 2002. <http://www.un.org/ageing/coverage/statements.htm>

Kinsella, A. *et al.*, eds. *An Aging World II*. Washington DC: US Bureau of Census, 1993.

Kowal, Paul, Lara J. Wolfson, and John E. Dowd. *Creating a Minimum Set on Ageing in Sub-Saharan Africa*. 2000. [Mimeo]

Kuzmanovic, Bora. "Drustveno – politicki stavovi, glava 9." *Drustveni karakter i drustvene promene u svetlu nacionalnih sukoba*. Eds. Zagorka Golubovic, Bora Kuzmanovic, Mirjana Vasovic. Beograd: Institut za filozofiju i drustvenu teoriju "Filip Višnjić," 1995. 247-99.

Lazić, Mladen, ed. *Racji hod. Serbia in Transformational Processes*. Belgrade: Filip Višnjić, 2000.

Markov, Slobodanka. *Izvestaj istrazivackog projekta, Socijalni polozaj i potrebe starih zena u Vojvodini i Novom Sadu*. 2003. [Mimeo]

On-line Bulletin Board Discussion. "Ageing Aspects of the 12 Critical Areas." 2002. <http://un-instraw.org/discus/messages/38/38.html>

Priestley, Bo, Paul Hinchliff, and Nadia Saim. *Building a better future: older people in Serbia*. London: HelpAge International, 2001.

Randel, J., German, T., and Ewing, D. *The Ageing and Development Report: Poverty, Independence and the World's Older People*. Earthscan [in association with HelpAge International], 1999. <Papers, manuals, reports>

Sekelj, Laslo. "Realno samoupravljanje, realni nacionalizam i dezintegracija Jugoslavije." *Sociologija* 33. 4 (1991): 587-99; SGJ *Statistical Yearbook of Yugoslavia*. Belgrade: Savezni Zavod za Statistiku, 1991.

Strategija za smanjivanje siromastva u Srbiji. Beograd: Prvi nacrt SSS-a, 2003.

Sunhwa, Lee, and Lois Shaw. *Gender and Economic Security in Retirement*. Washington DC: Institute for Women's Policy Research, 2003.

Thane, P. "The muddled history of retiring at 60 and 65." *New Society* 45. 826 (1978): 234-6.

United Nations. "The International Plan of Action on Ageing." United Nations Publication, Sales No. E. 82. I. 16, chap. VI, sect. A, 1982.

—. "The Principles for Older Persons." *United Nations resolution* 46/91, 1991.

—. *Report on the Second World Assembly on Ageing. Madrid, 8-12 April*. New York: United Nations, 2002.

"U susret reformi penzijskog sistema." *Ekonomski ravnopravne*. (Beograd, 30-31 Dec. 2002). <http://www.danas.co.yu/20021130/ekonomija.htm> 7 Jan. 2003.

Vesti b92 za 24.05.2003. "Vojvodjani na devetom mestu u svetu po starosti." <http://www.b92.net/>

Willmore, I. "Universal Pensions in Low-income Countries." [Paper prepared for the annual meeting of the International Association of Pension Fund Organizations, Costa Rica, 2001].

World Bank. *Review of the PRSP Experience: An Issues Paper for the January 2002 Conference*. <http://www.worldbank.org/poverty/strategies/review/>

Zakon o osnovama penzijsko invalidskog osiguranja Republike Srbije. 2002. [Law on Pensions and Disability] <www.propisi.com>

Zarkov, D. *The Silence which is not One: Sexuality, Subjectivity and Social Change in a Feminist Rethinking of Research on Peasant Women*. Den Haag: Institute of Social Studies, 1991. [MA thesis]

The Hourglass of Time:

Life Cycle in the Digital Era

Carles Feixa Pàmpols

The temporal construction of life

> Everything happens as if the ritualising of [social] interactions had the paradoxical effect of offering all its social efficiency to time, never as active as when nothing happens, just the time itself: "Time is said to work for itself."
> Bourdieu 1980: 81

It is difficult to deal with the social history of cultural construction of biography, of the ways by which every society organises the life cycle and relations among generations, using the common academic language, since it refers to deeply changing terms, conceptions and values in time and space.[1] This is the reason why it might be more appropriate to reflect on this process by using some metaphors. These invite us to look into reality from moving images and comparisons, from a film being mounted rather than a series of fixed pictures. I suggest that we consider the metaphor of the clock, which will help us interpret the different mechanisms, used at different times and in different places to measure the access of young people into adulthood. The clock measures the chronological passing of time, but it can also symbolise biological time and, especially, social time. As far as ages are culturally-constructed biographical stages making up more or less flexible borders and more or less institutionalised forms of passage through stages, we can consider the clock as a marker of these borders and passages. From this perspective, the

---

[1] Although my argument refers to the complete life cycle, the examples and reflections are focused on youth as one of the age grades where the metamorphoses of life course are more dramatic.

historical evolution of the clock can serve to illustrate the historical evolution of the life cycle.[2]

When we look into our watches, we observe a condensed – metaphorical – version of the history of civilisation: the division of the day into twenty-four hours comes from ancient Egypt where sundials and hourglasses were invented; the division of the hour into sixty minutes comes from the sexagesimal mathematical system used in old Mesopotamia; the face and the hands driven by a complex clockwork from medieval Europe were perfected during the modern time and were widely diffused by industrialisation thanks to American and Swiss clockmakers. Nowadays, the electronic circuits that are the basis of digital watches started to be used in the second half of the twentieth century and became popular thanks to Japanese trademarks. For my purposes here, therefore, three types of clocks are considered: the hourglass, the analogical watch and the digital watch, as symbols of three cultural modalities – the hourglass is derived from a natural or cyclic conception of time, dominant in pre-industrial societies; the analogical clock springs from a linear or progressive conception of time, dominant in industrial societies; and the digital watch is based on a virtual or relative conception of time, emergent in post-industrial society. The three types of clock can be related with three different ways of social construction of biography.[3]

In her classic essay *Culture and Commitment* (1970), Margaret Mead suggests a typology of cultural forms according to the modalities of transmission between generations. Thus, 'post-figurative cultures,' corresponding to primitive societies and to small religious or ideological groups, would be the ones in which "small children learn basically from the elder" – time is repetitive and social change is slow; 'co-figurative cultures,' corresponding to large State civilisations, would be the ones in which "both children and adults learn from their contemporaries" – time is more open and social change is accelerated; and 'pre-figurative cultures,' that according to Mead were emerging at the time when she wrote her essay towards the end of the 1960s, would be the ones in which "adults also learn from children" and "youths assume a new authority through their pre-

---

[2] The Castilian term *reloj* comes from the medieval Catalan *relotge* which was adapted from the Latin *horologium*. I will summarise the history of this time machine schematically, of course. The bibliography about this subject is extensive. I will refer only to three extraordinary works for their lucidity and diffusion: Whitrow (1990), Cipolla (1999), and Barnett (2000).

[3] Manuel Castells devotes a section of the first volume of *The Information Age* (1996) to the transformations in the concept of time, totally converging with the metaphors of the clock used in this text. I am going to make particular use of the notions of 'intemporal / timeless time' and 'culture of real virtuality,' elaborated to describe the relativity of time in the information society.

figurative grasp of a still unknown future" (1977: 35).[4] Mead's pseudo-evolutionist pattern runs the risk of simplifying too much, but is useful when thinking about the clock as metaphor. In post-figurative cultures, as with the hourglass, a circular vision of the life cycle prevails, where each generation reproduces the cultural contents of the previous one. In co-figurative cultures, as with the analogical watch, a linear vision prevails, according to which each generation sets up a new range of cultural contents. Finally, in pre-figurative cultures, as with the digital watch, a virtual vision of inter-generation relationships is established whereby connections betweeen ages groups are inverted and biographical structures overlap.

If the clock symbolises the individual measure of time, then we can consider inter-generation relationships as a metaphor of social time. That is to say, the ways in which every society constructs divisions and passages between ages are indicators used to conceptualise transformations of their lifestyles and values. I have suggested in other places that we analyse the concept 'youth cultures' from two complementary perspectives: 'social conditions' and 'cultural images.' On the level of social conditions, understood as the set of rights and duties that define every individual's identity within a social structure, youth cultures are constructed from identities of generation, gender, class, ethnicity and territory. On the level of cultural images, understood as the set of ideological and symbolic attributes assigned or appropriated by each individual or social group, youth cultures are translated into styles integrating heterogeneous material and non material elements, that can be translated into languages, styles, music, cultural creations and focal activities. Social conditions are configured from the interaction between the 'hegemonic culture' that reflects the distribution of cultural power at the scale of the wider society and 'parental cultures' that can be considered as the large cultural traditions that young people share with their parents and their original social environment. On the other hand, cultural images are configured from the interaction between 'macro-cultures' – the resorts, in the wider society, that form and inform individuals, like churches and media, and 'micro-cultures' – small groups that filter and semanticize forms and contents of the strategies of formation and information, like voluntary associations and friendship networks.

In every clock, time measurement reveals the connection between social conditions and cultural images, which are translated into different modalities of transit – borders and passages between different age categories. This brings about three types of rituals that symbolically represent these transits: the passage rites, fundamental in pre-modern societies, based on the mechanism of social reproduction; those that can be named rope rites, fundamental in modern societies, based on the mechanism of social transition; and the ones I suggest be called

---

[4] Page references for Mead, M. (1970) correspond to the translation into Castilian by Eduardo Goligorsky – *Cultura y compromiso. El mensaje a la nueva generación* (Barcelona: Granica, 1977).

holoselection rites, fundamental in post-modern societies, based on a mechanism of social nomadism.[5]

* * *

The hourglass

> Sand clepsydrae appeared rather late. They were very used on board of vessels to measure the duration of the sailors guard services and the speed of the vessels.
> Cipolla 1999: 15 [6]

The hourglass has been used for centuries to measure the passing of time. It seems that the first ones came from old Egypt, where also sundials and water clocks – the sophisticated clepsydrae – were found. These three types of clock spread later into classical Greece and ancient Rome. These tools use natural sources of energy – gravity and sunlight – where the degree of precision is low and depends to a large extent on environmental conditions and the observer's standpoint. The advantage of the hourglass is that, unlike the sundial, it can be used to measure time at night and, unlike the water clock, it does not depend on temperature. Its small size and usefulness explains its persistence throughout history, despite a design weakness which meant that the friction of the sand wore it away, and its limited capacity in that it can measure only short fractions of time.[7]

A natural conception of time, the hourglass functions thanks to natural laws; the law of gravity allows the sand to fall and, once all the sand has fallen to the bottom, human strength turns the hourglass upside down. Like the sundial, its mechanism reflects the cyclical nature of time, symbolised by the succession day-night, sunshine-shade, up-down. Most conceptions of time existing in primitive societies and states are based on a cyclical vision that compares the life phases with the changing of the seasons and the movement of the planets. There is a sense of transit in biological time. The passing of seasons corresponds to age awareness;

---

[5] For more explanations of these concepts, see Feixa 1998. The concept 'rite of passage' was proposed by Arnold van Gennep in a classic essay (1909). The concept 'corda rite' is inspired in films such as Charlie Chaplin's *Modern Times* (1935) that show industrial machination. The concept 'holosection rite' is inspired by television series such as *Star Trek* that generate youth subcultures, for example, the 'trekkies.'

[6] Page references for Cipolla, C.M. (1981) correspond to the translation into Castilian by Antoni Martínez – *Las máquinas del tiempo y de la guerra* (Barcelona: Crítica, 1999).

[7] In 1957, the German philosopher Ernst Jünger published a fascinating book about the meaning of time entitled *Das Sanduhrbuch*, translated into Castilian by Andrés Sánchez with the title *El libro del reloj de arena* (Barcelona: Tusquets, 1998). In fact, the hourglass has been used in the history of art as a kind of metaphor for the fugacity of life, as expressed in the pictorial genre of *vanitas*.

infancy is the springtime of life, youth is the summer, adulthood is the autumn and old age is the winter. The ancient Greeks identified time with Chronos, a god represented by an old man carrying a sickle and a clepsydra – a water clock – or an hourglass, and who ended up by devouring all of his children. According to this representation, time is an individual on whom years have piled up, bearing a tool used by peasants to cut plants that have already borne their fruit. The hourglass can be used, then, to represent a cyclic vision of the life cycle based on the generation wheel, each of them repeating *ad infinitum* the behaviour of the previous one. It is the type of cultural construction of ages that has existed in most tribal states and farming societies throughout the history of mankind. The predominance of the past corresponds to a low degree of economic mercantilism. Young people – a life stage often not socially-acknowledged – not only are not present in the cultural consumption – since there is no feed-back between supply and demand – but they also make little contribution to cultural innovation, being, in effect, socially repressed.

Each individual sets his own hourglass in motion [see Figure 1], departing from a set of relatively rigid social conditions, determined by origin: age (chronological), gender (biological), rank (social), descent (family) and place of living (locale). These markers are transmitted through three major social pillars – family, community and power structures – that mediate in more or less conflictive relationships between 'parental culture' – the ways of living and values existing in the original social environment, identified with the network of kin – and 'hegemonic culture' – ways of living and values suggested as dominant model in each society, imposed by military, religious or political institutions. All these elements converge in the moment of the rite of passage, which normally takes place together with physical or social puberty and usually indicates transit into adulthood, although this is often limited to men, or even only to those coming from privileged classes. After the rites of passage by which, following the ritualised passage through a sequence of three phases – separation, transition and reintegration, the individual achieves a kind of re-birth and returns to society with a new status: professional, marital, reproductive, political and festive. Role-status systems corresponding to every age are legitimised and justified through a series of 'cultural images,' expressed in the mythic-ritual systems, and internalised by means of different macro-cultural spheres that exist at societal level and are usually expressed through religion, and micro-cultural spheres that exist in reduced social spheres and are usually expressed through groups of equals, as happens in age class systems in certain primitive societies.[8] In this way, the social energy prevailing in the hourglass is symbolically translated into the so-called rites of passage ceremonies – puberty, marriage, access to citizenship – that affirm the mechanisms

---

[8] These observations could apply to studies about time experience in primitive societies, as well as to contemporary ethnographies about 'total institutions' – prisons, sects or mental hospitals. See, for example, E.E. Evans-Pritchard (1940).

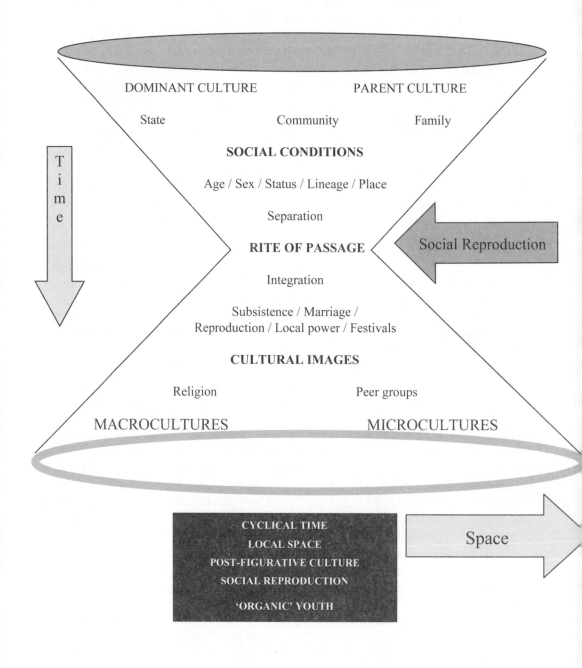

FIGURE 1: THE HOURGLASS

of generation solidarity on the societal scale.

What is interesting about the metaphor is that, when the cycle closes, the clock is turned upside down so that cultural images can pour down again onto social conditions and the genealogical wheel of generations is completed. A conception of 'cyclic time' – such as sacred, mythical or mystical – displayed in local space – tribal, rural, municipal – is therefore prevailing. According to Margaret Mead's terminology, children learn from parents and grandparents, the sole authority reference, and repeat in a post-figurative way, with few changes, life phases, rites of passage and biographical conditions as followed by their parents. It is an 'organic' view of age working as a mechanism of social reproduction: life cycle is a condensed image – a metaphor – of social continuity.[9]

* * *

The analogical clock

> The decisive machine in the modern industrial age wasn't the steam engine. It was the watch.
> Lewis Mumford 1934 [10]

The first mechanical clock appeared at the end of the eighteenth century, invented by anonymous European craftsmen. It was the first totally automatic machine. Its cogs were an example for later machines, like the ones that made possible the industrial age. They used to be large public clocks, based on a complex mechanism that regularly struck a bell and moved the hands around a clock-face divided up into twelve hours. For many centuries, clocks strategically placed on local bell towers marked the community's daily time, announcing working and praying times as well as those of births and deaths. With the rise of the trading bourgeoisie, personal pocket-watches complemented public clocks. The invention of the more regular and ductile pendulum clock in the seventeenth century also contributed to the personalisation of timepieces and its diffusion needs to be related to the birth of the new urban civilisation, from cathedral time to market time.[11]

---

[9] The contrast between the 'organic' and 'mechanical' youth models is inspired by Émile Durkheim's concepts of social solidarity (Durkheim 1893), although it does not exactly correspond to the French sociologist's original formulation.

[10] This quotation from Lewis Mumford's *Technics and Civilization* (London: Routledge, 1934) is taken from J.E. Barnett's *El péndulo del tiempo. De los relojes de sol a los atómicos* (1998. Barcelona: Península, 2000) 67.

[11] Jacques Le Goff devoted his classic essay "Au moyen âge, temps du marchand et temps de l'église" (*Annales ESC*, 1960: 417-33) to this subject in which he drew a distinction between church time that is dominated by a cyclical and spiritual conception of time and the merchants' time that pre-figures a secular, regular and foreseeable conception of time.

Not until after the beginning of the nineteenth century, with the arrival of industrial civilisation, did the mechanical watch begin to spread throughout the population. Swiss clockmakers, who specialised in the mass production of exact and cheap personal watches, were partly responsible of this success. Demand came from the manufacturing sector that required much more precise and generalised time synchronisation. E.P. Thompson (1979) has demonstrated how the imposition of a working discipline carried essential changes in the perception of time. While traditional handicraft and the first home industries valued the principle of a salary for the amount of work done, manufacturing work imposed payment by the hour. The watch enabled the coordination of the movements of men and machinery; since time was divided into precise units, it could be measured. The omnipresence of time and its direct link with workers' salaries gave rise to the idea that it was time that was being sold rather than labour. Time could become money, or, as the saying goes, "time is money." Just like money, time could be measured, earned, saved and consumed. The concept of leisure time followed the same pattern; quantified in terms of clock time, it is earned, saved and consumed. The history of industrialism is the history of the imposition of clock time and resistance to it. Another consequence of the spread of the clock was the universalisation of time zones. While, like the sundial, the first mechanical clocks measured only local time, by the end of the nineteenth century a world time network was agreed, based on Greenwich Mean Time. In this way, the measurement of time became an international matter. The wristwatch is an even more modern invention. Although bourgeois ladies had started to wear one, they did not spread until soldiers during World War I discovered how useful they are when worn in a visible place. Today this is such a deeply-rooted habit in our culture that if in the future archaeologists were to study our remains, they might well name us the "wristwatch people" (Barnett 2000: 298).[12]

The mechanical or analogical watch – 'analogical' given that it measures time on the basis of a continuous numerical system established analogically with the day's division into twenty-four hours – is derived from a linear or progressive conception of time, emblematic of modern, industrial civilisation. Its operation comes from a mechanical contrivance: it needs periodical winding up, just as a steam engine needs the feeding of coal. By so doing, time always flows onwards, just as society moves in a forward progression without pause. From this perspective, the present replaces the past as a source of authority, with the look into the future as symbolic horizon and faith in progress as the new civil religion. If we transfer this conception to the age system, we realise that every generation seeks to live better than the previous one and not to reproduce its cultural models. Generation succession reflects the process of modernisation, but also carries

---

[12] The first country to adopt an official time was Great Britain, in 1848. The USA did the same in 1883 and Spain in 1901. J.E. Barnett has observed that this diffusion was closely related to the extension of railway networks and the need to unify timetables (2000: 139).

generation gaps and conflicts; with a different understanding of the conception of time, age groups have different expectations concerning the past and the future. Just as the mechanical clock detached 'time' from its link to the rhythm of nature and made of it something abstract – an autonomous being in itself, we can also assume that the invention of 'youth' as a new-age category, with tendency towards autonomy and the creation of a world of its own, could mean the consolidation of progress toward an artificialisation of age divisions.[13]

The analogical watch operation as represented in Figure 2 is based on the action of winding up, either manually or mechanically. This is symbolic of the process of social insertion, by which the individual socialises by taking on a series of new roles and social status. A person reaches this point by overcoming a series of life phases – infancy, adolescence, youth, adulthood, old age – that usually correspond to other institutionalised roles – play, education, work, family, retirement. Social conditions constitute the inner mechanism, usually invisible, which operates the whole system. The strong borders of pre-industrial society, based on birth, slowly fade away, but far from disappearing, they can actually become stronger.

The social concept 'generation' replaces biological age; 'gender,' as a cultural construct, replaces sex; 'class,' based on the position within the productive system that allows social promotion or descent replaces the more rigid rank or strata system. The notion 'ethnicity policy' replaces lineage based on kinship systems; nation-state 'territory' replaces locality – tribal lands, village, city – as a place for coexistence. In the meantime, the 'family' becomes increasingly nuclear and the 'neighbourhood' increasingly urbanised and yet they continue to configure parental cultures that become more intensively heterogeneous, evolving from divisions based on the notion of social class. Hegemonic culture is expressed mainly through the 'school' – that large-scale, highly-universalised invention of modern times. Closely aligned with the age system and the labour market as a mechanism of social-role assignation, the school's predominance is wholly dependent on the distribution of economic resources and political power that converge in market institutions, either competitive and monolithic, and within the State, either authoritarian or democratic.

Cultural images express social changes that take place as the clock's hands show the time. They reveal the breaking-off of the existing monolithism in post-figurative cultures, with the emergence of segregated codes according to age group:

---

[13] Even today, some rites of passage, like the Roman Catholic Church's first communion and confirmation ceremonies, are marked by the presence of a clock that symbolically turns the individual into an adult.

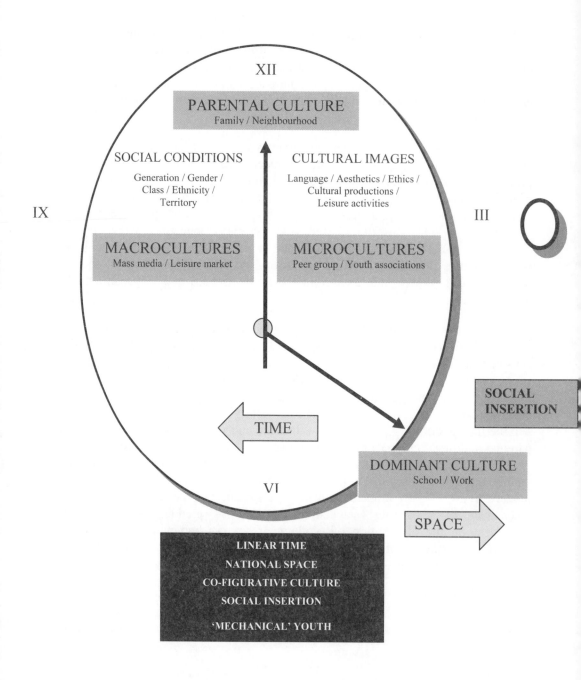

FIGURE 2: THE ANALOGICAL CLOCK

differences in verbal and non-verbal language, body and external aesthetics, popular and mass music, written and visual cultural productions, and progressively leisure time-oriented focal activities slowly create the conditions not only for the invention of new-age categories, like adolescence, but also for the emergence of cultures based on generation, as evidenced by the 'generation gap' after World War II. Although the culture of young people has an increasing number of spaces for expression, they still have two privileged spheres: on the one hand, 'macro-cultures'– those cultural networks of general or universal range that concern young people beyond the local space, as occurs with mass culture, the leisure market and rock music as a first generation, international, popular language, and on the other hand, 'micro-cultures' – localised cultural networks that influence young people in their daily interactions, as happens in youth associations that appeared at the beginning of the twentieth century and have increased throughout the century, and informal groups, ranging from gangs to urban tribes.

The social energy prevailing in the analogical watch is, then, symbolically translated into the so-called winding-up rites. Generation-based activities and ceremonies like military service, starting work and juvenile protests are all feedback from the clockwork of social change. A conception of 'linear time' – progressive, regular, continuous – prevails in such rites, displayed in a 'national space' – regional, state, international. According to Mead's terminology, children learn from their contemporaries, which make up a new authority referent and innovate in a co-figurative way, with constant modifications, the life phases, the rites of passage and biographical conditions experienced by their parents. It is, after all, a 'mechanical' vision of age, based on a mechanism of social insertion, that operates like the hands on the clock of modernisation, including generation gaps. In this way, the life cycle becomes a condensed image – a metaphor – for social change.[14]

* * *

The digital watch

> In a digital watch there isn't a single moving piece. Nothing is to be seen, except a small battery, a small capsule with the quartz crystal. A small electronic circuit.
> Barnett 2000: 153

---

[14] These observations can be applied to the whole tradition of studies about gangs and youth subcultures that, from the school of Chicago to the one in Birmingham, have taken an interest in the frequently conflictive relationship between youth and society (*cf.* Hall, and Jefferson 1983; Feixa 1998).

The digital watch has imposed its hegemony during the last third of the twentieth century, in association with advances in computer technology and the need for precision not dependent on external factors. The source of energy is now an electric battery feeding some electronic circuits. The system is not the numerical division into twelve hours any more, as is the case for the analogical system, and is now binary, that is, digital. This has been made possible thanks to the discovery of quartz crystal oscillations and later on to the cesium atom that can regulate time-measurement machines with extraordinary precision. The first quartz clock was manufactured in 1928; the first atomic clock in 1953. But the true popularisation of the digital watch had to wait until the 1970s, when Japanese brands flooded the market with today's well-known wristwatches. Some authors have seen this phenomenon as one of the first signs of world-wide diffusion, that is, globalisation.[15]

The most characteristic feature of the digital watch is that it has not one moving component. The traditional face and hands have been replaced by a numerical display. It is provided with a memory that codifies time information into a binary language and a decoding circuit that turns this information into numbers. It is a microchip-based system, progressively miniaturised, with the purpose of measuring time with great precision – the frequency of alternating current is about 50 cycles per second, whereas that of the microchip is 300 million. While the hourglass measured minutes and the analogical watch presented seconds and tenths of a second, the digital watch measures hundredths and thousandths of a second with high precision. Along with personal computers, the digital-based time conception is widespread. The digital watch is being progressively built into all sorts of electronic devices, controlling their internal operation – television sets, radios, timers, safety systems, and so on.[16]

In a way, the digital watch brings to daily life the revolutionary conception of time implicit in Einstein's theory of relativity. Along with post-modernity, time-measurement is much more precise, universal and ubiquitous – watches are omnipresent in every corner of our daily lives – but, at the same time, time-measuring is a lot more relative, off-centred and ambivalent, depending on space as

---

[15] It might not be by chance that IBM started at the beginning of the twentieth century as a company specialised in manufacturing clocking-in machines (Barnett 2000: 164).

[16] In recent years, digital watches have been transformed and personalised, spreading a 'philosophy of deceleration,' based on a less agitated and more plural conception of time: watches can now be enjoyed. There are design watches and ecological watches, with built-in condensers instead of a battery, and so on. In order to solve the Internet time disparity, Swatch has suggested introducing a World Digital Time as a substitute for the time zones based on the Greenwich meridian, dividing the day into ten exact 'hours,' operative anywhere on the globe and in cyberspace. Of course, the new digital 'centre of the universe' would be the headquarters of this Swiss company.

much as on the subject. One of the attributes of digitalised time-keeping is that the beginning, end, duration and pace of an activity can be constantly reprogrammed. A truly 'virtual' time is created, whose 'reality' depends on the environment where it is produced and the objectives pursued. Video-games, for instance, generate their own space and time that set down the conditions for the actor's social perception. The maximum example of this virtual conception would be the so-called Y2K problem that, by the end of 1999, threatened the operation of all built-in systems based on the operation of one or more microprocessors, thus preparing for what could be called a truly virtual millennium.[17]

The digital watch is the emblematic symbol of post-industrial or post-modern civilisation, based on a conception of time that we could call virtual. Time is also denationalised, becoming more global. As airline flight schedules replace train timetables as the agent of time unification, world-reach digital electronic networks – television, telephone and text-based systems – contribute to creating the sensation that we are all living at the same time and that everything happens in real time, the impression given by video-conferencing or chats. From a symbolic point of view, the digital conception of time has its maximum expression in a series of ludic devices – video-games, virtual reality games, simulators, holograms, and so on – omnipresent in home computers and their many substitutes. All these devices create simultaneous, but not continuous times; they create an artificial simultaneity where there is no past and no future, just present. As Castells says, "the network society is characterised by the breaking-off of both biological and social pace, associated to the notion of life cycle" (1999: 480).[18]

---

[17] At the end of 1999, the Internet was filled with pseudo-apocalyptic messages about the so-called Y2K problem. As an example, here are two emails I received at the time:

> 1. Built-in systems are the ones where one or more parts consist of micro-processors. They usually operate, control, protect or monitor vital processes. Any device showing or processing dates or time values can be affected by the so-called Y2K problem.
> 2. The Public Administrations Ministry informs that there is a new virus associated to the Y2K problem. An electronic message sending a supposed regressive counter of Y2K, but really containing a virus, has been detected. Microsoft appears falsely as the sender.

Although the Y2K problem could be seen not as an example of collapse itself, it did invoke an unjustified *fear* of collapse, of an announced catastrophe that never arrived, and of big business, in this case with a suspicion of fraud (Amparo Lasén, personal communication).

[18] Holograms are purely mathematical constructions, ways to render an unstable thing stable, a moment of order inside chaos. I owe these observations to the Mexican mathematician Linda Suárez, who suggested that all the ideas explained in this section be related to the theory of chaos. Some authors like Ulrich Beck (1998) have tried to apply this theory to social sciences, using the concept 'risk society.'

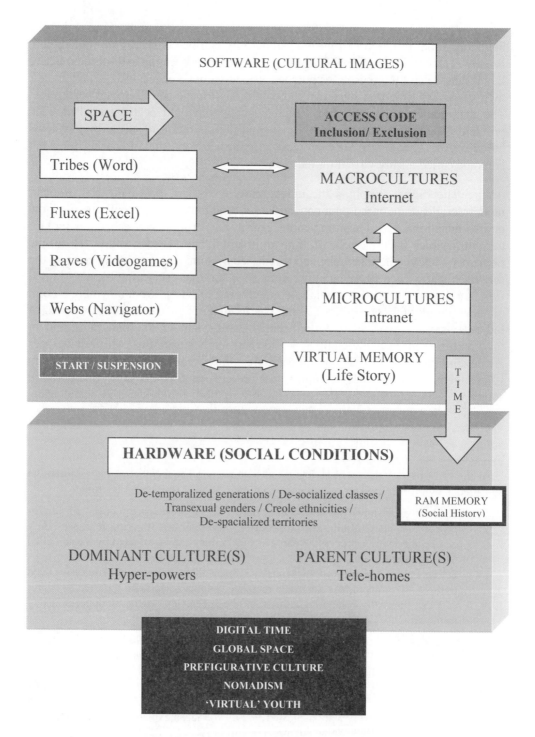

FIGURE 3: THE DIGITAL WATCH

In Figure 3, digital watch is represented through the image of the personal computer (PC), one of the emerging instruments in the post-modern society, whose operation is based on a microchip. In this metaphor, social conditions make up the computer's hard disk. Miniaturisation and indivisibility have in no way led to their disappearance. On the contrary, as differences between people and groups have widened, they have become more subtle and imperceptible and the external signs that expressed them have disappeared. For example, generation differences are not always translated into different ways of dressing or talking any more. Some adults dress like young people, and some children share aesthetic or playful tastes with adolescents. As major historical events that marked generation identity such as occurred in Russia in 1917 and in Europe in 1968 fade from collective consciousness, generations detemporalise, that is, lose their temporal dimension, and "non-events" arise[19] equivalent to "non-places,"[20] authentic social limbos that can be likened to passing through airports or railway stations towards nowhere. Social classes are declassed, dependent not on wealth or power only, but mainly on the more intangible cultural capital.[21]

With slow but irreversible women's emancipation and the emergence of gay and lesbian movements, genders become transsexual, favouring the process of both physical and symbolic transvestism. From the point of view of ages, this implies a revolutionary implosion of borders between masculinity and femininity in the transit to adulthood and old age. With the crisis of the nation-state, ethnicities become creole and hybrid with an accompanying increase in xenophobia and racial conflict. With the emergence of global space and cyberspace, territories have become deterritorialized as the influence of geographical milieu in the configuration of social identitites decreases. Social conditions challenge everything, from structures to more flexible networks, interconnected within the hard disk, building the challenging 'habitus' of social actors. Those processes are supported by the increasing complexity of hegemonic cultures – hyper-powers in which governance is mostly in anonymous and invisible hands, and parent cultures – tele-homes where father and mother figures progressively delegate their functions.[22]

Thanks to RAM memory – social history within every life history – social conditions connect with cultural images that are stored on the soft disk, the one you

---

[19] See Balardini (2000).

[20] See Augé (1993).

[21] See Bourdieu (1980).

[22] These observations can be related to the notion of 'disanchorage,' used by Giddens for describing "the 'taking off' of social relations from its local contexts and its restructuration in specific space-time intervals" (1999: 32). For Castells, network society is characterized by the breakdown of rhythmicity, as biological as social, associated with the concept of life cycle (1999: 480).

can see on the screen. It is an artificial space – cyberspace – constantly recreated by the programmes that all computers have. Word processors allow speech-making in Babelian languages, favouring the emergence of the 'time of tribes,' data-bases manage real empires, the multinationals of the new economy and the new politics, invoking the concentration of information; spreadsheets enable material and symbolic flows on planet scale; video-games recreate virtual realities through the combination of holograms, music and new drugs, as in the case of rave parties in the techno culture; and browsers generate virtual communities that only exist on the Internet. These cultural images, progressively fragmented by age groups, are translated into a macro-cultural system – the Internet network – that embraces the whole planet, and into many micro-cultural systems, no longer limited to a specific place, that link actors of very different tastes – intranet networks.

There are three elements in the PC metaphor that should be explained further. First, the little clock on the lower right-hand corner of the screen monitors the operation of the whole system. System operation or its collapse – for instance, if caused by the Y2K problem – conditions all operations of all social subjects within the system framework. Second, this temporality is not regular – it is subject to each programme's 'beginning' and 'suspension,' being a decision taken by an actor and his social environment, thereby allowing for ways in and out of youth to be univocal processes. Third, a 'password' is required to access the Internet, providing inclusion or exclusion from the system. This generates a dual society, in which an important section of the population cannot even access the system.

The social energy in the digital watch is symbolically translated into the so-called holosection rites[23] – generation ceremonies like virtual reality games, role-play games, rubbish contracts, night raves or new-youth violence – to represent the anarchic, autarchic and sometimes virtual character of transitions into adult life. A conception of digital time – pendular, irregular, non-continuous – prevails in such rites, displayed in a global space that is trans-national, cyber-spatial, but not necessarily universal. According to Margaret Mead's terminology, parents start to learn new referents of authority from their children and, in a post-figurative way, dismantle biographical phases and conditions that define the life cycle, suppressing or displacing most of the rites of passage that divide them. It is a 'virtual' vision of age that favours 'social nomadism,' that is to say, the constant transit and exchange of generation roles and status.

* * *

---

[23] Holosection is a room in the spaceship *Enterprise*, from the TV series *Star Trek*, where crew members can have fun with virtual reality games based on holograms that reproduce scenes from the past or imaginary spaces and times, although in some episodes they threaten to become real.

The generational construction of time

> See a world in a grain of sand . . . and eternity in one hour.
> William Blake

> Time is always divided into innumerable futures.
> Jorge Luis Borges

Not only does time socially construct age; age also socially constructs time, to the extent that it models, readapts and projects new modalities of temporal experience. As the quotations from these two visionary writers suggest, sand and time can be appropriate metaphors for understanding worlds and visualising futures, necessarily polymorphous. These suggestions have been used here to reflect on youth culture and its transformations at the end of the millennium. However, the suggested model should be interpreted not as an evolutive pattern, but rather as a transversal metaphor with which to investigate the contemporary complexities of time conception. From this perspective, it is useful to analyse interconnections and hybridisations between different modalities of the life cycle that interweave in different institutions of the same society, or at different stages of the same biography.

In every place and time, different conceptions of time coexist. It is not just about grandparents still living with the hourglass, parents with the analogical clock and children experimenting with digital time; young people live on the borders of the three clocks. Depending on the institution they find themselves in, the moment in their lives and their personal tastes, and in the knowledge that life is a game, and that the important thing is to participate, rather than win, young people play with one another. In our society, for instance, chronological time is still important in institutions like schools, military barracks, churches and traditional professional institutions in which hierarchical, authority structures are deep-rooted and where age and seniority are still pillars of power and knowledge. The mechanical clock also prevails in those institutions, such as leisure time, juvenile groups and market associations, where authority structures are shared and where age hierarchy is diminished, while age group affiliation is still a referent for social classification. For its part, however, the digital clock expresses itself mainly in institutions like mass media, new information technologies and means of digital diversion, where authority structures are non-existent and where age is transmuted into changing symbolic referents and subjected to constant feedback.[24]

---

[24] As today's young people combine their temporalities by articulating the three clocks, members of other societies also needed to manage with different time experiences. See classic contributions by Norbert Elias (1997) and a reading of this author's work by Amparo Lasén (2000).

In order to view the metaphor from another perspective, this time one which draws parallels with the film industry; three major models or syndromes are identified which correspond to three types of accounts of youth or youth stories. The first model, *the Tarzan syndrome*, was invented by Jean-Jacques Rousseau at the end of the eighteenth century and lasted until the middle of the twentieth century. According to this model, the adolescent is the noble savage who inevitably needs to be civilised, a being in whom the full potential of the human species remains undeveloped because he keeps pure and uncorrupted. Faced with oncoming adulthood, the young person shows the same confusion as Tarzan when he confronts civilisation, a mixture of fear and fascination. Does the adolescent need to be isolated in his child's jungle, or should he be integrated into adult civilisation? Rapid transitions from play to work, the first insertion into a profession and marriage, participation in rites of passage such as induction into military service, would all be features that characterise a model of adolescence based on an 'organic' insertion into adult society. This is a youth story, a textual odyssey, that explains the passing from oral culture to written culture – in *the Guttenberg galaxy*.

The second model, *the Peter Pan syndrome*, was invented by happy postwar teenagers and became hegemonic in the second half of the twentieth century, aided by the potential of consumer society and mature capitalism. According to this model, the adolescent is the new revolutionary subject, the new consumer hero, who rebels against adult society and resists becoming part of its structure – it is better to be or appear young than old. The accelerated process towards schooling, the slow transitions towards adulthood, the creation of adolescent micro-societies, both in education and leisure time, the increase in young people's purchasing capacity, the disappearance of rites of passage into adulthood, the emergence of 'tribes' and youth subcultures, are features that characterise a model of 'mechanical' insertion into society. This is a story about youth, a contextual odyssey, that tells of the passage from a written culture to a visual culture – in *the McLuhan galaxy*.[25]

Finally, the third model, *the Blade Runner syndrome*, has emerged at the change of century and is destined to hegemony in future society. Like Ridley Scott's replicants, adolescents are artificial beings – half robot, half human – split between obedience to the adults that have fathered them and the will to emancipate themselves. Since they have no memory, they have no consciousness and, therefore, they are not free to construct their futures. Yet they have been programmed to use all the potential of their technologies and, therefore, they are

---

[25] Enrique Gil Calvo (2001) maintains that what is characteristic about the twentieth century is age invention, and particularly the invention of youth, that is, the enlargement of biographic stages as a consequence of the enlargement of life expectancy, which has as a sub-product the emergence of youth culture centred on cinema, music, fashion and sport.

better fit to adapt to changes and to confront the future without their parents' prejudices.

But their rebellion is condemned to failure; they can only carry out sterile and episodic uprisings, while they wait to acquire, one day, the consciousness that will turn them into adults. Like replicants, adolescents have all the world within their reach, but they are not the owners of their destinies. And like Blade Runner, adults hesitate, caught between their fascination for their offspring and the need to eradicate any deviation from the norm. The result is a hybrid, ambivalent model of adolescence, on the border between increasing social infantization, translated into economic dependence, lack of spaces for responsibility, and an increasing intellectual maturity expressed in the access to new information technologies, new aesthetic and ideological criteria, and so on. Discontinuous transition toward adulthood, social infantization of adolescents, permanent delay in accessing labour markets and residence, the emergence of artificial worlds like Internet surfer communities, the configuration of adolescent networks on planet scale, are all features that characterise a 'virtual' model of insertion into society. This, once again, is a youth story, a hypertextual odyssey, that tells of the passage from a visual culture into a multimedia culture – in *the Gates galaxy*.[26]

The three models should not be understood as countered types in an evolution model, but as modalities of interaction between adolescents and society that can coexist in the same time-space within different institutions that condition young people's lives.

* * *

Of course, my suggestion[27] that today's young people be termed the 'generation @' is not to underscore the hegemony of the digital watch or the virtual conception of time. If this is not yet clear in Europe, it is a lot less clear on a universal scale, where social, geographical and generation inequalities not only do not disappear, but are reinforced with the current process of globalisation. This explains the active role of young people in anti-globalisation movements and demonstrations in centres in many parts of the world. As Margaret Mead has indicated, the young people's conception of time plays a central role in this transformation, as a sign and metaphor of new cultural consumption modalities. Today we are experiencing a moment of fundamental transit in the conception of time, similar to that encountered by the first factory workers when their lives started to be ruled by the clock. The consumption of audio-visual goods, particularly by young people, is

---

[26] For more on virtual youth communities and social links in cyberspace, see Finquilievich (2000) and Balardini (2000).
[27] See Carles Feixa. "Generación @. La juventud en la era digital." *Nómadas* 13 (2000): 76-91.

probably the sector of the market that best reflects these changed tendencies. In these practices, though still vague, ambiguous and contradictory, we can see oblivion from the past, paradoxes from the present and uncertainties from the future, as in one of Salvador Dali's 'soft' clocks.

Works cited

Amit-Talai V., and H. Wulff, eds. *Youth Cultures. A Cross-Cultural Perspective.* London: Routledge, 1995.

Augé, M. *Los no-lugares. Lugares del anonimato.* Barcelona: Gedisa, 1993.

Balardini, S. "Jóvenes e identidad en el ciberespacio." *Nómadas* 12 (2000): 100-11.

Barnett, J.E. *El péndulo del tiempo. De los relojes de sol a los atómicos.* 1998. Barcelona: Península, 2000.

Beck, Ulrich. *La sociedad del riesgo.* 1986. Barcelona: Paidós, 1998.

Bourdieu, Pierre. *Le sens practique.* Paris: Les Éditions du Minuit, 1980.

Castells, Manuel. *The Information Age: Economy, Society and Culture: The Rise of the Network Society.* Oxford: Blackwell, 1996.

Castells, Manuel. *La era de la información. La sociedad red.* Vol. I. 1996. Trans. Carmen Martínez, and Jesús Alborés. Madrid: Alianza, 1999.

Chisholm, L. "Els joves i la globalització." *Joves entre dos móns.* Eds. Feixa, C., and J.R. Saura. Barcelona: Secretaria General de Joventut, 2000. 11-26.

Cipolla, C.M. *Las máquinas del tiempo y de la guerra.* 1981. Trans. Antoni Martínez. Barcelona: Crítica, 1999.

Durkheim, Émile. *The Division of Labour in Society.* 1893. New York: Free Press, 1964.

Elias, Norbert. *Sobre el tiempo.* 1984. Mexico DF: FCE, 1997.

Evans-Pritchard, E.E. *The Nuer: A Description of the Modes of Livelihood and Political Institutions of a Nilotic People.* 1940. New York: Oxford UP, 1987. [*Los Nuer.* 1940. Trans. Carlos Manzano. Barcelona: Anagrama, 1977.]

Feixa Pàmpols, Carles. *La joventut com a metáfora.* Barcelona: Secretaria General de Joventut, 1993.

—. *El Reloj de Arena. Culturas juveniles en México.* Mexico DF: Causa Joven, 1998.

—. "Generación @. La juventud en la era digital." *Nómadas* 13 (2000): 76-91.

Finquilievich, Susana. *¡Ciudadanos a la red! Los vínculos sociales en el ciberespacio.* Buenos Aires: Ciccus, 2000.

García Canclini, N. *La globalización imaginada.* Buenos Aires: Paidós, 1999.

van Gennep, Arnold. *The Rites of Passage.* 1909. London: Routledge, 1977.

Giddens, Anthony. *Consecuencias de la modernidad.* 1990. Madrid: Alianza, 1999.

Gil Calvo, Enrique. *Los depredadores audiovisuales.* Madrid: Tecnos, 1985.

Hall, S., and T. Jefferson, eds. *Resistance Through Rituals. Youth Subcultures in Post-War Britain.* 1975. London: Hutchinson, 1983.

Jünger, Ernst. *El libro del reloj de arena.* 1957. Trans. Andrés Sánchez. Barcelona: Tusquets, 1998.

Landes, D. *Clocks and the Making of the Modern World.* London: Cambridge UP, 1983.

Lasén, Amparo. *A contratiempo. Un estudio de las temporalidades juveniles.* Madrid: CIS, 2000.

Le Goff, Jacques. "Au moyen âge, temps du marchand et temps de l'église." *Annales ESC.* (1960): 417-33.

Lévi-Strauss, Claude. *La pensée sauvage.* 1962. Paris: Plon, 1962.

Machado, J., ed. *Traços e riscos de vida.* Lisboa: Ambar, 1999.

Maffesoli, M. *Du nomadisme. Vagavondages iniciatiques.* Paris: Livrairie Generale Française, 1997.

Mead, Margaret. *Culture and Commitment: A Study of the Generation Gap.* New York: Natural History Press, 1970. [*Cultura y compromiso. El mensaje a la nueva generación.* Trans. Eduardo Goligorsky. Barcelona: Granica, 1977.]

Tapscott, D. *Growing Up Digital: The Rise of the Net Generation.* New York: McGraw-Hill, 1998.

Thompson, Edward P. "Time, Work-Discipline and Industrial Capitalism." *Past and Present.* 38 (1967): 56-97. ["Tiempo, disciplina de trabajo y capitalismo industrial." *Tradición, revuelta y conciencia de clase.* 1979. Trans. Eva Rodríguez. Barcelona: Crítica, 1984. 239-318.]

Whitrow, G.J. *El tiempo en la historia.* Barcelona: Crítica, 1990.

Willis P. *Common Cultures.* Boulder: Westview, 1990.

"'Aware too late,' said Beauty as she passed."

The *Expiry Date* to be Liked and to Love: Some

Medieval Views on Old Age and Sexuality[1]

Edurne Garrido Anes

S.J.H. Herrtage's edition of "Caclides, Of a Young Knight Who Slew an Old Knight and Married his Widow" (1879: 61-3) presents a Middle English translation of one of the stories in the medieval collection of anecdotes known as the *Gesta Romanorum*. The title does not provide much information about the woman, that is, the Old Knight's widow. However, even before reading the tale we can venture to guess that as the young knight killed the old knight to marry his widow, then the widow is either young, as is the case here, or rich. In the absence of youth and beauty, in medieval literature a good economic and social position is considered the only reason for an old person to be worth marrying, killing, or both.[2]

In his rewriting of Ovid's *Ars amandi*, the anonymous Norman author of a French poem *La Clef d'Amors* (ca.1280), translated into Modern English as *The Key to Love*,[3] deals with this fact. The advice the speaker gives to his male readers is to find a woman who is either young and pretty or, alternatively, old and rich:

> Whom you must seek in your pursuits,
> and what should be her attributes:
> she must be simple, sweet and fresh,
> tender of years and fair of flesh
> [. . . .]
> Or if, indeed a more mature,
> somewhat more seasoned paramour
> is what you chance to have in mind
> [. . . .]
> If you are wise, then pay your court

[1] This paper has been undertaken with the support of the Spanish Ministry of Science and Technology, MCYT Project I+D: "Vejez y Literatura." BFF2002-02763.
[2] See B.A. Hanawalt. "Widows" (C. Dinshaw, and D. Wallace, eds. 2003. 58-69).
[3] See Norman R. Shapiro's translation in *The Comedy of Eros: Medieval French Guides to the Art of Love* (Chicago: U of Illinois P, 1997) 9-42.

> In circles of the noblest sort,
> Where, if you will, you may select
> A woman worth the world's respect,
> Of proper birth and pedigree [. . .] .
> (*The Comedy of Eros: Medieval French Guides to the Art of Love* 14-5)[4]

With a good pecuniary situation being the only justifiable reason for someone's involvement with an aged person, there was always the underlying assumption that the elderly were out-of-date as far as other-than-money based relationships were concerned. Thus, contrary to the present-day dictum that love and sexuality are good and healthy at any age, philosophical, scientific and literary writings from the Middle Ages used to warn that only in youth was it right, natural and healthy to have sexual relationships.

* * *

The advocacy of youth and beauty and rejection of the old for sexual matters were not simply grounded in aesthetic principles. To continue clinging to sexual love in old age was generally regarded as ridiculous and unnatural behaviour. Apart from being sinful and immoral, or maybe because of that, late-in-life love-making was also seen as a dangerous deviation from one's psychological and physical integrity. Not only was it thought to be punished with madness or blindness,[5] but it was also believed to threaten and to shorten a man's life. It is no wonder, then, that many medieval authors endeavoured, more or less seriously, to take some care over this issue.

For these reasons, in literary, moral and philosophical writings, the love-related *carpe diem* topos, sanctioned while one was still young, was replaced immediately by widespread condemnation if intended to be put into practice during later ageing. Medieval works urged readers to make the most of love in youth and, by contrast, to restrain themselves in old age, a period in life for which other more appropriate activities were recommended. Some authors tried to establish an expiry-date or age deadlines to demarcate limitations for the times during life to be liked and to love. In literature, this attitude contributed to constructing stereotypes of old people and the sexuality of the aged. However, whereas moral and philosophical writers gave physiological reasons for keeping the elderly away from sexual intercourse, the compilers of practical medical manuals often collected remedies that could serve both as an alternative and as a last resort when other suggestions did not achieve the desired effects.

Contemporary studies support the contention that an individual's sexuality does not age. In "Human Sexuality and the Aging," M.J. Pompeo holds that "the

---

[4] From *La Clef d'Amors*. See N.R. Shapiro (1997).
[5] See M.J. Carrillo Linares (2002).

sexual needs and desires of a human being do not undergo an abrupt change with advancing age" (*Social Casework* 57. 4 1979: 237). Nevertheless, it was generally assumed in classical literature that old age ought to imply parting with physical pleasures and that was, in fact, one of the *vituperationes* or complaints about this stage of life that Cato had to deal with in Cicero's dialogue *De senectute*.[6] We know, too, of Aristophanes' jokes on the sexual desires of old women[7] and, as C.C. Esler points out in "Horace's Old Girls: Evolution of a Topos," the Latin author was "unable to see beyond the assumptions of his culture to the possibility of sexual love in old age" (Falkner, and De Luce, eds. 1989: 179). This idea survived into medieval works, many of which are also full of ironic allusions to the incompatibility between old age and a fulfilling sexual relationship. For example, in Geoffrey Chaucer's *The Canterbury Tales*, the Wife of Bath comments on her three old and, of course, rich husbands, saying:

> The three were kindly men, and rich, and old.
> But they were hardly able to uphold
> The statute which had made them fast to me.
> You know well what I mean by this, I see!
> So help me God, I can't help laughing yet.
> Thinking of how at night I made them sweat
> [. . . .]
> Their land and wealth they had by then conferred
> On me, and so I safely could neglect
> Tending their love or showing them respect.
> (*The Canterbury Tales* 212-3)[8]

Likewise, in Rodrigo de Cota's *Dialogue Between Love and an Old Man*, a Spanish dramatic poem from the late-fifteenth century, the old man is subjected to scornful comments uttered by Love who, after having persuaded him to love again, laughs at the old man for being so naïve as to believe that he could still perform at his age:

> ¿Tú no miras tu figura
> y vergüenza de tu gesto?
> ¿Y no ves la ligereza
> que tienes para escalar?
> [. . . . .]
> ¡Quién te viese entremetido
> en cosas dulces de amores,

---

[6] See T.G. Parkin "Ageing in Antiquity. Status and Participation" (P. Johnson, and P. Thane, eds. 1998) 24. See also J. Pimentel Álvarez, ed. (1997).

[7] See M.I. Finley "Introduction" (T.M. Falkner, and J. De Luce, eds. 1989) 11. See also E. Henke, and M. Janek (2002).

[8] See Geoffrey Chaucer *The Canterbury Tales. The Portable Chaucer* (T. Morrison, ed. 1997). All further references are to this edition.

y venirte los dolores
y atravesarte el gemido!
¡O quién te oyese cantar:
Señora de alta guisa,
y temblar y gagadear,
los gallinos engrifar
tu dama muerta de risa!
¡O maldad envejecida!
¡O vejez mala de malo!
¡Alma viva en seco palo,
viva muerte y muerta vida!
Depravado y obstinado,
deseoso de pecar,
mira, malaventurado,
que te deja a ti el pecado,
y tú no le quieres dejar.
(*Biblioteca de Autores Españoles* 227)[9]

Isidore of Seville[10] and Ambrose[11] both agreed that the senses begin to diminish with man's decrepitude.[12] In *Growing Old in the Middle Ages*, Shulamith Shahar informs how in the fourteenth century, in his *Secretum*, Petrarch entered into an imaginary conversation with Saint Augustine of Hippo who wanted to convince the poet to keep himself apart from love and physical pleasures because he was an old man (1997: 19). Shahar also comments on how Christine de Pisan wrote that women's desires also cool in old age "because nature no longer inclines you to them" (1997: 78), and how Philip of Novare declared that "old women who continued to indulge in the sins of flesh were those who refused to acknowledge the fact of their ageing and kept sinning to prove themselves and to others that they were not yet old" (1997: 78). Hence, according to medieval moral and medical standards, it was the laws of nature that would make old people feel inclined to abandon sexual pleasures.

This was, in turn, desirable because, apart from the belief in the dangers of becoming blind or mad as a punishment from God for having out-of-date sex, in the Middle Ages sexual intercourse was also perceived as a life-threatening activity

---

[9] See Rodrigo de Cota's *Diálogo del Amor y un Viejo* (C. Aribau, ed. 1944. 226-7). All further references are to this edition.

[10] Born in Cartagena, Spain, ca.560; died 4th April 636. Isidore, Bishop of Seville, was one of the Latin Fathers. He exercised great influence on the educational life of the Middle Ages. The most important and best-known of all his writings is the *Etymologiae*, which gathers, systematizes, and condenses all learning from his time.

[11] Bishop of Milan from 374 to 397; born probably 340, in Trier, Arles or Lyons; died 4th April 397. He was a Doctor of the Church together with St. Augustine, St. John Chrysostom and St. Athanasius.

[12] See M.E. Goodich (1989) 146-7.

for elderly people. In "Physiology and Etymology," A. Blamires remarks that Andreas Capellanus[13] recalls "once reading in a medical treatise that sexual activity makes men senile earlier" (1992: 38), which suggests that the contention of Averroes[14] that "castrati outlive those who copulate" (Goodich 1989: 151), and of Arnold of Villanova[15] that mules outlive horses (Shahar 1997: 78), were commonplace ideas in medieval times. An explanation for this can be found in Peter of Spain's commentary on Aristotle in the thirteenth century; life was supposed to be supplied by sperm, in such a way that while men are young, they can retain, without much trouble, all the warmth and humidity they need to continue living. But after the age of forty-eight, he believed, along with other medieval writers like Arnold of Villanova, that the excessive emission of sperm was responsible for bringing about loss of blood, dryness and consequently, for accelerating death (Goodich 1989: 151). Therefore, those who preserved and did not waste sperm after that age were considered to be prone to enjoying better health and living longer than those who behaved otherwise. Moreover, it was women who were blamed for this; like Albert the Great[16] in his *On the Secrets of Women* (*De secretis mulierum*), many medieval writers held the common belief that "in an older woman whose menstrual system was deteriorating, baneful fluids seeking an outlet could be transmitted through the eyes and could poison."[17] To this was probably related the fact that, when procreation was no longer possible, sexual relationships with the ageing woman were negatively portrayed.

Bearing all these ideas in mind, it is not surprising that authors from the Middle Ages insisted on transmitting in their writings the assumption that the time span for men and women to be involved in sexual relationships should end with the coming of old age. In Rodrigo de Cota's *Dialogue Between Love and an Old Man*, the old man's initial, though not lasting, resistance to allegorical Love's charming temptations is the only reasonable attitude that will allow him to avoid getting into trouble at his age:

> Cerrada estaba mi puerta,
> ¿a qué vienes? ¿por dó entraste?
> Di, ladrón, ¿por qué saltaste
> las paredes de mi huerta.

---

[13] André le Chapelain, in Latin Andreas Capellanus, was the twelfth century author of a treatise entitled *De amore* (*On Love*).

[14] Arabian philosopher, astronomer, and writer on jurisprudence; born in Córdoba, 1126; died in Morocco, 1198.

[15] Medieval physician from the Crown of Aragon who taught at Montpellier (ca.1238-1311).

[16] Scientist, philosopher, and theologian; born ca.1206; died in Cologne, 15th November 1280. He is called "the Great" and "Doctor Universalis" (Universal Doctor) because of his genius and extensive knowledge.

[17] See A. Blamires (1992) 38.

> La edad y la razón
> ya de ti me han liberado
> [. . . . .]
> Tú nos metes en bullicio,
> tú nos quitas el sosiego,
> tú con tu sentido ciego
> pones alas en el vicio.
> Tú destruyes la salud,
> tú rematas el saber,
> tú haces en senectud
> la hacienda y la virtud
> y la autoridad caer.
> (*Biblioteca de Autores Españoles* 226)

Also to be found in Rodrigo de Cota's *Dialogue Between Love and an Old Man* is a melancholy description of a *locus amoenus*[18] that no longer exists. Vividly evoked, the *locus amoenus* is a bitter symbol of the ephemeral beauty and transitory character of youth and, consequently, of the time for love-making:

> Cuánto más que este vergel
> no produce locas flores,
> ni los frutos y dulzores
> que solías hallar en él.
> Sus verduras y follajes
> y delicados frutales
> [. . . . .]
> La beldad de este jardín
> ya no temo que la halles,
> ni las ordenadas calles,
> ni los muros de jazmín,
> ni los arroyos corrientes,
> de aguas vivas notables,
> ni las albercas y fuentes,
> ni las aves producientes
> de cantos tan consolables
> [. . . . .]
> Sal de este huerto, miserable;
> ve buscar dulce floresta;
> que tú no puedes en esta
> hacer vida deleitable,
> ni tú ni tus servidores
> podéis estar conmigo.
> (*Biblioteca de Autores Españoles* 226)

---

[18] *Locus amoenus* means 'pleasant place' in Latin. By Ovid's time it had become a poetic convention consisting in the description of an idyllic setting, where romantic encounters usually occur.

* * *

But old age was, and still is, a vague and imprecise term that greatly depends on personal perceptions and, therefore, on subjective factors. In "Ageing in Antiquity. Status and Participation," T.G. Parkin notes that in Plato's *Republic*, Cephalus observes that "most old people complain about their old age, but he puts their troubles down not to old age but to their characters" (Johnson, and Thane, eds. 1998: 23). In "Old age in the High and Late Middle Ages. Image, expectation and status," Shulamith Shahar states that in legal texts medieval people are considered to be entering old age at sixty (Johnson, and Thane, eds. 1998: 43), and in "The Merchant's Tale" in Geoffrey Chaucer's *The Canterbury Tales*, January rejects the idea of marrying a thirty-year-old woman, considering her to be too old.[19] By contrast, in *Julian of Norwich. A Revelation of Love*, it is reported that God infected Julian with a "bodily sickness in youth at thirty years of age"[20] and, again in *The Canterbury Tales*, the Wife of Bath does not really consider herself old at forty:

> He was, in fact some twenty winters old
> And I was forty to confess the truth;
> But all my life I've still had a colt's tooth.
> My teeth were spaced apart
> [. . . . .] and became me well.
> So help me God, I was a lusty one,
> Pretty and young and rich, and full of fun.
> (*The Canterbury Tales* 223)

Maybe not at forty, but by the time she joins the pilgrimage to St. Thomas Beckett's tomb at Canterbury, the Wife of Bath becomes nostalgic about former times in which she could fully adhere to the dictum of *carpe diem*. At her current, more advanced age, however, the *ubi sunt* topos that applies to youth and beauty takes its place instead, as a lament on their ephemeral nature:

> But, Lord Christ, when it all comes back to me,
> Remembering my youth and jollity,
> It tickles me to the roots. It does me good
> Down to this very day that while I could
> I took my world, my time, and had my fling.
> But age, alas that poisons everything,
> Has robbed me of my beauty and my pith.
> Well, let it go! Good-bye! The devil with what cannot last.
> (*The Canterbury Tales* 220)

---

[19] See T. Morrison, ed. (1997) 269.
[20] Translated from the Middle English "bodily sekenesse in youth at XXX yeeres of age." See M. Glasscoe, ed. (1976) 1.

Maimonides[21] said that "an old woman is one who is called old and does not protest" (Shahar 1997: 13). The same could apply to men, as may be inferred from authors calling themselves old from the ages of thirty, forty-five, fifty, sixty or much later.[22] Notwithstanding these subjective impressions, or perhaps because of them, many attempts were made in the Middle Ages to guide people in the task of deciding what the *expiry date* for love was. Sometimes the preservation of health would be the authorial purpose while at other times a moral reason would underlie the argument. More often, both physical and spiritual preoccupation would merge. In the twelfth century, Andreas Capellanus wrote:

> And now let us see what people are apt for love [. . .]. Age makes love impossible after the age of 60 in men and after the age of 50 in women [. . .]. Similarly, a woman should not love before the age of twelve,[23] and a man should not love before he is fourteen. And I also say firmly that a boy cannot be a real lover before the age of eighteen. (*De Amore* I.V, 1-4)[24]

Generally concurring with these beliefs, the French poet Jean Froissart[25] declared that although old age actually began at fifty-eight, one is too old for love earlier, at thirty-five, and, according to Vincent of Beauvais,[26] despite the fact that some women are able to conceive a child up to the age of fifty, thirty-six is the average age for them to stop having children, after which a woman is old and not suitable for love.[27]

* * *

Perhaps more significant than these figures is the fact that old age was invariably associated with repulsive physical traits, clearly incompatible with any idea of

---

[21] Jewish commentator and philosopher, born of Spanish Jewish parents in Córdoba in 1135.

[22] See S. Shahar (1997) 19.

[23] "At *adolescentia*, regarded as twelve for girls and fourteen for boys, young people could marry according to canon law [. . .]." See D.T. Kline "Female childhoods" (C. Dinshaw, and D. Wallace, eds. 2003: 13).

[24] Translated from Latin: "*Est nunc videre quae sint aptae personae ad amoris arma ferenda* [. . .] . *Aetas impedit, quia post sexagesimum annum in masculo et post quinquagesimum in femina* [. . .] . *Similiter ante duodecim annos femina et ante decimum quartum annum masculus non solet in amore exercitu militare. Dico tamen et firmiter assero quod masculus ante decimum octavum annum verus esse non potest amans.*" See A. Le Chapelain, ed. (1964).

[25] Late fourteenth-century / early fifteenth-century French historian and poet.

[26] Thirteenth-century priest and encyclopedist.

[27] See S. Shahar (1997) 16-9.

desirability. As suggested by the Middle English poem "Tale of Florent" in John Gower's *Confessio Amatis*,[28] old age made women look more like men:

> Her lips for age were shrunk,
> There was no grace in the visage,
> Her front was narrow, her locks were gray with age
> [. . . . .]
> Her neck is short, her shoulders humped
> That might a man's lust disturb
> Her body great and nothing small,
> And shortly to describe her all,
> She has no limb without defect.
> (*Confessio Amatis. Book I.* 146)[29]

And, according to Roger Bacon,[30] old men were characterised by the following features: "White hair, pallor, wrinkling of the skin, excess of mucus, foul phlegm, inflammation of the eyes and general injury of the organs of sense, diminution of blood and spirits, weakness of motion and breathing in the whole body" (Shahar 1997: 37). As Rodrigo de Cota advises in his *Dialogue Between Love and an Old Man*, when physical or biological deterioration becomes so apparent, it is high time to refrain from sexual pleasures:

> ¡Viejo triste entre los viejos,
> que de amores te atormentas,
> mira cómo tus artejos
> parecen sartas de cuentas;
> y las uñas tan crecidas,
> y los pies llenos de callos,
> y tus carnes consumidas,
> y tus piernas encogidas
> cuales son para caballos!
> (*Biblioteca de Autores Españoles* 227)

Indulging in sexual pleasures in old age would have denoted devious behaviour and endangered the elderly person's physical and moral integrity. Hence, the natural attitude for an aged person to adopt was to find pleasure somewhere else – for example, in philosophy, as Plato suggests in his *Republic*;[31] in gardening and agriculture, as stated by Cicero in *De senectute* (Rosenthal 1996: 178); in

---

[28] See G.C. Macaulay, ed. (1900-1901) and R.A. Peck, ed. (2000).

[29] Translated from John Gower's Middle English "Tale of Florent," lines 1683-1691. See R.A. Peck, ed. (2000).

[30] Philosopher, surnamed *Doctor mirabilis*; born in Ilchester, Somerset, ca.1214; died in Oxford, perhaps 11th June 1294.

[31] See T.G. Parkin "Ageing in Antiquity. Status and Participation" (P. Johnson, and P. Thane, eds. 1998) 23.

eating and drinking, as recommended by Andreas Capellanus (Shahar 1997: 16), and in music and reading the Scriptures, according to Arnold of Villanova (Shahar 1997: 40). If none of these worked, remedies based on medicinal plants and other natural substances were then available to assuage unnatural sexual desires. Some examples can be drawn from the *Circa instans* or *Book of Simple Medicines*, which was a popular manual on simple drugs in the Middle Ages. One of its Middle English translations states that *Agnus castus*, more commonly known as the chaste tree, helped to make "a man chaste, [for] a bed made thereof abates a man's lust and liking,"[32] that is, it suppresses sexual desires. Another cure "to abate a man's liking that he has to women" consisted in letting him "smell camphor, and it will abate his lust."[33] But even though abstinence was the most efficient as well as the most highly-encouraged solution, when the old person did not stick to it, which was probably not infrequent, the plant *satirion*[34] and the fish *stincus*[35] were thought to be able to increase man's *kynde* or sperm, in order to counteract the loss of it, which was believed to shorten life.

* * *

The young knight in the story from the *Gesta Romanorum* killed the old knight because "it had been more convenient for me to have had this young woman, and the other man my wife."[36] Marriages between people with a big age difference were morally and medically discouraged in the Middle Ages. Had the Wife of Bath married the three old men while she was still young, it would have been for neither love nor sex; only money would have given any sense to such relationships. In the same way, now as an elderly woman, the situation is inverted because, as she herself says, although "my fifth (husband) [. . .] / I took for love not money," it was he, the young one, who benefited from her possessions: "To him I gave lands, titles, the whole slate / of goods that had been given me before" (Morrison, ed. 1997: 221). In his *Dialogue between Love and an Old Man*, Rodrigo de Cota aimed at showing that nothing can make an old man enjoy youthful pleasures again, let

---

[32] Translated from the Middle English: "Agnus castus: [. . .] his vertu is to make a man cast. A bed imad þerof abatiþ a mannys lust and liking." See M. Platearius. *Middle English Circa instans*. MS. CUL Ee. 1.13, f. 4r.

[33] Translated from Middle English: "To abate a mannys likyng þat he haþ to wymmen, let him smil to camphor and hit woll abat his luste." See M. Platearius. *Middle English Circa instans*. MS. CUL Ee. 1.13, f. 20r.

[34] "Satirion: His vertu is to enkrece a mannes kynd." See M. Platearius. *Middle English Circa instans*. MS. CUL Ee. 1.13, f. 83v.

[35] "Stincus is a fisch [. . .] and his vertu is to enkrese a mannys kynd, but he schal not be vsed in grete quantite for harmyng." See M. Platearius. *Middle English Circa instans*. MS. CUL Ee. 1.13, f. 84v.

[36] Translated from Middle English: "þat hit had be more conuenient me to haue had this yonge woman, and þe oþer man my wif." See S.J.H. Herrtage, ed. (1879) 61.

alone love-making. This is probably Pandarus's underlying reason in Geoffrey Chaucer's *Troilus and Criseyde* for warning Criseyde by saying:

> Think that in each of you, from hour to hour,
> There is some part of beauty laid to waste
> By the advance of age; ere Time devour
> You, *love!* When you are old, there's none will haste
> To love you; there's a proverb to my taste:
> "'*Aware too late,' said Beauty, as she passed*"
> And age will cure disdain in you at last.
> (*Troilus and Criseyde* II. 57)[37]

Works cited

Aribau. C., ed. *Biblioteca de Autores Españoles*. Madrid: Atlas, 1944.

Blamires, Alcuin, ed. *Woman Defamed and Woman Defended: Anthology of Medieval Texts*. Oxford: Clarendon Press, 1992.

—. "Physiology and Etymology." *Woman Defamed and Woman Defended: Anthology of Medieval Texts*. Ed. A. Blamires. Oxford: Clarendon Press, 1992: 38-45.

Carrillo Linares, María José. "Pecados y penas: vejez y pensamiento científicos medieval." [Paper read at the XIV Congreso de la Sociedad Española de Literatura General y Comparada (SELGYC). Alcalá de Henares: Universidad de Alcalá de Henares, 2002.]

Chaucer, Geoffrey. *Troilus and Criseyde*. Trans. N. Coghill. Harmondsworth: Penguin, 1971.

—. *The Canterbury Tales. The Portable Chaucer*. Trans. and ed. T. Morrison. Harmondsworth: Penguin, 1997.

Coghill, Nevill, trans. *Troilus and Criseyde*. Harmondsworth: Penguin, 1971.

de Cota, Rodrigo. "Diálogo del Amor y un Viejo." *Biblioteca de Autores Españoles*. Ed. C. Aribau. Madrid: Atlas, 1944: 226-7.

Dinshaw, Carolyn, and David Wallace, eds. *The Cambridge Companion to Medieval Women's Writing*. Cambridge: Cambridge UP, 2003.

Esler, C.C. "Horace's Old Girls: Evolution of a Topos." *Old Age in Greek and Latin Literature*. Eds. T.M. Falkner, and J. De Luce. Albany: State U of New York P, 1989: 172-82.

Falkner, T.M., and J. De Luce, eds. *Old Age in Greek and Latin Literature*. Albany: State U of New York P, 1989.

Finley, M.I. "Introduction." *Old Age in Greek and Latin Literature*. Eds. T.M. Falkner, and J. De Luce. Albany: State U of New York P, 1989: 1-20.

Glasscoe, Marion, ed. *Julian of Norwich. A Revelation of Love*. Exeter: U of Exeter, 1976.

Goodich, M.E. *From Birth to Old Age. The Human Life Cycle in Medieval Thought, 1250-1350*. Lanham, New York and London: UP of America, 1989.

---

[37] See N. Coghill, trans. (1971).

Hanawalt, Barbara A. "Widows." *The Cambridge Companion to Medieval Women's Writing*. Eds. C. Dinshaw, and D. Wallace. Cambridge: Cambridge UP, 2003: 58-69.

Henke, E., and M. Janek. "Women and Aging in Antiquity." <http://www.muohio.edu/~delucej/senectus/essays/henke.html> 26 May 2002.

Herrtage, S.J.H., ed. "Caclides. Of a Young Knight Who Slew an Old Knight and Married his Widow." *Early English Versions of the* Gesta Romanorum. London: Trübner, 1879: 61-3.

Johnson, P., and P. Thane, eds. *Old Age from Antiquity to Post-Modernity*. London and New York: Routledge, 1998.

Kline, D.T. "Female childhoods." *The Cambridge Companion to Medieval Women's Writing*. Eds. C. Dinshaw, and D. Wallace. Cambridge: Cambridge UP, 2003: 13-9.

Le Chapelain, A., ed. *Andreas Capellanus. De Amore*. Munich: Eidos Verlag, 1964.

Macaulay, G.C., ed. *Confessio Amatis. Book I. The English Works of John Gower*. London: Early English Text Society, 1900-1901.

Morrison, T., trans. and ed. *The Canterbury Tales. The Portable Chaucer*. Harmondsworth: Penguin, 1997.

Parkin, T.G. "Ageing in Antiquity. Status and Participation." *Old Age from Antiquity to Post-Modernity*. Eds. P. Johnson, and P. Thane. London and New York: Routledge, 1998: 19-42.

Peck, R.A. *John Gower. Confessio Amantis. Vol. 1*. Kalamazoo: TEAMS, 2000.

Pimentel Álvarez, J., ed. *Catón el Mayor: De la Vejez (Marco Tulio Cicerón)*. Mexico DF: Universidad Nacional Autónoma de México, 1997.

Platearius, M. *Middle English Circa instans*. MS. CUL Ee. 1.13, ff.1-91.

Pompeo, M.J. "Human Sexuality and the Aging." *Social Casework* 57. 4 (1979): 237-44.

Rosenthal, J.T. *Old Age in Late Medieval England*. Philadelphia: U of Pennsylvania P, 1996.

Shahar, Shulamith. *Growing Old in the Middle Ages. "Winter Clothes us in Shadow and Pain."* Trans. (Hebrew) Yael Lotan. London and New York: Routledge, 1997.

—. "Old age in the High and Late Middle Ages. Image, expectation and status." *Old Age from Antiquity to Post-Modernity*. Eds. P. Johnson, and P. Thane. London and New York: Routledge, 1998: 43-63.

Shapiro, Norman R., trans. *The Comedy of Eros: Medieval French Guides to the Art of Love*. 1971. Notes and commentaries James B. Wadsworth, and Betsy Bowden. 2nd edition. Chicago: U of Illinois P, 1997.

Ripeness is Gall:

Images of Ageing in the Theatre of Edward Bond

Pere Gifra Adroher

Over the last few decades Edward Bond has been one of the British playwrights who has intensively cultivated a politically committed drama whose progressive views, constant experimentation and multiple registers trigger reflections and point towards a gradual transformation of society.[1] The main themes in his plays often revolve around issues that affect us both as individuals and as a group: power, injustice, tyranny and all forms of violence, whether personal, social or institutionalised. Furthermore, one of his lifelong goals has been to denounce the dehumanisation of society and the alienating effects of capitalism on the individual, and he has done so through the cultivation of what he terms "rational theatre," that is, a theatre of ideas not only geared at presenting situations but at proposing ways of transforming them.[2] Through prologues, essays and stage debates, as well as through the observation of his characters both as individuals and representatives of a given social class, Bond has been particularly concerned with the social and political factors that domesticate, brutalize or numb citizens' critical consciousness. In short, he has painstakingly focused on the oppression and the transformations

---

[1] Despite its apparent bitterness, Edward Bond's theatre is positively humanistic rather than despairingly nihilist. "We begin to lose our humanity. The affluent Utopia becomes a prison," Bond has warned in a recent collection of essays. "In earlier times stories of gods and demons related their people to their world in a more humane way than our supermarkets and machines relate us to ours. Perhaps we will go on being less cruel but we are no longer the guides to our own existence" (2000: 4).

[2] Edward Bond provides a succinct description of this type of drama in one of his notebook entries. "By R[ational] T[heatre] I do not mean that we should have discussion plays. Nor do I mean that we should abolish emotion from our plays, either between the people on the stage or between the audience and the stage. On the contrary, the RT can be very emotional," he observes. "To understand RT we have first to go outside the theatre. We have to look at the physical nature of the universe, and at our species and our societies . . . . The RT is founded on the proposition that human beings can understand themselves and their society rationally – and that the solutions to these problems can be understood" (2001: 36).

that from childhood to old age human beings suffer under the hidden mechanisms of power or the inertia of the great historical processes.

For Edward Bond, old age is one of the phases of life that remains more exposed to the unjust social order that prevails in many other spheres of society, and even though on certain occasions the representation of his ageing characters appears linked to familial or institutionalised power, in general his images of old age resist sublimation, idealization or stereotyping and rather take the audience to a universe where ageing men and women alike fall prey to injustice, neglect and mistreatment. Ageing, in other words, is not for Bond what Paul and Margaret Baltes have termed "successful aging," that is, "an opportunity to begin again, to regain control over one's life and to reacquire one's own voice" (Baltes, and Baltes, eds. 1990: 4). On the contrary, it is rather just another one of the many trials that his characters have to endure throughout their lives in a hostile, capitalistic world seeking regeneration. In one of the most quoted lines from Shakespeare's *King Lear*, Gloucester affirms that "Ripeness is all."[3] Conversely, for many of the old characters in Edward Bond's best-known plays ripeness is affliction, it is gall. The bitterness present in Bond's representations of male and female elders, however, far from constituting a bleak perspective on the ageing process itself, becomes the playwright's own way of renewing our attention to an often neglected stage of life, one which he aptly endows with meaning by making his elderly characters play out acts of resistance whose mission is to transfer wisdom, hope and social responsibility to the upcoming generations.

* * *

Bond's first images of ageing date back to the early years of his dramatic career, a period marked by a crude naturalism and several polemical cases of censorship. *The Pope's Wedding* (1962),[4] his first performed play, set in a small community of East Anglia, presents the character of Alen, a seventy-five-year-old recluse living in a remote shack cluttered with tins and newspapers. Alen is looked after by Pat, who once promised her dying mother that she would take care of him, but at the end of the play she cannot avoid his murder by her husband Scopey, a by-product of a sick social environment capable only of generating gangs of careless derelicts. The negative social perception of ageing reflected in Scopey and his friends and revealed through their mockery of Alen not only affects the old man's identity but eventually claims his life. Similarly, in *Saved* (1965),[5] which chronicles the grim life of a modest South London family, Bond includes sixty-five-year-old Harry as the person who tries to bring some stability into a shaken household. His daughter's neglected baby has been killed by a gang of hooligans in the park, the

---

[3] William Shakespeare. *King Lear* V. 2.
[4] See Edward Bond. *Plays: One* (1977) 226-308.
[5] See Edward Bond. *Plays: One* (1977) 19-133.

whole family sits mesmerized in front of the television, and yet by the end of the play he stands as an old representative, albeit a frail one, of the resilience of the working class in the face of adversity. If we leave aside the meaningless tragedies recounted in both texts, a common point already seems to be arising from Bond's early texts, namely, that the relationship between old and young people, for better or worse, will eventually change the life of the latter in a socially-significant manner.

One of the most sustained and memorable image of ageing in Bond's early dramatic career, however, appears in *The Sea* (1973)[6] through the fussy and domineering Mrs. Rafi. The leader of a group of gossiping ladies in a provincial coastal town where certain strange events have happened, Mrs. Rafi's perception of herself, her role in the community and of her influence is initially self-assured:

> I'm afraid of getting old. I've always been a forceful woman. I was brought up to be. People expect my class to shout at them. Bully them. They're disappointed if you don't. It gives them something to gossip about in their bars. When they turn you into an eccentric, it's their form of admiration. Sometimes I think I'm like a lighthouse in their world. I give them a sense of order and security. My glares mark out a channel to the safe harbour. I'm so tired of them. I'm tired of being a side-show in their little world. Nothing else was open to me. (*Plays: Two* 160)

Yet in contrast to this self-confidence and sense of empowerment, by the end of the play Mrs. Rafi comes to realize that her capacity to influence her fellow townsfolk is greatly diminished. She proceeds with a dreadful depiction of ageing that could appropriately exemplify what Richard Posner has termed the "pitiless" representation of the psychology of the old (1995: 100), for the loquacity she so admirably manifests throughout the play sadly betrays an acrid disillusionment:

> I'll grow old and shout at them from a wheel-chair. That's what they're waiting for. They get their own back for all the years that I've bullied them. They wheel you where they like. 'Take me there.' 'You went there yesterday. We want to go the other way.' 'Take me down to the beach. I want to see the sea.' 'You don't want to see the sea. You saw the sea yesterday. The wind's bad for your head. If you misbehave and catch a cold we'll shut you up in bed. You'll stay there for good this time.' . . . You give up shouting. You close your eyes and the tears dribble down your ugly old face and you can't even wipe it clean – they won't give you your hanky . . . . There you are: old, ugly, whimpering, dirty, pushed about on wheels and threatened. (*Plays: Two* 161)

While Bond no doubt makes Mrs. Rafi voice the powerlessness that some senior citizens may feel at the end of their lives, her dramatic description of ageing at the same time foreshadows the demise of a certain worldview – that of the social networks interwoven by the daily face-to-face interaction of townsfolk. Her evil

---

[6] See Edward Bond. *Plays: Two* (1978) 103-69.

forebodings notwithstanding, she still retains her independent spark of intelligence and by the end of the play advises Rose, one of the young characters, to leave and start a new life away from town – the one she herself would like to have lived – before it becomes too late.

* * *

The somewhat veiled pessimism present in *The Sea* turns into a much darker atmosphere in two other works premiered in the same year, *Lear* (1973)[7] and *Bingo* (1973),[8] in which Bond pays homage to and argues with one of the playwrights that have influenced his drama most significantly, namely, William Shakespeare. In Bond's *Lear*, the Shakespearean senile monarch is presented as a dictator obsessed with the construction of a wall to protect the country from his enemies. But his cruellest foes are his three daughters; Bodice and Fontanelle enjoy torturing Lear's counsellor, old Warrington, and Cordelia leads a populist movement that, in an attempt to free the people, paradoxically wreaks havoc and plunges the country into even greater chaos. Once his plight becomes utterly manifest, Lear exclaims:

> My daughters have taken the bread from my stomach. They grind it with my tears and the cries of famished children – and eat. The night is a black cloth on their table and the stars are crumbs, and I am a famished dog that sits on the earth and howls. I open my mouth and they place an old coin on my tongue. They lock the door of my coffin and tell me to die. My blood seeps out and they write in it with a finger. I'm old and too weak to climb out of this grave again. (*Plays: Two* 31)

The poetic language of his words cannot belie the terrible condition of the ageing man speaking here, turned into an outcast both of family and country. Lear's declamation shocks not only because what he describes is literally impossible but also because it shows the extent to which parenting is a sacrifice of everything and the greed and lack of gratefulness of the young generation. However, the frightening image of old age employed here – a man buried alive in a locked coffin – is even further reinforced later by means of yet another crude torture – someone being buried alive in a wall:

> What can I do? I left my prison, pulled it down, broke the key, and still I'm a prisoner. I hit my head against a wall all the time. There's a wall everywhere. I'm buried alive in a wall. Does this suffering and misery last forever? Do we work to build ruins, waste all these lives to make a desert no one could live in? There's no one to explain it to me, no one I can go to for justice. I'm old, I should know how to live by now, but I know nothing. I can do nothing, I am nothing. (*Plays: Two* 94)

---

[7] See Edward Bond. *Plays: Two* (1978) 1-102.
[8] See Edward Bond. *Plays: Three* (1987) 1-66.

Echoing the famous lines on nothingness from the opening scene of Shakespeare's *King Lear*,[9] the senescent tyrant certifies here both his political and personal obliteration, but by the end of the play he will muster enough strength against all odds to reach again the obsession of his lifetime, the wall, and once there dig into it with a shovel three times in an attempt to redress his own actions and set an example for the new generations.

Lacking the epic tone of *King Lear*, the final years in a person's life are represented less heroically in *Bingo*. In this play, Bond portrays Shakespeare as an old man, retired to his country estate, who supports the local landowners near Stratford in their attempt to enclose the land against the rights of the poorer farmers. Shakespeare sits passively at home doing nothing to change this social injustice, but at the end of his life he will pay morally for the consequences of his inaction with the breaking apart of his family. The rhetorical question "Was anything done?" that echoes now and then in key passages throughout the play, reflects the emptiness of the old bard. Bond's Shakespeare laments the wasted years of his youth – "I spent so much of my youth, my best energy . . . for this: New Place. Somewhere to be sane in. It was all a mistake," and he feels nauseous as he regrets his past, sensing "a taste of bitterness in my mouth. My stomach pumps it up when I think of myself . . . I could have done so much" (*Plays: Three* 62). After an apparently successful career, the writer-turned-capitalist entrepreneur realizes that, in old age, his former bliss has become loneliness and that he has failed society as an intellectual. The bitterness in the old man's mouth figuratively induces the gall that arises from mixed feelings experienced by an uncommitted man morally torn apart.

* * *

One of the best plays to examine Bond's views on ageing, however, is *Summer* (1982),[10] not only because it is located halfway in Bond's theatrical career and continues to examine some of the recurrent topics that characterize his drama – violence, death, war, injustice – but because the main characters in it are three senior citizens haunted by their experiences of World War II. Set in an indefinite coastal town of eastern Europe that begins to receive the impact of mass tourism, *Summer* poses serious questions through a simple, mysterious plot. Xenia, an old woman who resides in Britain, returns to her native town to enjoy the summer in the company of her daughter Ann. They are to spend the holidays in her old family house, which after the war was transformed into flats where now live Marthe, a former maid of the family, her son David, and other residents. In principle, this resembles a nostalgic episode out of a Chekhovian play, but what ought to be another placid summer sojourn this time becomes for the protagonists a poignant

---

[9] "Nothing will come of nothing: speak again." See William Shakespeare. *King Lear* I. I.
[10] See Edward Bond. *Plays: 4* (1992) 349-404.

trip full of painful revelations. Ann will discover silenced aspects of her family's past such as the fact that her mother saved Marthe from being killed by the Nazis; Xenia, on the outcome of an unexpected conversation with a German tourist who had been stationed in the town during the war, will be compelled to accept the role of her social class before, during and after the war. In the meantime, sapped by a terminal illness before the helplessness of her son, a doctor at the local hospital, Marthe will ineluctably live her last summer revising a past still laden with bitterness.

The protagonists' secrets emerge slowly in the seemingly quiet locale of *Summer*, where the inevitable presence of some islands that had been a concentration camp during the war keeps history alive. The horrors of the last major European war already belong to the past, but for the three older characters in the play the reminiscences keep living on, act as catalysts of the tragedy and become, in short, inductors of universal antagonisms between social classes, the living and the dying, the young and the elderly. Bond's dramatic action is magnetic and advances thanks to these binaries and to the contrast of such ideas as justice and pity, life and death, civilization and barbarism, or capitalism and socialism, which achieve special significance in dialogues where the author presents an explicit thesis. Yet, what furthers the action in the play is the tension between the two ageing female characters, Xenia and Marthe, whose energetic personalities and obsession with the past betray Bond's indebtedness to Ibsen's drama. Forty years have gone by since the end of the war and it seems as though the new generations are not much interested in the past conflict. However, the lives of Xenia and Marthe, now in their sixties, continue to be branded by these horrid events and by the post-war wounds that have not yet been healed. Though less important, another character equally affected by World War II is the German elder, a disoriented, almost doddering vacationer that Bond seems to include in the play merely to trigger the discussion of ethical and political issues.

Edward Bond puts on stage two women who have been ageing with pent-up bitterness and latent scores to settle, yet significantly he does so in a context where the past is omnipresent: in the old house, on the islands visible from the terrace, even in the old ironmongery where Xenia nostalgically purchases some brushes that her grandmother used to buy to make presents before the war. Marthe and Xenia, however, are ageing with resentment mainly because, for Bond, they incarnate opposed, almost irreconcilable ways of understanding society. As Jenny Spencer has noted, "Bond's characters are always determined, in the last instance, by their environment. They are shaped by the social, familial and economic relationships which Bond so carefully articulates onstage" (Bigsby 1981: 130). Far from overcoming the traumas of the past, they become ideologically hardened and defend passionately the social class they belonged to before the war. As early as in Scene One, for example, Bond makes Xenia express attitudes inherited from the education that she received as a member of the richest family in town: her complaints about the service at the airports, her criticism against the vulgarity of early tourism, her still condescending attitude towards Marthe.

Xenia still lives in a world where she feels everyone must be thankful to her and seems to seek a moral compensation in the summers she spends in her hometown. But her meeting with the German war veteran reveals her implication with the deaths that took place on the island during the war, and now she will have to exonerate herself in the name of goodness, just as the old tourist justifies the German occupation for the sake of civilization and culture. Marthe, on the other hand, has never abandoned her status of survivor from the holocaust. Proud of the "second life" (*Plays: 4* 394) that she has been enjoying for forty years and of the local achievements she has contributed to, she finally welcomes the arrival of a retribution that consciously or unconsciously she had been expecting for decades. Her spitting at Xenia, one of the most dramatically charged images in *Summer*, is not addressed to Xenia herself, but to the class system that begot her and at the same time contributed, directly or otherwise, to the horrors of the war. As Bond puts it in one of the notebook entries he jotted down before drafting the play, this scene stands for "fifty thousand generations of servants spitting at their masters," so that "once this is done Marthe is free. The one thing she'd left undone, the one remnant of the old life, is gone – the trace of servant still left in Marthe is erased, now she can die in peace and contentment" (2001: 75).

Bond approaches Xenia neither with hatred nor indifference, but rather with the compassion of seeing her as bound to the past by class ties as Marthe has been tied to the present by her rancour. The difference between both ageing women, however, lies in their capacity to adapt to new scenarios, a capacity more developed in Marthe. Aware of the fortune that saved her from a sure death at the hands of the Nazis, Marthe has managed to use the subsequent years to build up a humble yet worthy life.[11] Quite to the contrary, Xenia has resided for almost four decades abroad enjoying an enviable standard of living, but paradoxically doing so almost as living dead. "The world was taken away from me," she says to herself. "I can't begin again. I've spent years pointing at my dead body – and no one sees it" (*Plays: 4* 394-5). Like the Shakespeare in *Bingo*, her words are dominated by the

---

[11] In one of the notebook entries on *Summer*, dated 17th September 1980, Edward Bond provides his own views on Marthe's ageing: "M is an active woman. She is now at a stage where she cannot act. She must be in the world as it has been made." He notes further:

> Old people seem to withdraw from the world into their memories; the slowly aging body can be kind to the old – though as we chuck out the old from our families the kindness of their body may become an affliction to them. But M is not very old – early sixties or so. She wants to be of use? What can she do – bless the young ones with her grace and beauty. For herself, she must be at peace . . . . Her child was not snatched from her arms by the butcher. She did not fall down, dying or dead, among the dead and dying. (2001: 63)

discourse of dissatisfaction. Marthe, to the contrary, utters the most emotive and poignant sentences in the play, perhaps as a tribute to the resilience of the working class and its ancient oral culture. "I am worn out," says Marthe as she describes her mood. "I listen to the air going in and out of my body. Like footsteps in a corridor. It's not easy: it's as if a crowd had to die" (*Plays: 4* 394). Despite the suffering, Marthe struggles and defies death, as Eva Figes points out in "Confronting the Past," "with peasant stoicism" (*Times Literary Supplement* Feb. 5, 1982: 133). She does not give in, she fights her own battle against her disease with dignity and resigned endurance, like a Shakespearean character, and her silent death leaves the legacy of a sincere and melancholy speech about life. "Don't give yourself to your enemies or neglect anyone in need. Fight," she advises to a receptive Ann a few minutes before she passes away. "I die so that you may live" (*Plays: 4* 399). Like Mrs. Rafi, Marthe may have been struck and defeated by the inevitable consequences of ageing, but in her final moments onstage she hands on the torch of hope to the next generation.

Edward Bond uses these two characters' bitter ageing as well as their obsession with the past to criticise the perversity of capitalism through social injustice and the class struggles it generates. Its harmful effects persecute everyone in a world where, according to the text, only the well-off can afford to be generous. Bond nevertheless rejects this social order and instead proposes a message of equity and struggle of which Marthe is the main spokesperson. "You can live without kindness, you can't live without justice – or fighting to get it," says Marthe to Ann. "If you try to you're mad. You don't understand yourself or the world. And then nothing works. You and everyone else suffer the consequences of your madness. Whole generations bleed for it" (*Plays: 4* 370). Ian Stuart explains how this Manichean division of society between despicable bourgeois and good proletarians caused some disagreements between Anna Massey and Bond during the rehearsals before the London opening of the play; Anna Massey wished to show Xenia's positive traits whereas Bond insisted on the impossibility of redeeming her and forgiving her as a member of an oppressing class. What Xenia wanted to do did not matter, maintained Bond; facts are what really matters in the long run, and this is the reason why Marthe judges her so strongly several decades later.[12] The same attitude pressed James Fenton in "The Deadly and Divided World of Edward Bond" to write a scathing review of *Summer* in which he termed Bond a pessimist devoid of clear ideological goals to build a new society, also accusing him of having a "Khmer rouge mentality" in a world where "you are to be condemned . . . not for what you do but for where you come from" (*The Sunday Times* Jan. 31, 1982: 40).

* * *

---

[12] See T. Shank, ed. (1996) 69-70.

The representation of ageing both as a powerful dramatic issue and effective ideological battleground has continued to be present in Bond's subsequent works, albeit never with the intensity displayed in *Summer*. Ironically, many of his later plays, such as *Jackets* (1990),[13] *Tuesday* (1993) and *At the Inland Sea* (1996), address instead the world of children and youngsters in an attempt to make the new generations conscious of the need to transform society. This of course does not necessarily entail Bond's rejection of the elderly as useless agents of social change, but possibly reveals strategic ideological changes as well as a certain degree of disenchantment experienced by the playwright himself on the threshold of old age. He has nevertheless come up now and then with characters or scenes associated with the problems of ageing. Take, for example, the ferocious realism of *In the Company of Men* (1989),[14] a play dealing with the cynicism and power struggles in the world of top executives. Oldfield, a weapons manufacturer in his early sixties, cannot do anything to avoid the takeover of his business by his adopted son Leonard, who is ill-advised by his stepfather's main competitor and his cunning secretary. Bond once again represents his ageing character following the Lear paradigm, that of the oppressor oppressed, for Oldfield is a ruthless executive obsessed with a lifelong, Spartan mission of public service, but such candid ideals eventually make him vulnerable among big business sharks. "Young people must turn against their elders, everyone knows that," Oldfield tells Leonard at one point. "They fight each other to the finish so they can get away from each other. It's like a curse on us" (*Plays: 5* 391). Ironically, what he does not know is that his words will prove prophetic and he will lose not only his business but ultimately also his life.

* * *

The theatre of Edward Bond contains numerous instances of physically and emotionally distressed old people, but on the whole it does not succumb to the hopelessness present in other forms of modern drama. In the "Introduction" to a recent book on literary representations of ageing, Maria O'Neill and Carmen Zamorano have stressed the optimistic message carried by many contemporary works which celebrate the human obstinacy to die. They remark how "it is appreciating and savouring the quality of the going and not merely the arriving that makes for successful ageing" (O'Neill, and Zamorano, eds. 2002: 10). Bond's plays fit quite suitably into this type of literature. His rational theatre sets his older characters up to take the blows of old age in order to argue two points of view about the ageing process, namely, that it is both a period of triumphant resolve and also a time of extreme vulnerability to whatever may come after. His old characters for the most part are tenacious, obstinate men and women who stand fast and even in the last moments of their lives take action; however, they are victims, anti-

---

[13] See Edward Bond. *Plays: 5* (1996) 239-328.
[14] See Edward Bond. *Plays: 5* (1996) 329-428.

heroes on a hostile journey with hardly any respite on the way. They may not age successfully, but they surely age in a courageous, sometimes epic manner. As Michael Mangan has observed, "Bond's plays comprise in effect one long, and as yet unfinished poem," that is, "the story of what it costs to find our humanity" (1998: 95-6). In a western world increasingly affected by the dehumanization as well as by the gerontification of society, Bond's images of ageing, for all their negativity and despite their tinge of gall, stand as a tribute to the human condition and its capacity to endure the personal and collective setbacks that ceaselessly shape our lives.

Works cited

Baltes, Paul B., and Margaret M. Baltes, eds. *Successful Aging. Perspectives from the Behavioural Sciences*. Cambridge: Cambridge UP, 1990.

Bigsby, Christopher W.E. *Contemporary English Drama*. London: Arnold, 1981.

Bond, Edward. *Plays: One*. London: Methuen, 1977.

—. *Plays: Two*. London: Methuen, 1978.

—. *Plays: Three*. 1992. London: Methuen, 1987.

—. *Plays: 4*. 1992. London: Methuen, 2002.

—. *Tuesday*. London: Methuen, 1993.

—. *Plays: 5*. London: Methuen, 1996.

—. *At the Inland Sea: a Play for Young People*. London: Methuen, 1997.

—. *The Hidden Plot. Notes on Theatre and the State*. London: Methuen, 2000.

—. *Selections from the Notebooks of Edward Bond. Vol. Two: 1980 to 1985*. Ed. Ian Stuart. London: Methuen, 2001.

Fenton, James. "The Deadly and Divided World of Edward Bond." *The Sunday Times* (Jan. 31, 1982): 40.

Figes, Eva. "Confronting the Past." *Times Literary Supplement* (Feb. 5, 1982): 133.

Mangan, Michael. *Edward Bond*. London: Northcote House, 1998.

O'Neill, Maria, and Carmen Zamorano Llena, eds. *The Aesthetics of Ageing: Critical Approaches to Literary Representations of the Ageing Process*. Lleida: Edicions i Publicacions de la Universitat de Lleida, 2002.

Posner, Richard A. *Aging and Old Age*. Chicago: U of Chicago P, 1995.

Shank, Theodore, ed. *Contemporary British Theatre*. London: Macmillan, 1996.

Spencer, Jenny S. "Edward Bond's Dramatic Strategies." *Contemporary English Drama*. Ed. C.W.E. Bigsby. London: Arnold, 1981: 123-37.

Stuart, Ian. "Edward Bond and the Royal National Theatre." *Contemporary British Theatre*. Ed. T. Shank. London: Macmillan, 1996: 62-78.

Problem Columns and the Discourse of Masculine Ageing Anxieties in Britain

Eduardo de Gregorio Godeo

For some time now, men in Western societies are becoming more and more concerned about questions to do with their physical appearance and personal looks. As Mark Mishkind remarked in "The embodiment of masculinity. Cultural, psychological and behavioural dimensions" during the late eighties, "men are likely experiencing more body dissatisfaction, preoccupation with weight, and concern with physical attractiveness and body shape now than they did even two decades ago" (Kimmel 1987: 45). In particular, preoccupation with the physical and aesthetic effects of ageing and the progressive loss of young glamour is turning into an issue of apprehension and distress for many men, especially if one bears in mind "that these things do not start falling off at a late age, but early. From the age of 20 onwards there is a steady decline" (Rowman 1997: 155). As John Rowman stresses, many young men in Britain and America opt for individual counselling to overcome the psychological and social effects of early ageing. However, counselling about this topic is similarly prominent in other genres, including popular self-help books, TV shows, male-grooming commercials or problem pages in men's lifestyle magazines. Questions about masculine insecurities and social fears caused by the physical effects of age recur again and again in the counselling pages of these publications. In the United Kingdom, discourses on masculine ageing anxiety are constructed in part in the advice columns of men's magazines. Drawing upon Critical Discourse Analysis (henceforth CDA), close examination of a case study will shed light on the constitution and articulation of such discourses, highlighting the fundamental role of language in this process.

* * *

Men's magazines, problem columns and masculine anxieties in contemporary Britain

As evidenced in a number of market-research studies (*cf.* Smith 1996: 1-2; Jackson, Stevenson, and Brooks 2001: 30), men's lifestyle magazines have become the fastest-growing print-media sector in the UK since their inception in the mid-

1980s.[1] Titles like *Arena*, *Esquire*, *FHM*, *GQ*, *Maxim*, *Men's Health*, *Stuff for Men* and *XL for Men* have become most popular among men in Britain. These general-interest publications specialise in the masculine lifestyle, incorporating features on sport, health and fitness, fashion and grooming, sex and women, cars and travel. In "Boy's Own. Masculinity, style and popular culture," an early article on the subject, Frank Mort estimates that when this editorial sector started developing in Britain, men's lifestyle magazines were targeted at young male readers of twenty-five to thirty-five years of age[2] and, in *Men's Magazines. Market Report*, Phillippa Smith's trade research confirms this trend regarding the age of male consumers, reporting that as many as fifty-nine percent of the twenty-five to thirty-four-year-olds buy and read these magazines in the UK (1996: 32).[3] In *Men in the Mirror. Men's Fashion, Masculinity and Consumer Society*, Tim Edwards substantiates these opinions regarding the nature of the targeted readership when he maintains that the genre is marketed by means of:

> a quite specific and often fixed targeting of single, affluent, city-dwelling, high-earning and high-spending, primarily heterosexual men to the exclusion of all others: that is, all those who do not at least primarily aspire to this way of living or its values. (1997: 96)

In addition to interviews with famous male icons, how-to sections and advertisements for men's wear and accessories, drink, tobacco and high-tech, these magazines feature problem columns that emulate the longer-standing tradition of 'agony aunts' in women's magazines. Readers' questions delve into conflictive relationships, health matters, body care and personal looks. In fact, the repeated appearance of questions on ageing signifies men's concern about this matter. Male readers tend to look for suggestions on how to mitigate the effects of age both on the body, for example, hair loss, wrinkles, genital dysfunctions and decrease in sexual drive, and psychologically, manifested, for instance, in questions dealing with fear of fathering or reluctance to commit oneself to consolidating relationships through marriage.

* * *

---

[1] As reported by the Audit Bureau of Circulations in Britain on its website <http://www.abc.org.uk>, at the beginning of 2002 titles like *FHM* achieved a circulation of over 570,000 magazines per month.

[2] See Chapman, and Rutherford (1988) 211.

[3] According to the study, the number of readers diminishes considerably among older men. However, Phillippa Smith (1996) points out a significant increase in the number of younger male readers, reporting that sixty-five percent of the men consuming these magazines are in their early twenties.

Age, gender, identity and discourse: the instrumental value of CDA

The construction of discourses on masculine ageing anxiety in the problem columns of contemporary men's general-interest magazines in the UK is characterised by a close interrelationship between age and gender. Together with other variables such as class, race and ethnicity, age and gender are two fundamental factors in the constitution of an individuals' identity. In *Unmasking the Masculine. Men and Identity in a Sceptical Age*, Alan Petersen claims that, "increasingly, identity is seen as a discursive construction [. . .] and acts as a normative ideal for regulating subjects" (1998: 14) and, in *Discourse and Social Change*, Norman Fairclough has observed that, "discourse contributes first of all to the construction of what are variously referred to as 'social identities'" (1992a: 64). Identities, thus, come into being as individuals take up or resist the subject positions which are created by discourses.[4] In "Who needs 'identity'?" Stuart Hall expresses the view that "identities are thus points of temporary attachment to the subject positions which discursive practices construct for us" (du Gay, *et al.*, eds. 2000: 19).

Following the strong Foucaultian influence on contemporary discourse and cultural theory,[5] discourse may be envisaged as a form of socio-cultural practice of a linguistic nature or, as Christopher Candlin has put it in his "General editor's preface" to *The Construction of Professional Discourse*, as:

> a means of talking and writing about and acting upon worlds, a means which both constructs and is constructed by a set of social practices within these worlds, and in so doing both reproduces and constructs afresh particular social-discursive practices, constrained and encouraged in the overarching social formation. (Gunnarsson, *et al.*, eds. 1997: ix)

Discourses may be said to emerge as institutionalised uses of language occurring at different levels such as the disciplinary, the political or the cultural. However, as Bronwyn Davies and Rom Harré point out in "Positioning: the discursive production of selves," "there can also be discourses that develop around a specific topic, such as gender or class" (*Journal for the Theory of Social Behaviour* 20. 1

---

[4] Stuart Hall maintains that "discourse produces 'subjects' – figures who personify the particular forms of knowledge which the discourse produces. These subjects have the attributes we would expect as these are defined by the discourse: the madman, the hysterical woman, the homosexual [. . .]" (1997: 56). But in "The work of representation," Hall points out that the discourse also produces a *place for the subject* (i.e. the reader or viewer, who is also 'subjected to' discourse)" (1997: 56). As a result, different types of discourse construct different subject positions, which "are specific to discourse types and ideologically variable" (Fairclough 1989: 102).

[5] Considering Michel Foucault's classical and pioneering definition, discourses designate "the practices that systematically form the objects of which they speak" (1972: 49).

1990: 45). Therefore, if, as Jean Stilwell Peccei posits in "Language and age," ageing is "a socially constructed process" (Thomas, and Wareing, eds. 1999: 108) and if, as Heidi Hamilton maintains in "Discourse and ageing," ageing "is more complex than a simple biological category" (Schiffrin, Tannen, and Hamilton, eds. 2001: 569), then this may well account for the constitution of discourses structured around the meaning of ageing in different social formations.[6] This would explain the special sort of articulation of discourses on masculinity and age that takes place in the arena of men's magazines' counselling columns.

* * *

In this context, CDA has become a powerful instrument with which to investigate "how discourse is shaped by relations of power and ideologies, and the constructive effects discourse has upon social identities, social relations and systems of knowledge and belief" (Fairclough 1992a: 27). CDA will thus be an appropriate analytical tool to examine the constitution of discourses on masculinity and ageing in present-day Britain, considering the basic assumptions that, as Margaret Wetherell has observed, "masculinities are constructed through power relations" (Wetherell, ed. 1996: 323). On similar grounds, CDA may also be an invaluable analytical resource for examining discursive constructions of ageing as social processes subject to changing power relations in social formations. As Nikolas Coupland, Justine Coupland and Jon Nussbaum have put it in "Future prospects in lifespan sociolinguistics," "lifespan representations of the self [are] a negotiative arena in which competing and multidimensional formulations of personal and social experiences are set in opposition and worked through [discourse]" (Coupland, and Nussbaum, eds. 1993: 287).

In Fairclough's model of CDA,[7] "every discoursal instance has three dimensions: it is a spoken or written language text; it is an interaction between people, involving processes of producing and interpreting the text; and it is a piece of social action" (1992b: 10). In order to unveil the construction of discourses and the role of language in this process, critical discourse analyses describe textual features that happen to be significant in the interpretation of the production and consumption of discourses, which discourses are finally explained considering their social matrix and underlying ideology.[8]

* * *

---

[6] Jean Stilwell Peccei (1999) and Heidi Hamilton (2001) provide updated and thorough overviews of the different directions in research on the relations between ageing, language and discourse.

[7] See Fairclough 1989, 1992a, 1992b, 1995a and 1995b.

[8] "Critical discourse analysis itself has three dimensions: *description* of the text; *interpretation* of the interaction process, and their relationships to the text; and *explanation* of how interaction process relates to the social action" (Fairclough 1992b: 11).

Discursive constructions of masculine anxieties over ageing: case study

In order to examine the constitution of the discourse on masculinity and ageing in men's lifestyle magazines' counselling columns, a sample from an *FHM* problem page will be examined to reveal the structure of such a discourse at various discursive layers.[9]

a) The language of ageing apprehension: discourse as text

Various textual features account for the construction of a type of discourse to do with young men's deep preoccupation with the mitigation of the effects of age as a result of external pressures to keep young. To begin with, *lexis* is articulated on the basis of classification schemes to do with, for example, age – "I hit 25," "are the same age," "pass for younger," "I'm well into my thirties"; healthy or unhealthy lifestyle habits – "exercise," "hobbies," "social activities," "sleep," "wholesome and varied diet," "general well-being," "stressful lifestyle," "poor sleeping and eating habits," "too much booze," "lack of exercise," "workload"; facial decay – "knackered," "saggy [face]," "tired-looking," "double-chin," "jowls"; and the solutions to these problems – "firm up my face," "facial exercises," "cardiovascular workouts."

Verbal processes are significant within the discursive representation of young men's preoccupation with the effects of age on their personal looks.[10] The abundant use of relational processes in the male reader's question is indicative of his attempt to describe his anxiety regarding facial deterioration, as evidenced, for example, in expressions such as "I've *become* aware," "my mates *are* the same age," "but could easily *pass for* younger," "whereas my face *has become* saggy and tired-looking," "I'm well into my thirties," "I'm very conscious of my double-chin and jowls," "how knackered I *look*." In contrast, the counsellor's reply makes a more copious use of *material processes*, which provide readers with specific keys to act upon this problem, in recommendations such as "*scrutinise* your workload," "*aim for* a balance," "facial exercises *will help*," "*ensure* you *eat* a wholesome and varied diet." In fact, different aspects of modality in the reader's question have a key role in his representation as highly unconfident as a result of his facial decay.[11]

---

[9] The *FHM* problem page under study is presented in the Appendix.

[10] According to Michael Halliday, "our most powerful impression of experience is that it consists of 'goings-on'" (1994: 106) or processes. These verbal processes may be of different kinds: material, which have to do with acting and creating; mental, related to sensing and consciousness; relational, which refer to being and becoming; existential, representing that something exists or happens; of verbal type, which are processes of saying; and behavioural, typical of physical or psychological human behaviour.

[11] Following a classical definition by John Lyons, "modality is used by the speaker in order to express, parenthetically, his opinion or attitude towards the proposition that the sentence expresses or the situation that the proposition describes" (1977: 452).

That is the case of the hypothetical attitude projected by *could* in the formulation of his questions – "Are there any exercises I *could* do to firm up my face?" – and in the presentation of further information – "My mates are the same age but *could* easily pass for younger."

Directive speech acts in the form of imperatives – "*Scrutinise* your workload in relation to exercise, hobbies and social activities [. . .] and *aim* for a balance," "*Ensure* you sleep at least six hours per night and *eat* a wholesome and varied diet" – not only serve to provide the male reader with specific recommendations for improving his facial appearance, but also to make him aware of a number of social factors intervening in this process, namely, leisure, exercise, work, sleep and eating habits.[12] However, retaining something of its second-person meaning, the utilization of the generic "you" by the counsellor provides an impersonal tone to the reply, which contributes to the editorial board's attempt to extend the advice to a plurality of male readers who are assumed to have similar problems with early ageing, as with, for example, "*Your* appearance has a lot to do with general well-being," "A stressful lifestyle, poor sleeping and eating habits, too much booze and a lack of exercise have a hugely negative effect on how *you* look."[13]

Finally, various *cohesive resources* are also significant of this reader's anxiety due to the effects of early ageing on his face.[14] Thus, comparative reference such as "My mates are *the same* age but could easily pass for *younger*" helps the reader to contrast his premature ageing with his friends. In fact, ellipsis of the second term of comparative clauses to refer to himself constructs this man in a position of inferiority in relation to other men of the same age who do not suffer from this problem – "My mates are the same age [as me] but could easily pass for younger [than me]." Moreover, the use of adversative and concessive conjunctions is relevant in respect of the hindrances caused by the effects of ageing on his face at such an early age, as in, for example, "My mates are the same age *but* could easily pass for younger *whereas* my face has become saggy and tired-looking."

---

[12] According to George Yule, "actions performed via utterances are generally called speech acts" (1996: 47). In particular, "directives are those kinds of speech acts that speakers use to get someone else to do something" (1996: 54).

[13] "Generic *you* is typically an informal equivalent of *one* [. . .] . But *you* again retains something of its 2nd person meaning: it can suggest that the speaker is appealing to the hearer's experience of life in general, or else of some specific situation, as in: This wine makes *you* feel drowsy, doesn't it?" (Quirk, *et al.*, 1985: 354).

[14] Using an illustrative and metaphorical definition, Raphael Salkie compares cohesive devices with "the glue which holds different parts of a text together" (1995: x-xi).

b) Producing / interpreting distress over ageing in columns: discourse as interaction

Questions and answers like the sample analysed are published in men's magazines' advice columns as representative of ideal readers' concerns. Needless to say, the wide readership of men's magazines such as *FHM* contributes to the massive circulation of this form of discourse among young men in today's UK. Men's preoccupation with ageing and their subsequent clinging to the maintenance of a young appearance is consistent with the ideological repertoire of the 'New Man,' a prominent subject position constructed in various discourses on masculinity circulating in different forms of popular culture in Britain today, problem columns included. As Sean Nixon observes in *Hard Looks. Masculinity, Spectatorship and Contemporary Consumption*, in addition to adopting softer and more sensitive and caring attitudes towards women in the home, "this regime of looking was central to the distinctiveness of the 'new man' imagery as a whole" (1996: 201).

As David Wright claims in *A Textual and Ethnographic Study of Men's Magazines*, men's magazines in general, and counselling pages in particular, are "one cultural resource that provides young men with a means of doing the work of identity" (1999: 86). Individual questions and replies are selected and published by editorial boards as being representative of ideal readers' concerns.[15] Drawing upon the problem page as a genre, media discourse and the discourse of counselling, young men's early ageing and their preoccupation with physical attractiveness is thus problematized, assuming that many young men share the same worries and anxieties. Calling to mind the schemata articulating this genre, individual readers come to understand the conflictive situation experimented by young men undergoing the effects of anticipated ageing and having to resort to problem pages to overcome such crises of identity.[16] As it is, individual utterances activate the presupposition[17] that there exist social actors like friends, workmates and various other people – "*My mates* are . . . ," "*My boss* keeps teasing me and *people* quite often think . . . " – who exert great pressure on men so that they maintain a young appearance.

---

[15] In fact, the original questions are frequently manipulated, or even artificially produced, in an attempt to conform to a magazine's ideology. Ellen McCracken has detected echoes of similar editorial practice in women's magazines, where "the advice appears to be offered in the spirit of friendship as a means of remedying real problems when, in fact, the problems are often artificially stimulated or magnified" (1993: 57).

[16] "Schemata are said to be 'higher-level complex (and even conventional or habitual) knowledge structures,' which function as 'ideational scaffolding' in the organisation and interpretation of experience" (Brown, and Yule 1983: 247).

[17] "A presupposition is something the speaker assumes to be the case before making an utterance" (Yule 1996: 25).

c) Explaining men's anxieties over age: discourse as social practice

In order to understand the configuration of this type of discourse, it is imperative to consider the changing power relations between the genders in contemporary Britain, where men are undergoing an increasing pressure to keep a young look and pay attention to the effects of ageing on their bodies. As evidenced in the text, these tensions emerge in institutional settings like the workplace or in the course of conversations among male friends. Tim Edwards claims in this respect that:

> men are increasingly encouraged towards self-awareness via the impacts of the women's movements and gay movements which have equally challenged hegemonic notions of heterosexual masculinity [. . .]. It is easy to see feminism as the primary cause of male self-reflection. (1997: 73)

The social matrix of discourses like this may, therefore, be located in these challenges to patriarchal constructions of masculinity, as manifested, for example, in many heterosexual men's lack of interest in questions to do with personal looks, which traditionally have been associated with the realm of femininity. In popular-culture genres like men's lifestyle magazines, discourses like this embody ideological constructs of masculinity highly concerned about personal appearance, which has been accordingly reflected in consumption practices focusing on men. As stated by Laurence Goldstein in *The Male Body. Features, Destinies, Exposures*, "an explosive market economy has begun to prey upon male anxieties about growing older and losing that self-defining macho glamour" (1994: x). This emergence of questions about ageing, attractiveness or personal looks in genres like men's magazines' problem pages may, therefore, be contextualised within the constraints of cultures of consumption and spectatorship on contemporary masculinities in Britain.

* * *

Questions about ageing abound in the problem pages of men's lifestyle magazines in the UK, and the topic has also been recurrent in various popular-culture genres dealing with men and masculinity in the UK in the late nineties, for instance, in television series like *Men Behaving Badly* and *Men Only* (Channel 4) or radio programmes such as *The Locker Room Series* (Radio 4). In exploring the significance of attitudes towards ageing in the configuration of British cultural identities, Jo Croft considers in "Youth culture and age" that age is "an aspect of identity which powerfully reflects the particular character of life in any national culture and we can learn a lot about a nation's values and cultural practices by paying attention to the significance it attaches to certain life stages" (Storry, and Childs, eds. 1997: 165). Certain language mechanisms regulate the construction of discourses that have to do with contemporary men's deep preoccupation with ageing in institutionalised sites for the production of discourses on masculinity in Britain as are men's magazines.

Drawing upon CDA, the analysis of the sample from the *FHM* counselling column has shed light on the multidimensional constitution of the discourses of masculine ageing anxieties in contemporary Britain. In examining the interactions between discourse and age, Heidi Hamilton highlights the value of case studies and small-scale studies of discourse and cultural theory "as being able to investigate in a more in-depth fashion the interrelationships among a variety of discursive and social factors, leading to well-grounded research questions and methodologies that can be used in subsequent large-scale studies" (Schiffrin, Tannen, and Hamilton, eds. 2001: 572). Hence, a case study like the present one is validated in its attempt to unveil the internal mechanisms which conform discourses combining the interrelationship between masculinity and ageing.[18] As has been demonstrated, lexico-grammatical and cohesive options, together with coherence aspects of textual production and interpretation, not only reflect but also construct a discourse centred upon anxieties experienced by British young men as a result of early ageing. However, only a wider conception of discourse as social action may account for the inscription of masculine ageing anxieties into the practices of publication and the reading of problem columns in Britain today.

Works cited

Brown, Gillian, and George Yule. *Discourse Analysis.* Cambridge: Cambridge UP, 1983.

Candlin, Christopher N. "General editor's preface." *The Construction of Professional Discourse.* Eds. Britt-Louise L. Gunnarsson, *et al.*, London: Longman, 1997. ix-xiv.

Chapman, Rowena, and Jonathan Rutherford, eds. *Male Order: Unwrapping Masculinity.* London: Lawrence and Wishart, 1988.

Coupland, Nikolas, and Jon F. Nussbaum, eds. *Discourse and Lifespan Identity.* London: Sage, 1993.

Coupland, Nikolas, Justine Coupland, and Jon F. Nussbaum. "Future prospects in lifespan sociolinguistics." *Discourse and Lifespan Identity.* Eds. Nikolas Coupland, and Jon F. Nussbaum. London: Sage, 1993. 284-93.

Croft, Jo. "Youth culture and age." *British Cultural Identities.* Eds. Mike Storry, and Peter Childs. London and New York: Routledge, 1997. 163-200.

Davies, Bronwyn, and Rom Harré. "Positioning: the discursive production of selves." *Journal for the Theory of Social Behaviour* 20. 1 (1990): 43-63.

---

[18] As Norman Fairclough puts it, however reduced it may be, any linguistic instance counts as discourse and may be examined in terms of its three-dimensional nature, namely as text, interaction and social practice: "any part of any text can fruitfully be examined in terms of the co-presence and interaction of these constitutive processes" (1995a: 6).

Edwards, Tim. *Men in the Mirror. Men's Fashion, Masculinity and Consumer Society.* London: Cassell, 1997.

Fairclough, Norman. *Language and Power.* London: Longman, 1989.

—. *Discourse and Social Change.* London: Polity, 1992a.

—. "Introduction." *Critical Language Awareness.* Ed. Norman Fairclough. London: Longman, 1992b. 1-29.

—. *Critical Discourse Analysis. The Critical Study of Language.* London: Longman, 1995a.

—. *Media Discourse.* London: Edward Arnold, 1995b.

Fairclough, Norman, ed. *Critical Language Awareness.* London: Longman, 1992b.

Foucault, Michel. *The Archaeology of Knowledge.* London: Tavistock, 1972.

du Gay, P., *et al.*, eds. *Identity: A Reader.* London: Sage / Open University, 2000.

Goldstein, Laurence. *The Male Body. Features, Destinies, Exposures.* Ann Arbor: U of Michigan P, 1994.

Gunnarsson, Britt-Louise L., *et al.*, eds. *The Construction of Professional Discourse.* London: Longman, 1997.

Hall, Stuart "The work of representation." *Representation. Cultural Representations and Signifying Practices.* Ed. Stuart Hall. London: Sage / Open University, 1997. 13-64.

—. "Who needs 'identity'?" *Identity: A Reader.* Eds. P. du Gay, *et al.*, London: Sage / Open University, 2000. 15-30.

Hall, Stuart, ed. *Representation. Cultural Representations and Signifying Practices.* London: Sage / Open University, 1997.

Halliday, Michael A.K. *An Introduction to Functional Grammar.* 1985. London: Edward Arnold, 1994.

Hamilton, Heidi E. "Discourse and aging." *The Handbook of Discourse Analysis.* Eds. Deborah Schiffrin, Deborah Tannen, and Heidi E. Hamilton. Oxford: Blackwell, 2001. 568-89.

Jackson, Peter, Nick Stevenson, and Kate Brooks. *Making Sense of Men's Magazines.* Cambridge: Polity, 2001.

Kimmel, Michael S., ed. *Changing Men. New Directions in Research on Men and Masculinity.* London: Sage, 1987.

Lyons, John. *Semantics.* Cambridge: Cambridge UP, 1977.

McCracken, Ellen. *Decoding Women's Magazines. From* Mademoiselle *to* Ms. New York: St. Martin's P, 1993.

Mishkind, Mark E. "The embodiment of masculinity. Cultural, psychological and behavioral dimensions." *Changing Men. New Directions in Research on Men and Masculinity.* Ed. Michael S. Kimmel. London: Sage, 1987. 37-52.

Mort, Frank. "Boy's Own. Masculinity, style and popular culture." *Male Order: Unwrapping Masculinity.* Eds. Rowena Chapman, and Jonathan Rutherford. London: Lawrence and Wishart. 1988. 193-224.

Nixon, Sean. *Hard Looks. Masculinity, Spectatorship and Contemporary Consumption.* New York: St. Martin's P, 1996.

Petersen, Alan. *Unmasking the Masculine. Men and Identity in a Sceptical Age.* London: Sage, 1998.

Quirk, Randolph, *et al.*, *A Grammar of Contemporary English.* London: Longman, 1985.

Rowman, John. "Ageing men." *Healing the Male Psyche. Therapy as Initiation.* Ed. John Rowman. London and New York: Routledge, 1997. 155-60.

Rowman, John, ed. *Healing the Male Psyche. Therapy as Initiation.* London and New York: Routledge, 1997.

Salkie, Raphael. *Text and Discourse Analysis.* London and New York: Routledge, 1995.

Schiffrin, Deborah, Deborah Tannen, and Heidi E. Hamilton, eds. *The Handbook of Discourse Analysis.* Oxford: Blackwell, 2001.

Smith, Phillippa. *Men's Magazines. Market Report.* Hampton: Key Note, 1996.

Stilwell Peccei, Jean. "Language and age." *Language, Society and Power.* Eds. Linda Thomas, and Shân Wareing. London and New York: Routledge, 1999. 99-115.

Storry, Mike, and Peter Childs, eds. *British Cultural Identities.* London and New York: Routledge. 1997.

Thomas, Linda, and Shân Wareing, eds. *Language, Society and Power.* London and New York: Routledge, 1999.

Wetherell, Margaret. "Life histories / social histories." *Identities, Groups and Social Issues.* Ed. Margaret Wetherell. London: Sage / Open University, 1996. 299-361.

Wetherell, Margaret, ed. *Identities, Groups and Social Issues.* London: Sage / Open University, 1996.

Wright, David. *A Textual and Ethnographic Study of Men's Magazines.* Nottingham: U of Nottingham, 1999. [Unpublished PhD thesis]

Yule, George. *Pragmatics.* Cambridge: Cambridge UP, 1996.

Appendix

Sample analysed: *FHM*, September 1999, 304.

Q. Ever since I hit 25 last year I've become aware of how knackered I look. My mates are the same age but could easily pass for younger, whereas my face has become saggy and tired-looking. My boss keeps teasing me and people quite often think I'm well into my thirties. I'm very conscious of my double-chin and jowls – are there any exercises I could do to firm up my face?

TV, Northampton

A. Your appearance has a lot to do with general well-being. A stressful lifestyle, poor sleeping and eating habits, too much booze and a lack of exercise have a hugely negative effect on how you look. Scrutinise your workload in relation to exercise, hobbies and social activities, and aim for a balance. Facial exercises will help in addition to cardiovascular workouts. Ensure you sleep at least six hours per night and eat a wholesome and varied diet. (AL)

Willie's "Monkey Gland" or the Bio-Aesthetics of Ageing in the Poetry of W.B. Yeats

Rached Khalifa

> Yeats was one of those few whose history is the history of their own time, who are part of the consciousness of an age which cannot be understood without them.
> T.S. Eliot[1]

Age and sex are inescapable in Yeats. The poet's obsession with the debilitating effects of time and old age on poetic imagination and libidinal vigour is, curiously enough, expressed from the start of his poetic career. In an early poem "The Wanderings of Oisin" (1889),[2] Yeats relates a moving tale of a wandering hero, Oisin, who, following the Odyssean predicament, renounces a Circean world where "neither Death nor Change comes near us, [. . .] / Nor the grey wandering osprey Sorrow" (*The Poems* 363), that is to say, a world of immortality, and he chooses "to dwell in the [mortal] house of Fenians" and "be shaken with coughing and broken with old age and pain" (*The Poems* 386). Insofar as the poem adumbrates the poet's politics of "imaginative nationalism,"[3] it equally contours what would amount to an aesthetics and poetics of ageing in Yeats. Oisin insists that the "tale" of his deliberate preference for ageing and death over immortality must "live to be old like the wandering moon" (*The Poems* 355). In such a poetics, the story outlives history, the "tale" the "dusty deeds," as Yeats puts it in an earlier poem, "The Song of the Happy Shepherd" (*The Poems* 7). "The Wanderings of Oisin," in fact, comes to reinforce an early Yeatsian idea that "To the cracked tune that

---

[1] See Hall, *et al.*, eds. *The Permanence of Yeats* (New York: Collier Books, 1961) 307.

[2] W.B. Yeats. *The Poems*. Ed. Richard J. Finneran (New York: Macmillan, 1983) 355-88.

[3] "The Wanderings of Oisin" is a turning point in Yeats's poetic career. It adumbrates what he calls "imaginative nationalism" in contrast to what he denounces as "conscious patriotism" of the Young Irelanders. For further discussion of Yeats's aesthetic nationalism, see Edward Said's "Yeats and Decolonization" in *Culture and Imperialism* (London: Chatto and Windus, 1993: 265-87).

Chronos sings / Words alone are certain good" (*The Poems* 7). Yeats's wielding of aesthetic immortality and poetic autonomy as strategies against ageing and mortality prove to be most constant and consistent throughout his poetic career.

Another early poem, "The Lamentations of the Old Pensioner" (1890),[4] though drastically rewritten, presents once again a moving account of the ravages of time on the body and the community. The old persona has not only been corporeally disfigured by old age, but, more pathetically, has lost his place, his "chair," among the very same people who used to cherish his "company" before time had "transfigured" him. He has been ostracised by the community. That the account is placed in the mouth of an "old Wicklow peasant" (*The Poems* 621), as Yeats annotates, is not surprising in itself, but that the theme be poeticised by a poet in the prime of his youthfulness, that is, in full poetic blossom and sexual vigour, is no doubt striking and intriguing. It calls for investigation. We know that Yeats's belief in the poetic project bears something of messianic fervour, if not fanaticism, right from the outset of his career, while in his *Autobiographies* the awakening of sexual impulses in him at the age of seventeen are likened to the "bursting" of a "shell" (1980: 62). Yet this early obsession with old age and loss of imaginative stamina seems to operate within Yeats's juvenile solid conviction that "our intellects at twenty contain all the truths we shall ever find" (1980: 189). Nothing would reinforce this precocious awareness or truth more firmly in his poetic imagination than his own experience of ageing. In this early poetry, Yeats ostensibly hits upon an inexhaustible subject matter. In it, the poet's major themes are rehearsed before they are articulated more vigorously – if not so movingly – in the later poetry. The obsession with biological age and with the decline of both imaginative and sexual power would accrue with time.

* * *

The old peasant's "lamentations" about old age and "contemplations" of a Time disfiguring or, rather, transmogrifying the body into "a broken tree" in the "The Lamentations of the Old Pensioner"[5] are the expression of what would prove most obsessive in the Yeatsian imagination, that is, his "rage against old age" (*The Poems* 197). The "broken tree" in the following lines foreshadows the later "stick" in "Sailing to Byzantium" (*The Poems* 193) and "the old scarecrow" in "Among School Children" (*The Poems* 216). Yeats's xyloid metaphors of self-derision are tinted with a good measure of pathos. "The Lamentations of the Old Pensioner" ends with a vitriolic tirade on Time and old age:

> Though lads are making pikes again
> For some conspiracy,

---

[4] W.B. Yeats. *The Poems* (1983) 46.
[5] W.B. Yeats. *The Poems* (1983) 46.

And crazy rascals rage their fill
At human tyranny;
My contemplations are of Time
That has transfigured me.

There's not a woman turns her face
Upon a broken tree,
And yet the beauties that I loved
Are in my memory;
I spit into the face of Time
That has transfigured me.
(*The Poems* 46)

More accurately, Yeats should be talking of Time's "disfigurement" rather than "transfiguration" of the body in these lines. Mystical transfiguration and bodily self-transubstantiation would symbolically take place much later in the experience of the Byzantine "artifice of eternity" (*The Poems* 193). However, this should not conceal the fact that the poem does adumbrate the themes to come. It imposes temporality and rage "against old age" and "loss of theme" as fundamental issues in Yeats.[6]

The juxtaposition of the "lads" and the bitter old man in the quotation above, for instance, foreshadows quite obviously the exordium of the much later and ostensibly more mature "Sailing to Byzantium" (*The Poems* 193-4). Here the "aged man," though "but a paltry thing, a tattered coat upon a stick," still scornfully denounces those young "dying generations" because they are caught up in that "sensual music" of "whatever is begotten, born, and dies," and "all neglect monuments of unageing intellect" (*The Poems* 193). Although Yeats seems a little wisened with time here, and chooses to "whither into [the] truth" of aestheticism, as he states in an earlier poem tellingly entitled "The Coming of Wisdom with Time" (*The Poems* 94), this so-called state of wisdom and composure, does not always underlie the poetic mood of the old Yeats. Imaginative rejuvenation and vigour in him is something intimately associated with libidinal and sexual potency. Nowhere is this conflation of imaginative vigour with sexual prowess, "knowledge" with "power," more imaginatively portrayed than in the metaphor of

---

[6] In one of his last poems "The Circus Animals' Desertion," written about a year before his death, Yeats still complains about thematic penury:

I sought a theme and sought for it in vain,
I sought it daily for six weeks or so.
Maybe at last being but a broken man
I must be satisfied with my heart, although
Winter and summer till old age began
My circus animals were all on show.
(*The Poems* 346)

sexual communion in his famous sonnet "Leda and the Swan" (*The Poems* 214). The swan's beastly grip on "the loosening thighs" of the "staggering" Leda not only engenders the "shudder" of historical and political violence and destruction, but also charts the thrill and vibration of the imagination when it possesses the poet's mind. Supernatural and natural, *Spiritus Mundi* and individual genius are "with the self-same ring wed," as Yeats says elsewhere.[7] In "Leda and the Swan," the act of sexual insemination and impregnation, hackneyed an image as it may be, is metaphorically associated with poetic inspiration and production in the Yeatsian symbolic system:

> A shudder in the loins engenders there
> The broken wall, the burning of roof and tower
> And Agamemnon dead.
>   Being so caught up,
> So mastered by the brute blood of the air,
> Did she put on his knowledge with his power
> Before the indifferent beak could let her drop?
> (*The Poems* 214-5)

* * *

Yeats's "dream of a Leadean body" came true at the age of sixty-nine, in 1934. Full of ecstasy and expectations he announced to a Dublin friend that "[he] had it done!" The "it" of course referred to the Steinach Operation he had just undergone. The genital operation was elaborated by the Austrian Professor Eugen Steinach in the 1910s. It sought "the rejuvenation by experimental revitalisation of the ageing puberty gland."[8] The operation was based on the theory that the ligature of the sperm duct would augment the production of male hormones, which would consequently enhance male sexual performance. Needless to say, the operation was nothing other than a simple vasectomy with no hitherto reports substantiating its magical powers on sexual potency and performance. The operation obviously earned the poet enormous ridicule in the London and Dublin literary circles. The news went round like bush fire that Yeats had undergone a transplant of monkey glands. Gogarty joked that the poet had become "sex mad."[9] Frank O'Connor's joke is perhaps the most amusingly cheeky; he said that Yeats's Steinach Operation was like putting a Cadillac engine into a Ford car![10] In 1997, a book review in *The Scotsman* dubbed Yeats "The Gland Old Man" (Maddox 1999: 265).

Although it is quite doubtful whether the operation had any miraculous effects on Yeats's libidinal capacities, it did nonetheless quite palpably bolster his

---

[7] W.B. Yeats. *The Poems* (1983) 284.
[8] See Maddox (1999) 256.
[9] Quoted in Maddox (1999) 265.
[10] Quoted in Maddox (1999) 265.

poetic imagination. The Muse, in some Ledaean fashion, had certainly been fertilised by the "white rush"[11] – or rather, more precisely, by the interruption of it. The imagination had been rekindled afresh and the poet embarked immediately after the operation on one of the most interesting phases in his poetic career, both quantitatively and qualitatively. The impact of the operation on the poet's psychology and imagination was immense. It untied his poetic tongue and liberated his sexual fantasies. In his post-Steinach period, Yeats's increasing obsession with sexuality and bawdiness borders on the pornographic. Consider, for instance, the poem "The Wild Old Wicked Man" (*The Poems* 310-1). Here the old wicked man, with "his stout stick under his hand" and his "bawdy talk of the fishermen" (*The Poems* 310-1), recalls not only the "old lecher" of "The Tower," but also the even bawdier imagery of "The Chambermaid's Second Song":

> From pleasure of the bed,
> Dull as a worm,
> His rod and its butting head
> Limp as a worm,
> His spirit that has fled
> Blind as a worm.
> (*The Poems* 301)

The "worm" was too creepy for such a delicate lady as Dorothy Wellesley, Yeats's correspondent, protector and mistress. She disapproved of the metaphor and asked him to change it (Maddox 1999: 301). Yet Dorothy seems to have missed the point here. She failed to understand the real reasons behind this sudden emergence of bawdy and licentious language in the old Yeats. The upsurge is only a mask which, in my opinion, hides deep down a sense of incapacity and paralysis when confronted with the advent of the inevitable, that is, death. It is man's eternal inability to decipher the enigma of life and death, to answer the eternally nagging questions "Whence do we come, and whither do we go?" as Shelley once phrased it.[12]

Licentiousness does not so much reflect a sense of freedom from linguistic and social decorum as translate the libertine's profound consciousness of, and anxiety about, the approach of what Burke calls "the king of terror"[13] – death.

---

[11] W.B. Yeats. *The Poems* (1983) 214.

[12] Percy Bysshe Shelley. *Shelley's Poetry and Prose* (Eds. Donald H. Reiman, and Sharon B. Powers. New York and London: Norton, 1977) 476.

[13] Analysing the sublime, Burke explains: "As pain is stronger in its operation than pleasure, so death is in general is a much more affecting idea than pain [. . .] . Nay, what generally makes pain itself, if I may say so, more painful, is, that it is considered as emissary of this king of terrors." For further discussion of the notion of the sublime, see Edmund Burke. *A Philosophical Enquiry into the Sublime and the Beautiful* (Ed. David Womersley. London: Penguin, 1998) 86.

Libertinism as such is intimately associated with finality. It is the rhetoric, the psycho-linguistic structure, of the subject's consciousness of the ineluctability of mortality. Faced with this ineluctability, the ego loses control over things, that is, the reality principle. It gives way under the pressure of consciousness. Its grip on the Id slackens, and, hence, the latter partially floods the ego. A total collapse of the ego, however, would lead to neurosis or psychosis, that is, dementia and senility. Yet a partial collapse would engender what might be described as spots of blindness, *aporias*, in the domain of consciousness, following which the self experiences a sense of momentary liberation from the rigidity of social and linguistic decorum. This hyper-consciousness of finality obviously grows in intensity with the approach of death, despite the fact that it is sporadically punctuated by moments of bursting energy – some sort of defence mechanism, in the Freudian sense – to cope with the increasing pressure of depression and anxiety. Yeats's words in the following statement, however desperately they try to ward off such an anxiety and pressure, articulate perfectly well this complex psychological structure resultant from age-consciousness:

> As age increases my chains, my need for freedom grows. I have no consciousness of age, no sense of declining energy, no conscious need of rest. I am unbroken. (1954: 852) [14]

This is a perfect case of what Sigmund Freud would call after Otto Rank[15] "an energetic denial of the power of death" (1990: 356). Who speaks in the statement is Yeats's "double." The "unbroken" man here is Yeats's alter-ego, or "Daemon," or "Mask," to put it in the poet's parlance, which, according to Freud, is nothing other than a defence mechanism "invented" by the ego to preserve itself against "destruction" and "extinction" (1990: 356). Freud returns the rise of the "uncanny" (*Unheimlich*) in literature and reality to the ego's phantasmic invention of such an indestructible "double," an idea which, if seen in relation to Yeats's highly-valued notions of "Mask" and "Daemon," as well as of occultistic spiritism, would no doubt yield insightful discoveries.

The statement is also a perfect example of what might be described – or rather diagnosed – as Yeats's *cyclothemia*. Its apparent ecstatic elation and denial of the consciousness of ageing and death, is only another Yeatsian trick to deal with the anxiety. Within the gesture of denial or occlusion of the consciousness is already embedded an oblique recognition not merely of the presence of such an ontological consciousness, but, more alarmingly, of the gravity and complexity of its crisis and impact on the psyche. Denial or renunciation signifies repression of

---

[14] See Yeats, W.B. *The Letters* (Ed. Allan Wade. London: Rupert Hart-Davis, 1954).
[15] Otto Rank (1884-1939) was an Austrian psychoanalyst on whose book *Der Mythus von der Geburt des Helden* (*The Myth of the Birth of the Hero*) Freud draws to analyse the concept of the 'double.'

the anxiety and by no means eradication of it, as Freud would emphasise. Yeats's ecstatic denial of old age, no doubt, falls under the Freudian paradigm.

* * *

Old age and death are Yeats's problems *par excellence*. It would suffice to survey the titles of his poems which contain an over-determined recurrence of words such as "Old Age," "Death" and "Time." These suffuse his poetic text from the beginning, and orchestrate its fluctuating moods or cyclothematic states. Yeats's cyclothemia is perhaps best articulated in "The Tower." In this poem, the poetic mood alternates between gushes of ecstatic exhilaration and moments of depression and dejection. No sooner has "decrepit age" been declared a vital impetus to imaginative creativity than it is contemptuously denounced immediately after in the poem:

> What shall I do with this absurdity –
> O heart, O troubled heart – this caricature,
> Decrepit age that has been tied to me
> As to a dog's tail?
> > Never had I more
> Excited, passionate, fantastical
> Imagination, nor an ear and eye
> That more expected the impossible –
> No, not in boyhood when with rod and fly,
> Or the humbler worm, I climbed Ben Bulben's back
> And had the livelong summer day to spend.
> (*The Poems* 194)

Then, the excitement turns bitter:

> Did all old men and women, rich and poor,
> Who trod upon these rocks or passed this door,
> Whether in public or in secret rage
> As I do now against old age?
> (*The Poems* 197)

The consciousness of biographical time, or what might be seen as an ontological crisis, in the quotations above transcends the boundaries of class and gender. Yeats should have added 'race' as well. It is man's tragedy to be thrown into being and then die without solving the enigma of arrival in life, nor deciphering the mystery of death. With the collapse of the theological solace with modernity and The Enlightenment, the ontological problem could only increase in intensity and anxiety. Although the obsession with the issue of being-in-the-world, what

Heidegger calls *Dasein*,[16] reaches somewhat pathological proportions in such modernist authors as Kafka, Musil and Camus, as Georg Lukács has demonstrated,[17] it is seminal to underscore the fact that Yeats, though obsessed as he was with the problem of life and death, did not go so far as to psycho-pathologise the existential crisis. Rather, he circumvents the issue in some Nietzschean fashion. He, in other words, aestheticises the crisis.

* * *

Not only does Yeats propose aesthetic redemption as an alternative to sort out the existential mess, but he also envisages a crafty strategy, a strategy as old as tragedy. The strategy seeks to outdo death by emptying it of its essence and biological meaning. The aim is to outlive – or rather outdie? – death by willing and having a tragic death. The tragic hero, in other words, chooses his or her *memento mori*. This act of free will and choice of the moment of death and, more importantly, its immortalisation in memory and aestheticisation in a work of art, is what strips death of its violence and cruelty – of its terrorising *diktat* on the human mind and psyche. By mythopoeticising the *memento mori*, death ceases to be a finality, a biological *terminus* – an absence. The tragic hero, because he is a "character isolated by a deed," is rather transmuted into some omnipresent being, into a "superhuman" entity "To engross the present and dominate memory."[18] He becomes larger than life. This is what Yeats calls in "Byzantium" the poetics of "death-in-life and life-in-death" or, simply, tragic *sprezzatura*, both in the Castiglionian and Nietzchean senses:

> I hail the superhuman;
> I call it death-in-life and life-in-death.
> (*The Poems* 248)

Here death ceases to be a fatality. It becomes an act of free choice, like choosing to be or not to be. It becomes part of one's conception of one's being and becoming. Death is thus domesticated – neutralised. Whether this choice is totally free-willed is debatable. Both Georg Lukács and Jürgen Habermas admonish against such a celebration of subliminal self-sacrifice. Subliminal death, according to them, not only disrupts the subject's understanding of objectivity and the world, but also ruptures the communicative relation between subjectivity and alterity – what Habermas refers to as the "inter-subjective communicative action" fundamentally

---

[16] Martin Heidegger. *Being and Time* (Trans. John Macquarrie, and Edward Robinson. Oxford: Blackwell, 1962).

[17] For further discussion of the issue, see Georg Lukács (1962).

[18] W.B. Yeats. *The Poems* (1983) 347.

needed for any social contract or consensus. Self-sacrifice or suicide, in other words, puts an end to the I's social contract with the community.[19]

Yeats's *locus classicus* of such a poetics of mystico-subliminal self-sacrifice is articulated in two powerful poems, "An Irish Airman Foresees his Death" (*The Poems* 135) and "Sailing to Byzantium" (*The Poems* 193). If in the first poem he aestheticises the physical death in action of Major Robert Gregory, the son of Yeats's benefactor Lady Gregory, then in the second he rather exults in symbolic death. The *memento mori* in "An Irish Airman Foresees his Death" is presented as a unique experience of a "lonely impulse of delight":

> I know that I shall meet my fate
> Somewhere among the clouds above;
> [. . . .]
> A lonely impulse of delight
> Drove to this tumult in the clouds;
> I balanced all, brought all to mind,
> The years to come seemed waste of breath,
> A waste of breath the years behind
> In balance with life, this death.
> (*The Poems* 135)

In balance with the beauty of these lines are the following ones from "Sailing to Byzantium," wherein the experience of death is willed symbolically, mystically. By donning a Grecian form, in Keatsian fashion, [20] the persona not only dissociates himself from those "dying generations," but seems to halt the process of time passing and ageing by transfiguring himself into an omniscient static being, into

---

[19] Jürgen Habermas rejects the Romantic sublime, as well as postmodernism, because they are bogged down in the limited and limiting philosophy of the subject. He argues that there is freedom from this subjective insularity "only when the paradigm of self-consciousness, of the relation-to-self subject knowing and acting in isolation, is replaced by a different one – by the paradigm of mutual understanding, that is, of the intersubjective relationship between individuals who are socialised through communication and reciprocally recognise one another." For further analysis of this idea, see especially Jürgen Habermas's lecture XI, "An Alternative Way Out of the Philosophy of the Subject: Communicative versus Subject-Centred Reason." *The Philosophical Discourse of Modernity*. Trans. Frederick Lawrence. (Cambridge: MIT, 1987) 294-326. See also Georg Lukács (1962).

[20] Yeats's reference to the "Grecian goldsmiths" in "Sailing to Byzantium" no doubt recalls John Keats's "Ode on a Grecian Urn." Both poems celebrate artificial beauty, insofar as it is changeless and eternal, as opposed to nature's process of ageing and death. In Yeats, artificial beauty is symbolised by a metal bird ("of hammered gold"), while in Keats's poem, a "Grecian urn" becomes the symbol of immortal beauty. Apostrophising the ancient urn, Keats's famous lines run as follows: "When old age shall this generation waste, / Thou shalt remain, in midst of other woe / Than ours, a friend to man, to whom thou say'st, / 'Beauty is truth, truth beauty,' – that is all / Ye know on earth, and all ye need to know."

some "bird" of "changeless metal," which sings "of what is past, or passing, or to come." The persona here becomes a pure poetic voice sublimated from the "complexities of mire or blood" of Nature and Historicity:

III

> O sages standing in God's holy fire
> As in the gold mosaic of a wall,
> Come from the holy fire, perne in a gyre,
> And be the singing-masters of my soul.
> Consume my heart away; sick with desire
> And fastened to a dying animal
> It knows not what it is; and gather me
> Into the artifice of eternity.

IV

> Once out of nature I shall never take
> My bodily form from any natural thing,
> But such a form as Grecian goldsmiths make
> Of hammered gold and gold enamelling
> To keep a drowsy Emperor awake;
> Or set upon a golden bough to sing
> To lords and ladies of Byzantium
> Of what is past, or passing, or to come.
> (*The Poems* 193-4)

Here aesthetic ecstasy or gaiety transfigures all that dread of being, as Yeats explains in "Lapis Lazuli" (*The Poems* 294-5). The Byzantine paradigm has reinforced in the Yeatsian imagination something of a symmetry between immortality and architecture, or what Yeats simply describes as self-immortalisation through building "monuments of unageing intellect," both architectural and textual.

This is, of course, a commonplace idea in architecture. The poem "To be Carved on a Stone at Thoor Ballylee" (*The Poems* 190) is a perfect articulation of this alliance between architecture and text against ageing, evanescence and time. Yeats's Norman tower, Thoor Ballylee, in county Galway, becomes the recipient of such a poetic quest. It becomes the expression of such a desire for timelessness. Notice how the highly autobiographical and familial, that is, the particular, becomes inextricably confluent with the historical and the universal in the poem:

> I, The poet William Yeats,
> With old mill boards and sea-green slates,
> And smithy work from the Gort forge,
> Restored this tower for my wife George;

90

> And may these characters remain
> When all is ruin once again.
> (*The Poems* 190)

In so much as the carving of the characters represents an inscription in stone of man's eternal desire to survive temporality, it equally inscribes a stony testimony of the validity of poetic truth which the poem self-reflexively aspires to foreground. William Wordsworth is canonic in such matters.[21] More interestingly to observe here is the implication that, in the final analysis, the restoration of the tower serves no other purpose but to reinforce Yeats's Blakean idea of the immortality of the Imagination.[22] The tower is restored in order to perpetuate the presence of the written word. Architecture, after all, as Yeats insinuates in "Lapis Lazuli," is itself subject to the process of building and un-building, construction and destruction, following the undulations of historical "gyres," no matter how much gaiety accompanies such a childish, if cynical, game: "All things fall and are built again / And those that build them again are gay" (*The Poems* 190).

Ironically, Yeats's prediction about the fate of his tower would have come to pass had not the Irish government stepped in to save it from ruin. If architecture cannot escape apocalyptic *tabula rasa*, when "all is ruin again," then the engraved "characters," more as a poem than a mere sepulchral inscription, Yeats implies, survives all of Authoriality, Temporality and the Tower itself. This idea does not only recall the juvenile "words alone are good," as opposed to "dusty deeds" in "The Song of the Happy Shepherd,"[23] but also sends us forward to another Yeatsian epitaphial and almost death-bed poem, "Under Ben Bulben."[24] Here again the written word is testimonial of its own timelessness in the face of both historical and biological finitude. As in "To be Carved on a Stone at Thoor Ballylee," the written "words" are the surviving traces which record in their very laconic brevity the bitter truth about life and death:

VI

> Under bare Ben Bulben's head
> In Drumcliff churchyard Yeats is laid.
> [. . . .]
> No marble, no conventional phrase;

---

[21] See especially Wordsworth's two poems "Lines left upon a Seat in a Yew-tree" and "Lines Written with a Slate-pencil upon a Stone."

[22] To argue for the immortality of the imagination, Yeats quotes Blake's following dictum in "Symbolism in painting": "The world of imagination is the world of eternity. It is the Divine bosom into which we shall all go after the death of the vegetated body. The world of imagination is infinite and eternal, whereas the world of generation or vegetation is finite and temporal." *Essays and Introductions* (Dublin: Gill and Macmillan, 1961) 151.

[23] "The Song of the Happy Shepherd" *The Poems* (1983) 7.

[24] "Under Ben Bulben" *The Poems* (1983) 325-8.

> On limestone quarried near the spot
> By his command these words are cut:
> > *Cast a cold eye*
> > *On life, on death.*
> > *Horseman, pass by!*
> (*The Poems* 327-8)

If Yeats's epigraph is undoubtedly "no conventional phrase," insofar as it does not call for a moment of meditative repose at the grave, but rather prompts the "horseman" to carry on with the business of life, then the reason behind its presence is a well-known poetic manoeuvre. The self-mythologisation, or the subtle streak of pomposity embedded in its *mythos*, seems to belie the somewhat *ethos* of simplicity, if not asceticism, the poet envisages for his tomb. In the same poem, there is the Yeats who not only imposes himself as a poet-guru, who patronisingly preaches to "Irish poets to learn their trade"[25] by singing the themes he had indefatigably celebrated all through his *oeuvre*, namely, "the peasantry," Irish mythology, and aristocratic chivalry and magnanimity, and there is also the Yeats who establishes himself as *the* architect as well as a monument of the nation's unageing intellect – an avatar of its literary and imaginative culture. Comparing himself to Homer in the poem "The Tower," he transforms himself into something of a national cultural institution:

> the tragedy began
> With Homer that was a blind man,
> And Helen has all living hearts betrayed.
> [. . . .]
> *And I myself created Hanrahan*
> And drove him drunk or sober through the dawn
> From somewhere in the neighbouring cottages.
> (*The Poems* 195-6)[26]

Perhaps Yeats's most oblique expression of such a search for self-aggrandisement, or, better still, self-monumentalisation, is best articulated in the metaphorical symmetry or link he has created between his Norman Tower and his imaginative work. Both are "monuments of unageing intellect," set up in mockery of Temporality and finitude. In "Blood and the Moon,"[27] Yeats not only territorialises himself in the Miltonico-Shelleyan poetic tradition, in which the tower-symbol occupies a substantial place,[28] but he also ambitiously associates his Thoor Ballylee with archetypal towers such as those at Alexandria and Babylon, as

---

[25] W.B. Yeats. *The Poems* (1983) 327.

[26] My emphasis.

[27] W.B. Yeats. *The Poems* (1983) 237-9.

[28] For further discussion of Shelley's towers, see W.B. Yeats. "The Philosophy of Shelley's Poetry." *Essays and Introductions* (Dublin: Gill and Macmillan, 1961) 65-95.

well as with ethnic genealogy, namely, his Anglo-Irish identity. All of the textual – the poem as inter-text, the historical – Alexandria and Babylon, and the ethnic – "my ancestral stair,"[29] are yoked together in what Yeats so much values as the "Unity of Image" of the *symbolon*.[30] The synthetic and synaethesiac powers of the *symbolon* – the Greek etymon "*symballein*" literally means "throwing together" – are substantiated in the symbol of the "tower" in the following lines from "Blood and the Moon":

> Blessed be this place,
> More blessed still this tower;
> A bloody, arrogant power
> Rose out of the race
> Uttering, mastering it,
> Rose like these walls from these
> Storm-beaten cottages –
> In mockery I have set
> A powerful emblem up,
> And sing it rhyme upon rhyme
> In mockery of a time
> Half dead at the top.
>
> II
>
> Alexandria's was a beacon tower, and Babylon's
> An image of the moving heavens, a log-book of the sun's journey and the moon's;
> And Shelley had his towers, thought's crowned powers he called them once.
>
> I declare this tower is my symbol; I declare
> This winding, gyring, spiring treadmill of a stair is my ancestral stair;
> That Goldsmith and the Dean, Berkeley and Burke have travelled there.
> (*The Poems* 237)

Yeats's Tower is, then, another phallic emblem – Ezra Pound has amusingly called it Yeats's "Ballyphallus" – which, like the Steinach Operation, was brandished against the ravages of time and the process of corrosion of sexual and imaginative potency. What is interesting to observe in the lines above is that the tower has also been advanced as a counter-discourse to a Time which is itself, ironically, corroded "at the top." Yet what should be underscored is that "time" here is laden with historical meaning, and by no means a simple chronological concept. In other

---

[29] W.B. Yeats. *The Poems* (1983) 237.

[30] Yeats wrote two essays on symbolism – "Symbolism in Painting" and "The Symbolism of Poetry." He owes his initiation into the continental philosophy of symbolism to his friend Arthur Symons, who wrote a book on the subject and dedicated it to the poet himself. Symons entitled his book *The Symbolist Movement in Literature*, in which he advocates a new philosophy of literature alimented by "a revolt against exteriority, against rhetoric, against a materialistic tradition," much to the delight and excitement of an occultistic Yeats.

words, it is an epistemological configuration rather than a mere abstract temporality devoid of material sense. The "time half dead at the top," in other words, is nothing other than Yeats's demeaning reference to modernity and modernisation. The tower as discourse of traditional sanctity and fixity, or what might be simply referred to as Yeats's medievalism, is wielded against modern flux and change. It is Yeats's solid paradigm that refuses to melt into air. It is no surprise that the amalgamation of biological time – old age – with historical time – modernity – and vice versa, has not escaped the pertinent eye of another Irish fellow-poet, Seamus Heaney, who sees in Yeats's Tower and obsession with the possessive "my" associated with its paraphernalia "a symptom of a last ditch stand [whereby] the poet, thrown back within the final personal ring of defence, is forced into single combat with old age and with history and can employ as weapons only those things which lie most nakedly to his hand or most indelibly inside his mind" (1989: 26).

* * *

Yeats's fulmination against old age is, therefore, not purely ontological, biographical. It also originates from the poet's heightened consciousness of the importance of historical time. The autobiographical is historicised, inasmuch as the historical becomes autobiographical. In Yeats, autobiography and history are inextricably interwoven. They are interchangeable. Things get even more complex and complicated when we see that this historical time is itself interlaced with both national and international history. The experience of ontological finality in Yeats is almost always equated with the collapse of Western civilisation and the historical and political apocalypse ensuing from it. That such self-aggrandisement is part of poetic self-mythologisation is quite evident, as stated earlier; but this search for self-myth-making in Yeats, as Paul de Man has remarked, almost constantly slips into "pomposity." De Man argues that the poet's "pomposity" resides in the fact that he "heralds himself [...] as one of the last representatives of heroic grandeur in a decaying world" (1984: 137). The process of change in Ireland and the world is dramatised to apocalyptic proportions in Yeats, suggesting not only the imminent end of the aristocratic order with which the poet entirely identifies himself, but also the imminent collapse of the entire Western civilisation, as the poem "The Second Coming" ecstatically announces.[31] Here the historical "cone" reaches its apocalyptic climax before another turn of the historical "gyre" starts to unfold:

> Turning and turning in the widening gyre
> The falcon cannot hear the falconer;
> Things fall apart; the centre cannot hold;
> Mere anarchy is loosed upon the world,
> The blood-dimmed tide is loosed, and everywhere

---

[31] W.B. Yeats *The Poems* (1983) 187.

> The ceremony of innocence is drowned;
> The best lack all conviction, while the worst
> Are full of passionate intensity.
>
> Surely some revelation is at hand;
> Surely the Second Coming is at hand.
> (*The Poems* 187)

Yet Yeats here does not identify himself with the disintegrating order, or what he refers to as the *primary age*, which he associates with modernity and the Encyclopaedists.[32] He rather identifies himself with the birth of *the antithetical age*, the age of mythology, authority and "masculinity," which he describes a little further on in the poem using mythological imagery such as the "rough beast [that] / Slouches towards Bethlehem to be born" (*The Poems* 187).[33] If in "The Second Coming" Yeats associates himself with historical beginnings, then the opposite is true for the rest of the poetry which is most often associated with a sense of closure – an ending of both biographical time and historical time.

The conflation between biological finality and historical finitude, between a sense of belatedness and the collapse of the aristocratic order, is, for instance, unambiguously expressed in the poem "Coole Park and Thoor Ballylee, 1931"[34]:

> We were the last romantics – chose for theme
> Traditional sanctity and loveliness;
> Whatever's written in what poets name
> The book of the people; whatever most can bless
> The mind of man or elevate a rhyme;
> But all is changed, that high horse riderless,
> Though mounted in that saddle Homer rode
> Where the swan drifts upon a darkening flood.
> (*The Poems* 245)

---

[32] Reference to the philosophes associated with writing the French Encyclopedia (1751-1772), which was edited by Denis Diderot (1713-1784) and Jean le Rond d'Alembert (1717-1783).

[33] Yeats's juxtaposition of what he calls the centripetal and centrifugal movements in history is most clearly expressed in a newspaper interview for the *Irish Times* on 16th February 1924. In it, the poet uses the rise of the Italian fascist Benito Mussolini as evidence that "the centrifugal movement which began with the Encyclopaedists and produced the French Revolution, and the democratic views of men like Mill, has worked itself out to the end. Now we are at the beginning of a new centripetal movement." For further discussion of this view, see Elizabeth Cullingford. *Yeats, Ireland and Fascism* (London: Macmillan, 1981).

[34] W.B. Yeats. *The Poems* (1983) 243-5.

There is an element of truth in the process of self-mythologisation or self-Homerising in these lines. After all, the revivalist projects undertaken by Yeats and Lady Gregory were to Ireland what the *Odyssey* and the *Iliad* were to Greece. They forged the imagination of the nation, and substantially contributed to Ireland's liberation from the colonial yoke. Yet what calls for concern here is the apocalyptic vision upon which the poem closes. The image of the swan drifting upon the ominous darkening flood not only suggests a vision of historical and political apocalyptism, since the tidal (flood), as well as the aeolic (wind), are almost always synonymous with the unfolding of historical process in Yeatsian symbology, but it also recalls the image of the other swan in "Nineteen Hundred and Nineteen."[35]

In "Nineteen Hundred and Nineteen," apocalyptic destruction targets not the world solely, but, more tragically, the aesthetic act itself – the very act of writing poetry itself. It becomes self-oriented. The poem turns its destructive violence against itself. It becomes an act of poetic suicide. The apocalyptic vision transforms itself into a will to end at once historical reality and the poetic imagination:

> The swan has leaped into the desolate heaven:
> That image can bring wildness, bring a rage
> To end all things, to end
> What my laborious life imagined, even
> The half-imagined, the half-written page;
> (*The Poems* 209)

That the apocalyptic vision is scary when transposed onto politics has been cogently demonstrated by Frank Kermode in his book *The Sense of an Ending: Studies in the Theory of Fiction.*[36] But these lines do reflect an authentically tragic moment of consciousness in Yeats's poetic *œuvre*. This *prise de conscience* articulates quite sincerely an acute awareness of the crisis of poetry in the modern age, or more precisely, a crisis of legitimation. The consciousness is not so much about the paralysis and failure of the poetic dream to "mend whatever mischief" that "afflict[ed] mankind" (*The Poems* 209), that is, in other words, to change the world into something better, as it is a profound consciousness of the real threats that the modern age – or modernity – poses to the poetic act and to the survival of poetry altogether. Hence Yeats's legitimation of poetic violence and "rebelliousness" against bourgeois modernity:

> [The arts] are not radical, and if they deny themselves to any it can only be to the *nouveau riche*, and if they have grown rebellious it can only be against something that is modern, something that is not simple. (1961: 350)

---

[35] W.B. Yeats *The Poems* (1983) 206-10.
[36] See Frank Kermode (2000).

* * *

The "filthy modern tide" (*The Poems* 101), as Yeats prefers to refer to bourgeois modernity, seems to have engaged in a relentless process of marginalising the poetic project because it does not fall into line with its philosophy of consumerism, utilitarianism and functionalism. "Only the wasteful virtues earn the sun," Yeats asserts against bourgeois utility (*The Poems* 101). In order to subvert modernity's grand narratives Yeats had almost ineluctably to turn all its values upside down. Instead of rationalism, progress and scientism he exalted irrational phantasmagoria, nostalgia and prophetic apocalyptism. This is Yeats's predicament; he is a man of his time who chose to write against his time. In so doing he confirms the Eliotic assumption that his biographical history is the history of his age. He is, as T.S. Eliot continues to argue, a "part of the consciousness of an age which cannot be understood without [him]"(Hall, *et al.*, 1961: 307). Such subtle awareness of the confluence between biological age and historical age, autobiography and history, did not escape Yeats's eye; indeed, it furnished the basis upon which he founded his search for self-monumentalisation against finitude.

Works cited

Burke, Edmund. *A Philosophical Enquiry into the Sublime and Beautiful*. Ed. David Womersley. London: Penguin, 1998.

Cullingford, Elizabeth. *Yeats, Ireland and Fascism*. London: Macmillan, 1981.

De Man, Paul. *The Rhetoric of Romanticism*. New York: Columbia UP, 1984.

Freud, Sigmund. *Art and Literature*. Trans. and eds. James Strachey, and Albert Dickson. 1985. London: Penguin, 1990.

Habermas, Jürgen. *The Philosophical Discourse of Modernity*. Trans. Frederick Lawrence. Cambridge: MIT, 1987.

Hall, James, *et al.*, eds. *The Permanence of Yeats*. New York: Collier, 1961.

Heaney, Seamus. *The Place of Writing*. Atlanta: Scholars, 1989.

Heidegger, Martin. *Being and Time*. Trans. John Macquarrie, and Edward Robinson. Oxford: Blackwell, 1962.

Kermode, Frank. *The Sense of an Ending: Studies in the Theory of Fiction*. New York: Oxford UP, 2000.

Lukács, Georg. *The Meaning of Contemporary Realism*. Trans. John Mander, and Necke Mander. London: Merlin, 1962.

Maddox, Brenda. *George's Ghosts: A New Life of W.B. Yeats*. London: Picador, 1999.

Said, Edward W. *Culture and Imperialism*. London: Chatto and Windus, 1993.

—. "Yeats and Decolonization." *Culture and Imperialism*. London: Chatto and Windus, 1993. 265-87.

Shelley, Percy Bysshe. *Shelley's Poetry and Prose*. Ed. Donald H. Reiman, and Sharon B. Powers. New York and London: WW Norton, 1977.

Symons, Arthur. *The Symbolist Movement in Literature*. 1899. Intro. Richard Ellmann. New York: Button, 1959.

Yeats, W.B. *The Letters*. Ed. Allan Wade. London: Rupert Hart-Davis, 1954.

—. *Essays and Introductions*. Dublin: Gill and Macmillan, 1961.
—. *Autobiographies*. London: Macmillan, 1980.
—. *The Poems*. Ed. Richard J. Finneran. New York: Macmillan, 1983.

Grapholagia Poetica:
Ageing as Confrontation with or
Avoidance of Death

John Kinsella

From the point of view of this poet, ageing involves a paradoxical relationship between the *loss* of some knowledge and 'experience,' and the accumulation, increase, or awareness of other knowledge and experience. In some cases, it is the development of pre-existing, or evolving awarenesses; in others, it is something entirely new, that becomes translatable out of a form of dynamic equivalence – a comparison to what we have known until that point. Poetry, in many ways, exists in this liminal zone of change, in these places of comparison, and in the search for an articulation of the new experience without co-ordinates in available memory. Instinct, ritual, learned behaviour, commonsense, might help, but essentially we are on our own – take risks, test the waters in different ways.

As a writer, it has always bemused me, when other writers' works are collected, usually after death, that their early child and teenage writings are separated off as 'juvenilia,' presented apologetically, or is it done to 'throw light' on the mature, older writer? Is there a point when we cease being child-writers, in the same way that we can officially vote, or drink, or drive a car? Most juvenilia are divided according to both age and level of accomplishment. Clearly, it cannot be at thirty, but at twenty-two you might have written a poem so critically well-accepted that you have matured enough for subsequent work to be considered non-juvenilia. The line is arbitrary. For me, it is all one and the same line of work: voices change over life, and that is interesting, but the imposed separation is also about control, about not letting the purity of adulthood be tainted by the innocence of childhood.

Arthur Rimbaud – writing his poetry outside of innocence, we are led to believe by Rimbaud himself and by his biographers – is promoted as child-poet-genius, the genius being the reason he wrote poems that appeal to adult sensibilities, more, comes the implication, than any child of the age *he* was when he wrote them. This is called precocity. Yet at the age of fifteen I was reading

Rimbaud and felt he was talking directly to me, as I am sure many other young people have too.

The other argument, which we can share with Rimbaud across the divider of age, is one of the conveniences of packaging. Of course we can, if we are old enough, we have all been children and young people and adults and middle-aged and old. This exploitation of the child-self for the delectation of the older reader is reprehensible in its dishonesty, and in its marketing. I have often wished that poetry would come to us without any biographical reference-points. I could certainly show poems written by my daughter at six that could pass for poems written by an adult. It is all about content and range: if the emotion is a specific one, and the focus is singular, the utterance of the words itself creates the emotional environment – it translates across age. The more information, the more emotional fracturing, the more clearly it comes out of an emotionally and technically inexperienced voice that has, seemingly, less to offer the adult.

Let us reconsider a poem (in my translation) by Arthur Rimbaud – "*Le dormeur du val*" ["Sleeper in the Valley"] – a poem written in October 1870, when the poet was sixteen:

> It is a richly green hole where a river sings
> Hooking silver tatters – fantastical and bright –
> To the grass; where the sun shines down from the swelling
> Mountain; it is a small valley frothing with light.
>
> A young soldier sleeps with open mouth and bare head,
> The nape of his neck bathing in the cool blue stain
> Of watercress: stretched out in grass, beneath the clouds,
> Pallid in his green bed where the light falls as rain.
>
> Feet amongst the gladioli, he sleeps. Smiling
> The smile of a sickly infant, gently napping.
> Nature, you must cradle him warmly: he is cold.
>
> No scents or smells disturb his nose, make it tremble;
> He sleeps under the sun, one hand resting tranquil
> On his chest. He has two red holes in his right side.
> (*Collected Poems* 105)

Two points leap out. One, that it is a highly sophisticated viewing of death as a child, as an unhealthy infant who can quite look after itself; secondly, that the suggestion of a "young soldier" brings a sense of witnessing from a point of view that is experienced, and certainly older. What is remarkable is that the dead soldier is certainly no younger than Rimbaud, and probably some years older. Rimbaud casts his voice as a voice of aged authority, even of parental authority, but also allows the luxury of innocent indulgence in the richness of language. He merges the 'pure' and the 'corrupt.' He transgresses the rules of age, of juvenilia.

* * *

When I was fourteen, I started working weekends and holidays at Wim Smits philatelists, in London Court, Perth, Western Australia. With my first pay I bought a book of Banjo Paterson's verse[1] for my mother. The inscription in it, in my teenage hand, reads: "To Mum / my first pay Hope you enjoy reading / Love Your Son John / xxxxx Birthday '77." Now, this might not seem much in itself, but it tells me a few things about my writing practice. The capitalisations were to add gravity to my efforts, to my beneficence, and to my excitement. It was a sign of respect to my mum, but also a sign of respect to myself. The gift was evidence of an independence, a coming of age. The handwriting in that book is the template or core of my handwriting now, though I write faster, with more fluidity, and far less definition of letters. Still, I know that person by his hand. The signature is the signature of a consciousness of maturing, of growth. It is a confrontation with paternity, with a desire to bridge the age gap. My mother was good that way – she allowed us to be *people*, as well as children.

Drafting by hand has always been important to me. The handwritten, even manually-typed and hand-corrected poem becomes an engagement with where I am developmentally. The same, but different. To reiterate a fascinating motif: I treasure the knowledge that in banks, those who sign things all day have signatures on record for different points of tiredness. So if someone has been signing for five hours, their signature is compared to the five-hour signature. This change is not only an issue of age and time, but of experience, of emotional and physical tiredness. Being tired has a lot to do with changes we attribute to age. Now, one might feel tiredness more, getting older, but my grandmother spent her last twenty years wide awake. We have, or had, insomnia in common.

So often when we speak of writing to age, we speak of writing to experience. The younger woman's fascination with the observations, experiences, sufferings, and distillations into poetry of Sylvia Plath[2] are more about associations of feeling and experience, or of the imagination of what that experience might be like, than something solely related to age. People mature at different rates physically, but our emotional needs also have different schedules, and, furthermore, alter. It becomes a question of whom, say, Plath was writing for? To other young women of a specific social experience and cultural background? Her

---

[1] Andrew Barton (Banjo) Paterson (1864-1941). Australian poet and journalist. Composer of "Waltzing Matilda."

[2] Sylvia Plath (1932-1963). American poet and novelist. Committed suicide (London, England).

ventures in form are an illustration of the constraint that young women, especially of the era, faced in terms of sexuality and domestic freedom. This formality is offset by the savagery and haunting physicality of her imagery. There is a tension here. Yet it could speak to an older woman who has lived a life of confinement in all sorts of ways – one can translate across physical age into experience. But the suicidal youthful girl or woman, so often attracted to Plath, is that way for a reason. Like pop music speaking to its generation – but then there are always those who cross the boundaries.

Often the death-poetry of youth comes from a fear of life, of ageing. The rock band The Who say, "I hope I die before I get old" (1965); the Rolling Stones are notorious for it, and equally notorious for getting old. Do they now play youthful music or have they taken youthful music to all ages, or other ages? When they adapted the blues, were they taking music for an older generation from one culture to a younger generation of another? Of course, the blues know no age, as shown by the apparently possessed and brilliant blues guitarist Robert Johnson[3] – King of the Delta Blues – who died at age twenty-seven. The issues dealt with in the blues – that a woman has left me, or a man has done me wrong, for example – can happen at any time.

So the poetry of death of the young man and young woman reaches across gender divides often to express a fear of ageing, of its inevitable confrontation with mortality. By confronting mortality immediately, a catharsis takes place. Death, as John Donne shows us in his poetry,[4] comes with the act of consummation as much as by being struck down. They are similar moments of climax – and dénouement. The poetry of death – so common among youthful writers – does not go away with the experience of writing; it just becomes wider in its terms of reference, and speaks outside a particular age group. Writers have committed suicide at early ages, and not just from the despairs of youth!

* * *

My partner, the poet Tracy Ryan, lost a brother at a young age. In some ways, ageing stopped then for her. In other ways, the loss led to its acceleration. Such defining moments in our lives become fulcrums for fears or confrontations with mortality, and so much of ageing is about strategies for negotiating our relationship with our own mortality, that of those around us, and of humanity as a whole. Here is what Tracy had to say, first in her youth when writing in her late teens, about age and the issue of death. Her poem is called "Letting Go":

---

[3] Robert Johnson (1911-1938) – "King of the Delta Blues" – American blues composer, guitarist and singer. He died of poisoning after drinking whisky laced with strychnine.
[4] See, for example, John Donne's "The Flea." *Complete English Poems.* (Ed. A.J. Smith. London: Penguin, 1977) 36-7.

The day the bright balloon slipped from your hand
There was no sun. The clouds had caught my eye,
Streamlined hovercraft on unfathomed sky.
I cried because I could not understand

How something held so tight could still be lost.
But you let go. I wonder what it saw,
Trailing its tail above the here and now,
Tirelessly rising to the uppermost

World, a giddy angel. Perhaps the light,
Clouded from vision, somehow warmly called
To rise and shine, get up and walk, and healed
The breach between the realms of faith and sight.

It is the star that satellites the heart,
The final act that tears the spheres apart.
(Unpublished poem, 198-)

I asked Tracy Ryan to comment on how she viewed her subject matter, as far as she can recall, at the age when the poem was composed, and how she views and writes it now:

> The main difference in how I treated this subject matter – death – in my teens, and how I approached it later, is that in the earlier writing I used much more formal technique – the poems are stiff, clichéd, metrical. Partly this is because poetry was newer to me – I was still learning how to do those things – but also it is because the main catalyst for my writing poetry – my brother's death – occurred when I was sixteen, and was way too overwhelming for me to deal with directly. The stiff formalism was a means of distancing myself from the experience, trying to "sort it out," examine it, see what it could tell me. Later on it was the direct emotional aspects of it that interested me – the event, the loss, had retreated or receded with time – though not necessarily the intensity of feeling, which has never been exorcised – and I was more interested in the universal aspect of it – how it was like / unlike what others experienced of death and loss. Distancing still happens through metaphoric treatment, but the voice is more apparently *immediate*.
>
> In "Letting Go," that the image of the hand letting go of the balloon / the person giving up life, comes from the same fact that is mentioned in the second line of the Wungong poem [below]: Sean's girlfriend said he lifted up one hand and waved at her as he died – he was a fair way across the water. For a long time I could not deal mentally with the idea that he knew he was going to die, and he chose to "let go" when he "should have" hung on. In the early poem, that gets abstracted beyond recognition – only the sky turns into water by implication – the sole remaining trace of the death-place, though I did not see that at the time. My teacher at school who read this manuscript said that he felt my obsession with ordering and formalising the poems was getting in the way of their energy – back then I thought he was just a 'free-verser,' but now of course I understand what he meant – the imposition of a pattern was constantly leading me away from what I

wanted to do – the poem degenerates into increasingly abstract Biblical and religious imagery. (Tracy Ryan, personal communication, 2004)

A horror is implicit in the sign of the hand. It is commonplace, and yet it is invested with an ominous, portentous meaning. A symbol of affirmation and loss – greeting and departure. In Ryan's adult work "Wungong Dam,"[5] in which she looks back at the death of her brother many years after the incident, it is the hand that ties the loss together. It literally reaches across. The fact that Stevie Smith's humour in "Not Waving But Drowning" is being darkly inverted, strengthens our horror.[6] Life goes at any age, and a knowledge of its imminence might be as it happens. The idea that we can know our death, and yet be surprised by it, is where the power of Ryan's poem lies.

* * *

We may compare "Letting Go" to poems written by Tracy Ryan over twenty years later, as an adult, and as a parent. The parenting experience, more than the age, is probably pivotal to creating a distance of a kind from personal mortality. One's own life becomes a substitute for the child's, which one would readily exchange for the child should it become a choice. Loss of a child, or the loss of someone loved outside the nuclear family before having children of one's own, can, of course, lead to a desire to substitute the self for the dead, but it is less common. The environment of nurturing, and in the case of women, the extension of the physical self, brings a fear of the mortality of someone else, and not as definitively for the self, unless it be the fear of the child's thereby losing protection and care. These are generalisations, but they are certainly patterns we can establish in the poetry of Ryan and many others.

This is the poem "Wungong Dam" from the collection *The Willing Eye* (1999):

> I always dream he is down here
> where he waved one hand and sank
> in the still pool. I forget the real
> dank fistful of dirt and agapanthus
> we threw on him, I forget
> red clods that adhered to
> our soles and dust smeared
> on damp cheeks, the unjust softness
> of kangaroo paws. I forget HE IS RISEN

---

[5] See Tracy Ryan's "Wungong Dam" *The Willing Eye* (South Fremantle: Fremantle Arts Centre; Newcastle upon Tyne: Bloodaxe, 1999) 36.
[6] Florence Margaret (Stevie) Smith (1902-1971) – English poet and novelist. See Stevie Smith "Not Waving but Drowning" *The Collected Poems* (Ed. James MacGibbon. London: Viking, 1975) 303.

> clamped over the earth-mouth.
> In dreams I come back for him
> to the one dam you have never
> written of.
> (*The Willing Eye* 36)

Ryan makes an interesting point about the solidity of this later poem. It does not retreat into rhetoric, but still manages to flow and give the sense of the dream it invokes. This is a maturity of technique welded with the learned behaviours of coping with grief. The poem becomes a tool for decoding that grief, but it is also a celebration of her lost brother's memory:

> . . . it is almost entirely concrete. It is about how memory (via dreams) goes looking for the dead brother in the (more spiritual) element of water – even though I know he is buried in the earth, I always dream he is buried in the water. (Tracy Ryan, personal communication, 2003)

In an even later volume,[7] Ryan re-confronts her brother's ghost: her loss is always tinged with a celebration of memory – both its sensual pleasures and the sense of grief and wastefulness this loss invokes. The flower is fresh and fades fast, as the persona will also fade and in fading join the dead. The lines that follow are from a poem called "Hydrangeas":

> "under my brother's window
> as if you knew
> he'd die young and we'd strew
> that pit with just such blue"
>
> [and the petals of that flower, which grew under his window when we were children, are][8]
>
> "like the simple cells
> that form the complex
>
> that is my body
> that will simplify
>
> again, like his, the petals shed
> colourless and drifting."
> (*Hothouse* 46)

Finally, Ryan adds:

> As an adult I am more able to recall details from childhood than I was at sixteen and seventeen, to convey the relationship with the dead brother. In the early poem "Letting Go," everything was filtered through indirect references and symbols

---

[7] Tracy Ryan. *Hothouse* (South Fremantle: Fremantle Arts Centre, 2002).
[8] The poet's interpolation to abridge the poem.

unrelated to the core of feeling – kind of abstracted. I did not have an *emotional poetic language*. (Tracy Ryan, personal communication, 2003)

This last comment is vital. Not only is the emotional experience not there, but there is an inexperience in realising how aware the experienced reader will be of literary stock sayings, styles, and clichés. So the use of a symbol or expression or rhetorical device that might seem fresh, or subtextual with a poet from the canon, becomes laboured to the experienced reader, especially the emotionally experienced reader. This does not invalidate the original emotion, or the attempt to express it, and in a sense suggests context *is* relevant.

* * *

As part of ageing together, as a couple, Tracy Ryan and I share experience through our work, our children, our veganism, and various other interests and beliefs. But one of the keys to our sharing each other's journey, through reconciling our move towards death, is incorporating each other's sufferings and losses into our own lives. This is a delicate thing – too much burden-bearing can become compromising, crowding – but there has to be some level of attempt at understanding these processes.

Tracy Ryan has moved away from the death of her brother, an event around which all views of relationships were formed – the risk of the most solid ones being 'taken away' without warning, or with warnings we do not know how to read, with one's teenage years being 'deprived' of a belief in the possibility of an immortality – the stuff that makes children think they are superman. She certainly never felt this. I did feel this, and did things accordingly. Bullying dragged me down – the observation and experience of violence. Drugs and alcohol became a way of short-circuiting the youth I did not want to have. I was always a child who wanted to be an adult because that would give me more freedom, but would also protect me from other children. It seemed to indicate I was mature beyond my years, but I was not; in many ways; I missed out on a part of growing up.

In reconciling ourselves to each other's emotional stultifications, and efforts at ageing mentally, emotionally, and spiritually, as well as physically – or at least to sense the possibilities – we have written into each other's lives. Below is an example of a poem I wrote on visiting Tracy's brother's grave. Both poems refer to kangaroo paws – plants indigenous to Western Australia with red flag-like flowers with green and red stems, yellow anthers, and the plant becomes a way of bridging the gap, of communicating about the idea, and our own mortality. As Tracy Ryan says, she has changed, but her brother in her memory will always be eighteen. It stops her ageing process to some degree as well. I am told I look like him, and am similar in many of my interests. Perhaps subliminally this informed the consolidation of our relationship; perhaps I have become a way of her confronting this mortality. I lost a close friend to suicide when I was in my early twenties, and this loss is something Tracy has been able to understand. The vulnerability of the physical self has united rather than alienated us. We help each other age. Here is my poem which is called "Grave":

> Serpentine. Tracy asks me to stop
> at the cemetery – her brother
> who drowned in Wungong Dam
> is buried here. She clears
> dry leaves from the framed
> blue metal while I think
> of Craig whose grave
> I've never visited.
> It's just something I can't face.
> Though I'll wander almost happily
> amongst the tombs of those I've
> not known. I did not know
> Tracy's brother, and it shows.
> I set out in search of flowers.
> It is autumn and they are scarce.
> Behind the cemetery I come across
> lines of dead sheep. Wool, red
> with raddle paint, hangs
> dankly about the carcasses.
> I return empty handed.
> One can't transfer flowers
> from another's grave.
> At the right time of year
> Tracy says kangaroo paws
> are rampant – occasionally
> erupting from graves,
> bloody windchimes
> muttering under their breaths.
> (*Peripheral Light: Selected and New Poems* 60)

Recently, I found a poem of mine in one of my mother's school poetry books. It is about imprisonment and wears its influence – the Australian poet Judith Wright[9] – loudly. For as far back as I can remember, the issue of imprisonment, especially false imprisonment, has concerned me. The skills one develops as a writer, as much as the perceptions of age, delineate fundamental differences in the poems below which deal with this topic. The first was written sometime during the 1977/78 school holidays when I was fourteen, possibly just fifteen, and having just moved from a city school to a country school. The dislocation was both freeing and

---

[9] Judith Wright (1915-2000). Australian poet, critic and short-story writer. Environmentalist and Aboriginal land rights activist.

imprisoning, so personal experience informs it. For a child who was bullied, new hopes were on offer, but it was not long before it was a case of "out of the frying pan and into the fire." I would say I redrafted this in the first few months of 1978. The notion of revenge fascinated me, and here ageing has brought a fundamental difference. I am a pacifist now, but then I played war games, made explosives, and believed in a morality based on justice. 'Justice,' to me now, is just another word for violence – psychological and physical. The poem is called "A Call For 'Freedom'," and was written when I was about fourteen or fifteen:

> The silhouetted figures cry for help,
> And still the shadows die without a care,
> Mournful cries come from within the dead,
> Whose shadows wander fluted corridors.
>
> These souls of confined men that call "Revenge!"
> In the face of their oppressors and their guards,
> No freedom did they have to call for life . . .
> So sought instead the mercy of their death.
> (Unpublished poem, 1977/78)

On days when prisoners in the state of Ohio were to be executed, Kenyon College's Episcopalian church, in the American town where I have been teaching as an adult in recent years, would sound its bells as a form of protest. The bells would continue to ring until the protest ate into people's consciences. The death sentence is an appalling hypocrisy and travesty of justice, to my mind, so it is not surprising that with the bells ringing through my body I would respond as I did in the poem discussed below. Kenyon College is in an isolated place in mid-Ohio, the village of Gambier – surrounded by woods and cornfields. The management of the lands in relation to the college is distinctly pastoral. The church community's pastoral is of an ecumenical religious form, but the two traditions of pastoral overlap. In this community a few years ago there was an horrific murder. When the murderer was given the death sentence, even the victim's family protested.

With these factors resonating, and given that I write landscape in the same way I write the body, it seemed that there was a violation of both going on with execution. Technically, and certainly in terms of references and nuances in deployment of language, there is more to this poem than the one written out in my mother's poetry book when I was fifteen, yet the concerns are the same. The revenge here is inverted of course, because the implication is that the prisoners – convicts, the results of penal colonialism – were wrongfully or unjustly (in the word of my youth) imprisoned.

The fact that the prisoner being executed in Ohio committed his crime is presumably not in doubt, but the question remains the same: to be murdered for a crime, no matter how grievous, implicates those casting judgement. This entangled issue of ethics crosses over with the first poem, "A Call For 'Freedom'." Age has brought extra knowledge, but so-called maturity has brought in many ways no greater insight. Knowledge is relative; the truths we know as children are no less truths for being immature. We might not comprehend a situation, or might not be able to access certain information, but truths are relative to the information we have. A sense of right and wrong is usually instilled at a very young age, and seems often Platonic in its pre-presence. Poetry, the articulation of the inexpressible, becomes the gesture. Audience is the issue – in a sense, both poems are directed towards an unjust and uncaring world. This second poem is called "Death Sentence in Ohio: epicedium":

> And yet . . . to stay
> and plan this pastoral . . .
> families extend in both directions:
> an eclogue of courts and therapy,
> anger and cemeteries,
> default patterns rising
> and closing off the day,
> the emperor's thumbs down –
> all beginnings and endings
> and linking first light
> with total darkness.
>   Blackout,
> as the state you take as host
> executes another – the bell
> keeping steady pace
> for all its heavy going,
> weather dull then bright,
> hardly newsworthy.
> A temporal flexibility,
> aspect of grace . . . occasional
> as the angle of script
> on the warrant.
>   You condemn
> the action but live quietly
> in the shadow of *their* gallows –
> dressed as metaphor, half-
> wondering grammatical contexts
> and last meals with their special
> kind of half-life, and what prises
> the soul from the body it makes,
> what takes the place of a face
> to hate, to paint repeatedly
> on paper,
>   electronically.
> (*The Yale Review* 93. 2)

* * *

My daughter and I enjoy going on bush excursions. We both keep field notebooks /
journals. Beginnings are so important. Just as I did as a child, Katherine keeps a
locked diary, and a public diary. As she grows older, I wonder if the private will
become more public, as it most certainly has in my case. Our secrets become the
stuff of our writing. Georg Lukács begins his 1910 diary with the following:

> 25 April 1910, at night
> . . . How strange and exciting to begin a diary (even in my current state it affects
> me). There are questions and suggestions: who among my old friends will
> reappear? What new names will make me fill these terrifying white pages with my
> blood? (1995: 27)

The point is that the white pages, the unwritten blanks of our lives, are terrifying.
We write, we record, to fight ageing, to fight loss. By recording we seem to suggest
that we can keep it, that nothing is lost. We see all this in Shakespeare's notion that
in writing his lover he gives him or her immortality; in the Egyptians' belief in
taking one's earthly goods on the journey across the river of death; in the diary in
which teenagers keep secrets from their mothers, only to be traumatised, to be
desecrated and feel as if part of themselves has been removed on finding that the
hair placed across the pages has been disturbed.

As writers, and writers of all kinds – of emails, tax forms, Christmas or
Hanukkah cards, we record where we have been, what we would like to attain. It is
all sidestepping mortality. In *The Guardian* newspaper of November 1st, 2003,
there is an article by Neil McIntosh entitled "World drowning in a rising sea of
information": "Peter Lyman, one of the leaders of the research team, said the surge
in information was due to a new-found desire to document all that happens around
us" (*The Guardian*, Nov. 1, 2003).

I do not think the desire to document is "new-found" – and numeracy and
literacy are not the only ways of recording. When wandering in the bush with my
daughter, where I am interested in recording the specific names of things, she
makes up for a lack of that knowledge by writing about the moods things create,
and drawing pictures of them so she might increase her knowledge. She will ask
me, as someone with more experience, but the process of interest is ageless. In fact,
my nine-month-old boy is the most hungry for knowledge of all. He records with
plastic cups and the bars of his playpen. We make stories, create narratives and
novels out of our lives to show where we have been, and consequently, where we
are going. In *Writing Degree Zero,* Roland Barthes says:

> The Novel is a Death; it transforms life into destiny, a memory into a useful act,
> duration into an orientated and meaningful time. (1990: 39)

Barthes continues to point out that "society imposes the Novel" (1990: 39), and, indeed, in the light of the need to control ageing, to categorise and separate our lives' narratives, to profit from them, and for power to be extracted from them, the novel becomes a necessity, as do now the chatroom, the blog.

In creating the time and durational co-ordinates of a poem, we step outside Génette's rules.[10] The poem merges in its compaction of the moment, its being stretched out, condensed, recounted, projected, and so on. The poem, as a device, denies age. If Shakespeare is right, poems are a denial of death. However, the use of the sonnet itself, the confinement of language to form, is a recognition of the materiality of the word, and of life. It is like an urn, or the slab of a tombstone. In form, we apply the rules of physics. Tracy Ryan's loss poem juxtaposes the confinement of form with the apparent freedom of the balloon, of life, which the poem suggests is an illusion, a false freedom. It is as trapped as the poem itself.

There is a wonderful quotation from A.W. Raitt's *The Life of Villiers de l'Isle-Adam* collected in D.J. Enright's *The Oxford Book of Death*:

> In 1887, when Villiers de l'Isle-Adam and Léon Bloy were passing the flower-sellers, monumental masons and shops specialising in funeral accessories near the Père Lachaise cemetery, Villiers exclaimed in fury: "Those are the people who invented death!" (Enright, ed. 2002: 145)

In some ways, literature fetishises and invents death as well.

* * *

On one of our outings, Katherine and I explored a piece of reserve bushland near the family home in York, Western Australia. Getting there was an exercise in itself, for though it was easy enough to find the front part of the reserve via the main road down to the city, we wanted to go in from behind, along the extremely potholed gravel roads at the back of Mount Bakewell, where our home is, in the wheatbelt of Western Australia. The actual trail into the reserve is extremely rocky, and we could take the car only so far. My daughter found this exciting, but also slightly threatening. The unknown possibilities of getting stranded bothered her.

On the other hand, she was not really old enough to take this fear into the extreme, though morbid tendencies could potentially evolve later as she fused fiction with reality. At the time, however, the possibility of being shot by a stray bullet from an illegal hunter, or of coming across a drug plantation guarded by underworld figures, were distinct possibilities. The kind of knowledge she had did not lend itself to these possibilities, though if something had happened then

---

[10] See G. Génette's *Narrative discourse: An essay in method* (Trans. J.E. Lewin. Ithaca: Cornell UP, 1980).

obviously the possibility would have become part of her vocabulary of expectation, on future visits to such places.

Experience told me these were possibilities, so I entertained the thoughts. Our relative experiences of the visit would be coloured by our relative fears and expectations. Though it was mid-winter, she feared a snake might awake and attack her. This was more a phobia than a belief in it actually happening – so more information than necessary would cause cascading fears. We wandered further into the bush, through grevilleas, under the odd jarrah, past York gums and hakeas. As the soil varied, so did the vegetation. We heard kangaroos moving through the bush. It was overcast, and a little humid. Thick clots of sap had dropped from red gums. Yes, like blood.

We came across a vast granite outcrop, black, and alive. In a split in the rock, we found bones and skin, probably dropped there by a fox that had captured a native animal. My daughter asked me what it was: a quoll, I thought. We stared at it for a while, lost in our own thoughts, separate, found a place on the rock, and wrote. The poems are below; I have only just seen her poem at the time of writing this. Since the outing, I have realised that the skin was that of a brushtail possum, but my daughter has remained confirmed in the unwavering belief that it was a quoll. Still, we both independently sought for more than the death itself. It was symbolic, certainly, but it was more than that. For all my searchings in language, I saw little more than my daughter saw.

It is not a matter of clarity through simplicity, but of choosing the words that work for us at a particular time and place. We are different poets – she is twelve at the and I am forty – but we were affected by the same sense of the place, the same need for affirmation in a place of death. The fear we have of our mortality is offset by fears of threats even greater than death – loss of soul, pain, loss of loved ones, our sanity – but occasionally the poem lifts out of the referentiality of our vulnerability, and transcends.

If being twelve has anything going for it, it is the ability to do that. We spend our ageing trying to recall it, to escape down its path. The irony is that the twelve-year-old has no more purity of vision than the mature person; it is just a different kind of vision. Once we start talking about the corruption of ageing, we are patronising our earlier selves. Some things are not open to us as children, and neither should they be, but what we did know then was as valid and complex as what we would know later. My poem is called "Death of a Brushtail Possum":

> In the valley, on granite faces,
> cosseted by she-oak perimeters,
> lichen, moss, black run-off,
> a brushtail possum broken down,
> strewn over and into cracks –

a limb, vertebrae, envelope of skin and fur,
touched by a boot, an undoing
touching both, that makes the granite
as overcast as clouds already
infested by gravity, the pull-down
levity a host to temperature –
cold, yet sultry, the ghost-imaging
it engenders . . . more blood
in the emptied body than on
the distant road, ripping with traffic.
Yellow robins and dusky wood swallows
cite a ministry of antithesis over this island
of all that's been said, plus acacias, flowering dryandra,
the white-fleshed granite that uncaps
a grey expression, the blank ink
they sign in deflection,
all here with the remains
of the possum – fox victim.
(*The New Arcadia: Poems* 180)

Katherine's poem is called "Metaphor":

for Daddy, on our excursion to the bush

Having to write about
the
latest metaphor in
mind;
A granite graveyard
or
so it looks
I
find a corpse of
that
pink gloom, my father
inspects
and comes to think it was a quoll
although
later knowing it was a
brush-tailed
possum, I feel sorry that
I
was scared of an animal;
was it pink
gloom
or pink peace?
I
think of it now as

> where
> the earth
> is
> the sunset.
> (Unpublished poem, 2003)

In my version, there is a lot of peripheral material, a lot of implied possibilities, a lot of noise coming from without. In Katherine's, there is the honed, unadulterated moment. The rules of the imagist manifestoes are at work. Age brings the trappings, but it does not have to. However, it would be unusual for a child of that age to include so much distraction to clarify a point. Tangentiality, side-stepping, allusion and avoidance are the tactics of experience living in a world where responsibility brings its own vulnerability, where one imagines the system will consume the naïve. Children learn that, and that is how they age.

Works cited

Barthes, Roland. *Writing degree zero*. Trans. Annette Lavers, and Colin Smith. Boston: Beacon, 1967.

Donne, John. *Complete English Poems*. Ed. A.J. Smith. London: Penguin, 1977.

Enright, D.J., ed. *The Oxford Book of Death*. 1983. Oxford and New York: Oxford UP, 2002.

Génette, G. *Narrative discourse: An essay in method*. Trans. J.E. Lewin. Ithaca: Cornell UP, 1980.

Kinsella, John. *Peripheral Light: Selected and New Poems*. Ed. Harold Bloom. New York: WW Norton, 2003.

—. *The New Arcadia: Poems*. New York: WW Norton. [Forthcoming, July 2005]

—. "A Call For Freedom." [Unpublished poem, 1977/78]

—. "Death Sentence in Ohio: epicedium." *The Yale Review* 93. 2 (April 2005).

Kinsella, Katherine. "Metaphor." [Unpublished poem]

Lukács, Georg. *The Lukács Reader*. Ed. Arpad Kadarkay. Oxford and Cambridge MA: Blackwell, 1995.

Rimbaud, J.-N.-Arthur. *Oeuvres*. Paris: Garnier-Frères, 1960.

—. *Collected Poems*. Trans. O. Bernard. London: Penguin, 1997.

McIntosh, Neil. "World drowning in a rising sea of information." *The Guardian* (Saturday, November 1, 2003).

Raitt, A.W. *The Life of Villiers de l'Isle-Adam*. London: Oxford UP, 1981.

Ryan, Tracy. *The Willing Eye*. South Fremantle: Fremantle Arts Centre; Newcastle upon Tyne: Bloodaxe, 1999.

—. *Hothouse*. South Fremantle: Fremantle Arts Centre, 2002.

—. "Letting Go." [Unpublished poem, 198-]

Smith, Florence Margaret (Stevie). *The Collected Poems*. Ed. James MacGibbon. London: Viking, 1975.

"None of it adds up": Economies of Aging in Doris Lessing's *The Diary of a Good Neighbor*[1]

Cynthia Port

> Now I know what it costs, looking
> after the very old . . .
> Doris Lessing[2]

One of the jokes behind the title of Doris Lessing's anonymously-published novel *The Diary of a Good Neighbor* (1983) is that while its narrator is an extraordinarily good, considerate, and even loving neighbor to the over-ninety Maudie Fowler, she is precisely *not* an official "Good Neighbor," that is, she is not being *paid* by the borough council to assist the aged. Both women insist that the exchange between them is based on neither charity nor greed, but on mutual affection. The two women share a material exchange as well as an emotional one: Janna, the stylish editor of a women's magazine in her late forties, shops for Maudie and bathes her, and in return, Maudie "entertains" Janna with "little stories" about her experiences (95). Janna not only enjoys these stories; she also profits from them, using them as "material" informing her magazine articles, sociological essays, and the lucrative romantic novels she begins to write. While not equal, their exchange is reciprocal and is founded on a shared pleasure in each other's company. After Maudie's long history of exploitation and dispossession and Janna's experience of emotional isolation, their intergenerational and interclass friendship fulfills a profound need for each of them.

While Maudie often seems paranoid, distrustful, and argumentative, Janna recognizes her strong sense of fair play and generous capacity for love. In the closing scene of the novel, one of Maudie's nephews depicts her as "scrounging and begging" by narrating a story in which she engages in a petty, vindictive tit-for-tat. Janna corrects this image, however, with an anecdote that demonstrates Maudie's investment in reciprocity and mutual exchange. As Gayle Greene points out, Maudie's last utterance in the novel – "You've helped me, and now I'll help

---

[1] A version of this essay was published in *Doris Lessing Studies* 24. 1 and 2 (Summer/Fall, 2004) 30-5.
[2] Doris Lessing. *Diary of a Good Neighbor* (1983) 66.

you" (260) – "resonates beyond the immediate context to suggest a right relationship between youth and age, an exchange based on reciprocity" (1994: 194).[3] It appears, therefore, that there is a relentless economic logic through which the novel attempts to organize its moral and ethical concerns about aging and intergenerational exchange.

* * *

History, Gender, and the Economics of Aging

Janna's recognition of Maudie's capacity for generosity and her strong sense of fair play are particularly important in the light of Maudie's profound material poverty. In *The Coming of Age*, Simone de Beauvoir asserts that "[s]ociety inflicts so wretched a standard of living upon the vast majority of old people that it is almost tautological to say 'old and poor'" (1973: 15). While some recent studies of contemporary aging concentrate on the 'grey market' of retirees as a new and increasingly powerful consumer group seeking commodities and leisure activities, many also remind us that poverty remains a key danger for individuals past the age of "production and reproduction."[4] The economic challenges of aging are often especially problematic for women, who generally live longer and are usually poorer, having been paid less for their work and often employed in the unpaid labor of caretaking and housekeeping. This is particularly true of working class women, as Doris Lessing reminds us in her novel; Maudie repeatedly gives up employment she enjoys in order to take care of others – her sister's children, her husband, and her son – without pay, and ends her life in appalling poverty.[5]

During the early 1980s, when Lessing was writing *The Diary of a Good Neighbor*, the combination of a major recession, the Thatcher administration's cutbacks in social services, and widespread unemployment, along with anxieties about increasing life spans and lower birth rates, created a sense of impending crisis in Britain about the financial burden of the old on the resources of the young.[6] According to historian Pat Thane, "[a]bove all, the fears [about

---

[3] Gayle Greene's book goes on to offer an insightful analysis of the novel's emphasis on the value of women's work.

[4] Andrew Blaikie, for example, recognizes the emerging power of the "potentially lucrative grey market" (1999: 213), but points out that "retirement for many continues to be an economically dependent phase, characterised by poverty, material deprivation, and a dwindling quality of life" (1999: 77). For analyses of the political economy of aging, see Phillipson (1982) and Minkler, and Estes, eds. (1991).

[5] On interrelations between aging, gender, and class, see Phillipson (1982), Blaikie (1999), Estes (1991), and Thane (2000; 2001).

[6] The perception of the aging population as a looming crisis recently surfaced again in Britain. However, whereas in the 1980s older employees were urged to retire early in order to free up jobs for younger (and theoretically more efficient) workers, proposals announced

increasingly extended life spans] are about the economic outcomes; that increasing numbers of older people will be dependent upon a shrinking population of working age, imposing upon younger generations new and intolerable costs of pensions, healthcare, and personal care" (2000: 1). Rejecting what she considers exaggerated anxieties about the drain on the young of sustaining the old, Thane concludes her history of old age in England by asserting that "we should – and can – conceive of older people as a resource, not a burden" (2000: 493). The reciprocal relationship between Jane Somers and Maudie Fowler depicted in Lessing's *The Diary of a Good Neighbor* recasts that potential burden as a valuable gift by demonstrating the profound rewards that come to Janna in return for the "cost," as she puts it, "of looking after the very old" (66).

In both its literal and metaphorical registers, the notion of economy provides access to a number of models for understanding the experiences of aging. While advancing age can be registered in terms of accumulation – of years, memories and experience – or as a gradual loss – of vitality, beauty, continence and financial resources – aging is often marked by the increasing difficulty of social, financial, and emotional exchange. De Beauvoir suggests that the condition of old age became particularly degraded in the twentieth century, in part because of a shift in economic theory and therefore in determinations of value. In nineteenth-century France and Britain, she explains, "middle-class ideology [. . .] set a high value on age [because] economic theory that looked upon the accumulation of capital as the universal remedy reached out – mistakenly – into the realm of psychology, holding that accumulation was always good – accumulating years meant making a profit, acquiring the value called experience" (1973: 297). In the twentieth century, however, "[t]he standing of old age has been markedly lowered [because] the notion of experience has been discredited. Modern technocratic society thinks that knowledge does not accumulate with the years, but grows out of date" (1973: 313).

This shift from a system that values accumulation and experience to one that is built on the sell-by date of obsolescence has important implications for understanding the economics of aging in *The Diary of a Good Neighbor*. By placing Maudie's world of "scrimping and saving" in counterpoint to Janna's participation in a consumer economy of expenditure and obsolescence, Lessing highlights not only the material consequences of class difference, but also the instability and dangerous erosion of individual, financial, and social value over time, as well as the crucial importance of emotional and material exchange in countering that erosion. In a capitalist economy, value is generally expected to increase as time passes. However, the aged are no longer in the workforce and, considered incapable of either production or reproduction, their value ebbs rather

---

in December 2002 include provisions for raising the minimum retirement age and offering incentives to induce workers to *delay* retirement in an effort to minimize the number of years pensioners will be drawing on public funds.

than grows with the passing of time. By articulating economic dynamics such as the costs of maintaining health and physical appearance, the commerce of fashion, the debts incurred by both the young and the old, and the escalating difficulties of meeting fundamental needs and controlling the elimination of wastes, Lessing charts both the costs and benefits of change over time. Through her attention to the economics of aging, she calls on readers to recognize the moral economies that underpin these dynamics and challenges us to recalibrate our notions of material and moral value.

* * *

Jane Somers: Consumption in and by time

Jane (Janna) Somers, "[a] handsome, middle-aged widow with a very good job in the magazine world" (17), takes great pride in her expert sense of style and in what she calls "this business of being good at clothes" (83). In the opening pages of *The Diary of a Good Neighbor*, she tells us:

> Mother used to say what I spent on my face and my clothes would feed a family. True. It's no good pretending I regret that. It sometimes seems to me now it was the best thing in my life that – going into the office in the morning, knowing how I looked . . . the girls admiring and wishing they had my taste. Well, I've that if nothing else. I used to buy three, four dresses a week. I used to wear them once or twice, then into jumble. My sister took them for her good causes. So they weren't wasted. (15)

By describing herself through her *taste*, Janna identifies herself as a well-trained participant in consumer culture, for whom identity is constituted by the choices he or she makes in the marketplace.[7] Eventually, Janna graduates from these disposable "fashions," and invests in what she calls her "classical-expensive" style, which she values precisely for its effectiveness as conspicuous consumption. Janna's narrative highlights the profound investment of money, energy, and time that women are generally expected to make in their grooming and physical appearance.[8] In fact, the very word 'investment' has its etymological origin in the act of clothing a person in a garment or 'vestment.' But the word 'investment' also has a military sense; it means "the surrounding or hemming in of a town or fort . . . so as to cut off all communication with the outside" (*The Oxford English Dictionary*). For Janna, investment in her appearance has also served as a kind of

---

[7] Regenia Gagnier discusses the role of choice in consumer culture in *The Insatiability of Human Wants: Economies and Aesthetics in Market Society* (Chicago: U of Chicago P, 2000).

[8] As Barbara Frey Waxman notes, this is an inversion of Kate Brown's "liberating and empowering divestiture" from the standards of feminine beauty in Doris Lessing's earlier novel *The Summer Before the Dark* (1973). See Waxman (1990) 46.

blockade, a means of personal and emotional containment and control. With it she "armoured" herself against the illness and death of both her husband and her mother. A "madly expensive" new outfit (75), she explains, can provide "a bulwark against chaos" (102-3). In addition to training her assistant and later her niece to invest in a self-protective and self-defining style, Janna also instructs the readers of the magazine she edits to be good investors in style – that is, good consumers. Unprofitable images, like those of old women, are banned from the magazine. "They don't buy us for that kind of thing," Janna's colleague Joyce explains (29). Eventually, however, Janna has to point out that it is time for Joyce to "change her style, to fit not being young" (73). Fashion offers protection for the young and middle aged, perhaps, but that "bulwark" breaks down with the passing of time.

Through its erasure of the old and insistence on continual investment in the hope of renewal, the fashion industry reveals its foundations in the fear and denial of mortality.[9] In her essay "The Other End of the Fashion Cycle," however, Margaret Morganroth Gullette argues that fashion serves as a vehicle of what she calls "decline ideology," training women to see their own aging as a kind of decline. Gullette cites Roland Barthes who, in his book *The Fashion System*, describes fashion as "a vengeful present which each year sacrifices the signs of the preceding year" (1983: 289). But while Barthes sees this "murder of the past" (1983: 289) as fundamentally impersonal, seeking only to hasten the purchase of new items, Gullette argues that the violence of the fashion cycle damages the identity of the individual, who becomes to some degree personally invested in the items that she buys. What women learn is that "we [. . .] incur shame if we ally ourselves with the past, the unwanted, the 'old'" (Woodward, ed. 1999: 48). From Gullette's perspective, then, the culture of rapid consumption and disposal encouraged by an advertising-driven women's magazine like *Lilith*[10] serves as a way to prepare aging women to accept their own obsolescence and decline.

To guard against this (learned) obsolescence, Janna has always invested enormous amounts of time and money in the vigilant upkeep and maintenance of her body and wardrobe. However, as time passes, she becomes less and less able (or willing) to put in the necessary energy and time. "Once I did have real proper baths every night, once every Sunday night I maintained and polished my beautiful perfect clothes, maintained and polished *me*, and now I don't, I can't. It is too much for me" (135), she writes in her diary. Janna is keenly aware that the cycles

---

[9] My thanks to Jim English for this observation.

[10] Janna defends the magazine she edits by pointing out that "two thirds of *Lilith* is useful, informative, [and] performs a service," but she also acknowledges that women buy it because they are "conditioned to need glamour" (148). Suggestively, according to Judeo-Christian legend, Lilith, the figure after whom the magazine is named, was Adam's first wife who was deemed obsolete and replaced with Eve after she refused to be subservient to Adam.

of replacement promoted by the fashion industry are also at work in the rise and decline of people and ideas, and in the power shifts from generation to generation, and she begins to prepare for her own looming obsolescence.[11] At a fashion show in Munich, she writes, "I have spent four days wondering what is at work in me which will lead me to be thrown out, or to remain in the office at some less taxing job, while – who? – goes off on these trips" (54). Indeed, after her colleague Joyce leaves the magazine, Janna soon feels politically outmoded and alienated from her staff of "middle class revolutionaries," and within a year she "abdicates" her position as editor, although she retains a part-time position (169). The significance of what first seemed like personal and professional "obsolescence," however, is deeply affected by what Janna learns from her friendship with Maudie. Lessing charts Janna's passage through and away from the fashion market as she cuts back on both her career involvement in the magazine and her own scrupulous shopping and habitual "polishing" of her body and clothes. As several critics argue, through her intimacy with Maudie, Janna learns to accept mortality – something she refused to acknowledge when her mother and husband died.[12] But she also learns to resist the ideology of decline, and to value life in all its stages – including old age. Distancing herself from a world of consumption and disposal, Janna begins to value – and to profit from – Maudie's accumulation of experience.

* * *

Maudie Fowler's Economic Logic: "Scrimping and Saving"

The vast difference between Maudie's economic and social world and Janna's is highlighted at their first encounter, which takes place while shopping. Janna, the ideal consumer, is investing in her image with a basketful of make-up products; Maudie, on the other hand, is trying to buy aspirin to relieve her chronic pain, but has trouble making her purchase and has to ask Janna for help. Their different positions of power on the consumer market are clearly marked as related to their respective age brackets as well as their difference in class status. When Janna enters Maudie's squalid apartment, she is shocked both by Maudie's manifest poverty and by the accumulation of six decades' worth of dirt and "rubbish" (23). The filthy rooms are filled with piles of rags, old newspapers, unwearable old clothes, "everything you can think of" (23). Whereas Janna is both obsessively clean and an expert consumer, renewing herself through frequent luxurious baths and defining her identity by investing in and then discarding expensive goods, Maudie can be seen as a saver or hoarder, accumulating layers of filth on her person and belongings, and collecting the ruined remnants of her former garments

---

[11] Doris Lessing writes about the inevitable obsolescence of ideas and assumptions in *Prisons We Choose to Live Inside* (1987). See especially the essays "When in the Future They Look Back on Us" (1-16) and "Laboratories of Social Change" (63-94).

[12] See, for example, Sprague (1987) 218, and Waxman (1990) 64.

as though they offer her the kind of "bulwark against chaos" that Janna finds in new clothes. Maudie even retrieves from the dustbin and saves garments that Janna has thrown away because they were reeking and soiled with excrement. Indeed, much of what Maudie saves Janna (at first) sees only as waste, and the proliferation of rubbish in Maudie's apartment seems analogous to the bodily waste that Maudie struggles but increasingly fails to control and contain. The contrast between Maudie's thrift and Janna's own expensive "investments," however, leads Janna to reconsider her definition of waste and her participation in an economy of obsolescence; she admits: "I thought of how all of us [at the magazine] wrote about decor and furniture and colours – how taste changed, how we all threw things out and got bored with everything" (22). Janna recognizes a difference not only in class and age status but also in the economic logic that attends those categories.

The contrast between Janna's and Maudie's classes, ages and economic assumptions may be linked to a broader narrative strategy. In *The Insatiability of Human Wants*, Regenia Gagnier explains how one of the methods of sentimental fiction in the Victorian period was to juxtapose scenes depicting the lives of the rich with those of the poor. Believing that "the problems of political economy could be solved by sympathy," the Sentimentalists supposed that contrasting the luxuries of the wealthy with the deprivations of the needy in their novels would "ignite a chain of 'moral sentiment'" that would motivate social changes (2000: 214). The juxtaposition of Janna's wealth and extravagance, on the one hand, and Maudie's deprivation and desperate hoarding, on the other, suggests that Lessing self-consciously echoes this Victorian strategy. Indeed, Janna satirizes herself as a latter-day Victorian philanthropist, and she undertakes writing novels in a sentimental style, one of which, entitled *Gracious Lady*, centers self-consciously on a charitable Victorian woman.[13] However, Doris Lessing distinguishes her own narrative strategy from the sentimental novels she describes as Janna's work; while the class division between Maudie and Janna will never be breached, the other significant contrast between them – the difference in their ages and all that that entails, for example, relative health and mobility – is one that will in time be eliminated. Janna will eventually grow old herself and her realization of this encourages empathy based on identification that is distinct from the sympathy Regenia Gagnier invokes which entails merely pity. Thus, in addition to drawing on Maudie's youthful experiences for her journalism and fiction-writing, Janna writes a diary entry from Maudie's perspective and, subsequently, from the perspective of other characters. As Barbara Frey Waxman puts it, "[t]o be 49 years old and become 90 years old in mind suggests the invalidity of the polarity Anglo-

---

[13] Janna's identification with Victorian ladies is more than a fictional conceit on Doris Lessing's part. Andrew Blaikie has pointed out that owing to cutbacks in the public sector, Britain in the 1980s saw the promotion of "'Victorian values' – private and voluntary charity, self-help, and the 'return' to a system of informal care and unpaid support" (1999: 45).

American culture assumes between youth and age" (1990: 62). Janna's capacity for empathy enables her to reconsider her own economic logic and challenge the culture of decline and disposal. Moreover, it opens the way to a mutual exchange that benefits both women, rather than the unilateral charity suggested by the model of the virtuous Victorian lady.

To some degree, it is Janna's reciprocal attachment to Maudie, which exposes her to shocking material conditions and confronts her with new ways of thinking about obsolescence, waste and value, that enables her partial detachment from work at the magazine and a slight relaxation of her regime of self-maintenance. Whereas before she invested only in her own firm and attractive body, she learns to perform the physically-exhausting and emotionally-draining labor required for the minimal upkeep of an old body. Similarly, although she and Maudie both enjoy a sense of style and share the pleasure of Janna's elegant clothes, Janna's image of herself changes somewhat when she wears those clothes to empty Maudie's commode or to scavenge in a construction bin for bits of wood for Maudie's fire. While it might seem as though Janna trades in one stereotype of female behavior – the consummate shopper, for another – the self-sacrificing caretaker, she also begins to enjoy new and rewarding kinds of creative and professional success, publishing romantic novels and sociological work that draw on and transform what she learns from Maudie's stories. In addition, Maudie's experience as a talented but impoverished and exploited milliner helps Janna reconsider the ethics as well as the economics of consumption; her first novel, *The Milliners of Marylebone*, is a romanticized account of the exploited workers who produce the commodities of fashion.

* * *

Maudie's "little stories": Exchange and the Value of Experience

Simultaneously disgusted and inspired by the material link to the past manifested in Maudie's hoarding, Janna eagerly attends to the memories Maudie has accumulated over time. When Janna offers to pay for her expertise on fashions of the past, however, Maudie is insulted by the notion that she might take money for something she loves to do. "Oh no," she exclaims, despite her poverty, "How can you . . . I love thinking about those old days"(36). Just as she expects no payment for the things she loves to do, Maudie does not trust those who are paid to help her. In the absence of mutual affection and reciprocity, she assumes others are trying to take advantage of her in some way. This is why she particularly treasures her reciprocal friendship with Janna, and especially "value[s] [their] time of sitting and talking" (95). Although, when narrating her experiences, Maudie prefers to concentrate on discrete moments of happiness, most of her narratives end in loss and dispossession – her money is repeatedly stolen, her best-loved new dress is torn, her husband abandons her and later abducts their young son . . . . The litany of losses Maudie recounts serves as evidence of decades of exploitation by others. Yet, despite her continuous experience of loss, Maudie retains a stubborn sense of what things are worth, which is one of the things Janna most admires in her. Her awareness of and commitment to what she values – despite its devaluation by others – helps her sustain her precarious existence. When Janna suggests that the twenty-two shillings that Maudie pays each week for her rent-controlled flat is "not worth the trouble" for the landlord to collect, Maudie indignantly replies: "Worth nothing, is it? It is worth the roof over my head" (27).

The attempt to determine what things and people are worth and to negotiate the unstable nature of value is central to *The Diary of a Good Neighbor*. For many years, Maudie had denied herself food and comfort in order to ensure herself a proper burial, but by the time she dies the fifteen pounds she had so laboriously accumulated decades earlier "would hardly pay for the hire of a spade" (258) in the contemporary economy with which her financial strategies are out of step. Like her funeral benefit, which through inflation has lost rather than accrued value, Maudie herself is perceived by nearly everyone as having eroded in value over time. The question of a young electrician resonates through Jane's diary: "What's the good of people that old?" (32). On considering this question, Jane determines that it cannot be answered by the familiar "yardsticks and measures" (33), such as the individual's capacity for production and reproduction. Instead, Lessing's novel suggests that new notions of value, new "yardsticks and measures" of human worth, need to be established to account for and sustain the value of the old. One way to develop these recalibrated measures, she suggests, is by initiating new circuits of reciprocal exchange across the perceived boundaries of generation and class.[14]

Alongside new estimations of the value of age, however, come new questions about intergenerational responsibility. In conversations and diary entries, Janna tries to understand what one "owes" to the younger generation, to oneself, and to the old. When Janna's friend and colleague, Joyce, decides to move to the States with her philandering husband because her compliance is "owed to" her children, she remains unconcerned about leaving her father behind (90). Blithely assuming that he will "go into a Home," she denies that "we owe" anything to the old (143).[15] Challenging this assumption of the higher value of the young, Janna

---

[14] In this economic model, Doris Lessing echoes Georg Simmel who, in *The Philosophy of Money*, argues that all notions of value are determined only by reciprocal exchange (1990: 90).

[15] According to Alan Walker in "Community Care and the Elderly in Great Britain," the question of who owes what to whom, which is crucial in the development of social policy for the aged, reveals a "hierarchy of values" in British culture (Minkler, and Estes, eds. 1984: 85). As sociologist Chris Phillipson points out in *Capitalism and the Construction of Old Age*, while education and healthcare programs for children can be seen as "a form of

continues to puzzle over what an old woman "*ought* to have by *right*" (231).[16] To the end of her life, Maudie continues her habit of thrift, fighting to accumulate more time and cursing the forces that once again seek to dispossess her, even after she has "run out" of stories with which to entertain Janna and has to begin recycling her memories (214). Resisting all of Janna's assumptions about the diminishing returns of living past the age of ninety-two, Maudie refuses to regard herself as obsolete. After all, her final years – the time she has spent with Janna – are the ones she designates as "the best time of [her] life" (130).

* * *

"To cheer up young writers": Age and the economics of literary value

An additional joke in the title of Doris Lessing's novel is that the document is neither a real diary nor written by Jane Somers. The author's decision to masquerade as a "new writer" is often dismissed as a publicity stunt, but I would argue that the questions about economies of moral and material value raised throughout *The Diary of a Good Neighbor* – What is a good life? A good neighbor? A good investment? – are mirrored by the questions about aesthetic value introduced by the novel's anonymous publication. "I wanted to be reviewed on merit," Lessing explains in the preface that now acknowledges her authorship, "without the benefit of a 'name'." Moreover, she adds, "I wanted to cheer up young writers, who often have such a hard time of it" because their talent is undervalued in an increasingly commercialized literary marketplace.[17] The culture of disposal, aiming to speed the pace of consumption, now applies to novels as well, and new works by unknown writers are, as Lessing points out, reduced to "what publishers call a 'shelf life' (like groceries) of a few months."[18] Whereas the fashion cycle venerates that which is youthful and new, the publishing industry banks on the accumulated symbolic capital of successful authors. Indeed, by masking her identity in a cloak of youthful anonymity, Lessing restages the plot of the novel, demonstrating the generally underappreciated value of accumulated age and experience. At the same time, however, she calls attention to the dangers of rapid cycles of obsolescence and disposal, which skew estimations of aesthetic as well as material and moral value. As Doris Lessing reminds us through both her novel and its publication history, the effective readjustment of appropriate notions of value will require the pursuit of fruitful exchanges between the young and the old.

---

investment in human capital," providing for the elderly does not offer any future "pay off" (1982: 78-9).

[16] Italics in original.

[17] See Doris Lessing. "Preface." *The Diary of a Good Neighbor* (1984) 5.

[18] See Doris Lessing. "Preface." *The Diary of a Good Neighbor* (1984) 8.

124

Works cited

Barthes, Roland. *The Fashion System*. Trans. Matthew Ward, and Richard Howard. New York: Hill and Wang / Farrar, Straus and Giroux, 1983.

de Beauvoir, Simone. *The Coming of Age*. 1972. Trans. Patrick O'Brian. New York: Warner, 1973. [*La vieillesse*. Paris: Gallimard, 1970.]

Blaikie, Andrew. *Ageing and Popular Culture*. Cambridge: Cambridge UP, 1999.

Botelho, Lynn, and Pat Thane, eds. *Women and Ageing in British Society since 1500*. Harlow: Longman-Pearson, 2001.

Estes, Carroll L. "The New Political Economy of Aging: Introduction and Critique." *Critical Perspectives on Aging: The Political and Moral Economy of Growing Old*. Eds. Meredith Minkler, and Carroll L. Estes. New York: Baywood Publishing, 1991. 19-36.

Gagnier, Regenia. *The Insatiability of Human Wants: Economics and Aesthetics in Market Society*. Chicago: U of Chicago P, 2000.

Greene, Gayle. *Doris Lessing. The Poetics of Change*. Ann Arbor: U of Michigan P, 1994.

Gullette, Margaret Morganroth. "The Other End of the Fashion Cycle: Practicing Loss, Learning Decline." *Figuring Age: Women, Bodies, Generations*. Ed. Kathleen Woodward. Bloomington: Indiana UP, 1999. 34-55.

Lessing, Doris. *The Diary of a Good Neighbor. The Diaries of Jane Somers*. 1983. New York: Penguin, 1984. 13-261.

—. *Prisons We Choose to Live Inside*. New York: Harper and Row, 1987.

—. "Laboratories of Social Change." *Prisons We Choose to Live Inside*. New York: Harper and Row, 1987. 163-78.

—. "When in the Future They Look Back on Us." *Prisons We Choose to Live Inside*. New York: Harper and Row, 1987. 1-16.

Minkler, Meredith, and Carroll L. Estes, eds. *Readings in the Political Economy of Aging*. Farmingdale, New York: Baywood Publishing, 1984.

—. eds. *Critical Perspectives on Aging: The Political and Moral Economy of Growing Old*. New York: Baywood Publishing, 1991.

The Oxford English Dictionary. 2nd edition. Oxford: Oxford UP, 1992. [CD-ROM]

Phillipson, Chris. *Capitalism and the Construction of Old Age*. London: Macmillan, 1982.

Simmel, Georg. *The Philosophy of Money*. 1978. Trans. Tom Bottomore, and David Frisby. Ed. David Frisby. 2nd edition. London: Routledge, 1990.

Sprague, Claire. *Rereading Doris Lessing: Narrative Patterns of Doubling and Repetition*. Chapel Hill: U of North Carolina P, 1987.

Thane, Pat. *Old Age in English History*. Oxford: Oxford UP, 2000.

—. "Old women in twentieth-century Britain." *Women and Ageing in British Society since 1500*. Eds. Lynn Botelho, and Pat Thane. Harlow: Longman-Pearson, 2001. 207-31.

Walker, Alan. "Community Care and the Elderly in Great Britain: Theory and Practice." *Readings in the Political Economy of Aging*. Eds. Meredith Minkler, and Carroll L. Estes. Farmingdale, New York: Baywood, 1984. 75-93.

Waxman, Barbara Frey. *From the Hearth to the Open Road: A Feminist Study of Aging in Contemporary Literature*. New York: Greenwood, 1990.

Woodward, Kathleen, ed. *Figuring Age: Women, Bodies, Generations*. Bloomington: Indiana UP, 1999.

Love's Knowledge? Growing Old Disgracefully in Philip Roth's *The Human Stain*

David Rampton

Philip Roth's *The Human Stain* (2000) turns around three main characters: Coleman Silk, a retired academic who is seeking respite from the furies of political correctness who have torn his life asunder; Faunia Farley, a thirty-something graduate of the school of hard knocks whom life has forced to grow up too quickly; and Nathan Zuckerman, Roth's alter ego in a clutch of novels and, in this book, the writer Coleman Silk turns to when he wants to have his story told. These characters are all in their different ways acutely conscious of ageing, and ageing for Roth is all about carnal knowledge, what our bodies tell us as we get older and what we can say about that knowledge.

If all Roth had to say about this inexorable process was that, despite it, retired deans can still find solace in the sack with acrobatic young women, there would be no need to devote a whole article to documenting that relatively uncontentious claim. But ageing for Roth is about carnal ignorance as well – all the illusions we cherish, all the notions that we are deceived by, and all the things that we cannot know in conventional ways. Much of the text of *The Human Stain* is given over to what the older man and the inventive lover half his age get up to, but the subtext is, as so often in Roth, our imaginings about what constitutes others' intimacies, and here Nathan Zuckerman's narrative, his account of things he could not have witnessed, has pride of place. The "growing old disgracefully" in the title, then, is a reference to the sexual adventurousness encouraged by an America preoccupied with the advent of Viagra and the salacious tales of adulterous oral sex in the White House.[1] The question preceding it is an attempt to focus attention on Roth's complex treatment of the intricacies of our deeds and imaginings that make us violate notions of normalcy and disgrace ourselves.

* * *

---

[1] The novel is set in the late 1990s in an America obsessed by the scandal surrounding the relationship between White House intern Monica Lewinsky and President Bill Clinton.

For Roth, ageing is a version of what the late Stephen Jay Gould[2] called, in a rather different context, "punctuated equilibrium";[3] that is, it consists of a series of moments that mark and define the changes in a process, the salient points in a wealth of seemingly unchanging days. There are quite a number of such moments in the book, and Roth organizes them more skilfully and makes them resonate more forcefully than he has been given credit for. Studying the depiction of ageing in this way, as a series of sudden, hard-to-define understandings, can offer a new take on this novel, one that runs counter to what is threatening to become the critical orthodoxy insofar as Roth's late fiction is concerned, that it constitutes a formless, uncritical, monologic meditation on human multiplicity. At the end of "The Cost of Clarity," a detailed critique of the novel, for example, James Wood sums up the case Roth makes in *The Human Stain* for our ignorance of others' complexities in the following terms:

> Roth tells us how bottomless we all are, but he is contradictorily engaged in the creation of characters who are entirely controlled and voiced by Roth, and who thus seem the opposite of bottomless. He never seems to hit a real obstacle to his impressive lucidity. This is a late trap for late Roth: an anger that is in fact a sentimentality, a pessimism that is really an optimism, and a commitment to the bottomlessness of people and situations that is shallower than it wants to be. And running through it all is Roth's grinding, unappeasable intelligence, which in this novel is perhaps too easily appeased. (*The New Republic* 2000: 78)

James Wood is a sympathetic reader and he makes a strong case, but in what follows I propose to argue for a somewhat different reading by suggesting that the novel is organized around, not noisy recognition of our endlessly unavailable otherness by a bunch of ventriloquized puppets, but a much more attenuated and complex acquiescence in reconciling ourselves to mortality. The series of moments in which these acquiescences must be made constitutes, according to this view, precisely what Wood seeks to deny, that is, "real obstacle[s] to [Roth's] impressive lucidity." They are, in short, a series of anti-epiphanies – what the narrator describes at one point as the "pure state of something that is nothing" (257). The emphasis in such moments is on paradoxical formulations like "something that is nothing," on suggestive intertextual echoes, and on the importance of non-rational modes of communication. Studying these moments more carefully can help us understand better how Roth presents ageing in *The Human Stain*.

* * *

---

[2] Professor of Geology, Biology, and the History of Science at Harvard University, Stephen Jay Gould (1941-2002) was one of the best known and most widely read scientists of the twentieth century.

[3] See Niles Eldredge, and Stephen Jay Gould. "Punctuated Equilibria: an Alternative to Phyletic Gradualism" *Models in Paleobiology* (Ed. Thomas Schopf. San Francisco: Freeman and Cooper, 1972) 82-115.

At first glance, ageing for all three of the principal characters involves a series of experiences from which they learn how hard it is to learn anything. Someone Coleman Silk loves leaves him because she cannot finally marry a black man. Four years later, they meet by chance and we are told:

> Stunned by how little he'd gotten over her and she'd gotten over him, he walked away understanding, as outside his reading in classical Greek drama he'd never had to understand before, how easily life can be one thing rather than another and how accidentally a destiny is made . . . on the other hand, how accidental fate may seem when things can never turn out other than they do. That is, he walked away understanding nothing, knowing he could understand nothing, though with the illusion that he *would* have metaphysically understood something of enormous importance about this stubborn determination of his to become his own man if . . . if only such things were understandable. (125-6)

This is a difficult passage. Like Coleman Silk, we may understand nothing – even "metaphysically" understand nothing, whatever that means – after our first encounter with it. How can a "destiny" or "fate" be "accidental"? Was he doomed never to have this girl, or not? Is his illusion of a possible understanding illusory because no such understanding is possible? Or only because it is not possible for him? Or will what is not possible for him now be all the clearer to him later on? And what does classical Greek drama have to do with it? The passage concludes:

> He thought the same useless thoughts – useless to a man of no great talent like himself, if not to Sophocles: how accidentally a fate is made . . . . Or how accidental it all may seem when inescapable. (126)

More paradoxes, of course, and what are we to make of the distinction made here between the use of these truths by a literary artist and the haplessness of those who must simply live them? The characters' attempts to find answers to such questions are the driving force behind what happens in *The Human Stain*, and tracking such attempts will determine the succcess of our engagement with it.

* * *

In a sense, the novel, or at least Nathan Zuckerman's story, begins with the degree zero of explanation, a moment in which it would seem there is absolutely nothing left to learn, nothing to be communicated. I am thinking of the scene in the graveyard after the funerals of the two main characters, a scene in which he is trying to get started on his story – trying to "hear" Coleman Silk and Faunia Farley "talk" to each other, trying to animate his imagination. Nathan Zuckerman compares it to entering a "professional competition with death" (338), an evocative phrase that means presumably not only re-creating the voices of two dead people in ways that make them seem to be alive, replacing their silence with language, but also engaging in an attempt to write a story that works its way to a conclusion different from the ones death keeps churning out so successfully. So he focuses on individual scenes, created by hints and guesses.

Consider the scene in which Nathan Zuckerman sees Coleman Silk and Faunia Farley for the last time, the concert at Tanglewood where they and a bunch of elderly tourists listen to the Boston Symphony Orchestra play works by Sergey Rachmaninoff, Nikolay Rimsky-Korsakov and Sergey Prokofiev. Roth sets things up carefully. First, he has his narrator imagine that the assembled audience is on a pier built on the Atlantic coast to welcome ocean liners from Europe, a pier magically transported inland: "We were about a three-hour drive west of the Atlantic," Nathan Zuckerman recounts, "but I couldn't shake this dual sense of both being where I was and of having pushed off, along with the rest of the senior citizens, for a mysterious watery unknown" (206). The dual sense involves the in-between nature of this group of Americans who have come together to listen to three Russian composers, each of whom has a particular link with the United States, and the "between old age and death feeling" (209) that hits so hard in the New World precisely because that world works so strenuously to deny it expression. But this duality also gently introduces the idea of the tenuous links between a would-be perennially youthful America and an ageing Europe on which it has turned its back, a point to be taken up at various points in the novel. When the orchestra begins with Rimsky-Korsakov's *Symphonic Dances*, Nathan Zuckerman describes the music as laying bare for all these oldsters "the youngest, most innocent of our ideas of life, the indestructible yearning for the way things aren't and never can be" (207). And the stage is set for the great rant about our isolated individuality that James Wood and other commentators have rightly identified as the centre of the novel – the scene in which, while watching Coleman Silk and Faunia Farley, the narrator is struck by how little we know about each other.

Is this assertion of the redemptively messy obscurity of human life simply another cliché, as Wood suggests, a sentimental counter-ideology, hysterically insisted on but insufficiently dramatized? The passage is far too long to quote in its entirety, but let us reconsider the context for a moment. No sooner has Nathan Zuckerman sung his hymn in praise of how clearly he can see how little there is to see than he starts talking about the end to which all these human entities – these complex vehicles of hidden information – are moving. He says:

> I began cartoonishly, to envisage the fatal malady that, without anyone's recognizing it, was working away with us, within each and every one of us; to visualize the blood vessels occluding under the baseball caps, the malignancies growing beneath the permed white hair, the organs misfiring, atrophying, shutting down, the hundreds of billions of murderous cells surreptitiously marching this entire audience toward the improbable disaster ahead . . . . The ceaseless perishing. What an idea! What maniac conceived it? (209)

Note that the narrative has moved from acknowledging ignorance to flaunting knowledge, and what we know does away with knowing – the insane inexorability of a universal death march coolly cancels out whatever meaning we might be tempted to ascribe to it. All our unknowable complexities are suddenly one with the army of unseen cells hurrying us to our doom. This would seem to qualify rather sharply the celebration of ignorance in the novel's preceding paragraph.

In the throes of the emotions engendered by this moment, Nathan Zuckerman settles down to listen to Prokofiev's *Second Piano Concerto*, and immediately he shifts again. It should be noted here that this particular work is generally acknowledged to be the Prokofiev concerto most pianists prefer to play in concert. Its epic scale, its extraordinarily difficult cadenzas, the physical and emotional challenges it poses have a profound effect on audiences who respond to it as one of the great romantic statements of the early twentieth-century, the work in which the composer most fully exposes his heart, as problematic as that formulation is. Listening to it played by Yefim Bronfman, another Russian, Nathan Zuckerman suddenly feels what he calls redemption. Conveyed by the pianist's extraordinary skill, the music is so overwhelming that "our own lives now seem inextinguishable. Nobody is dying, *nobody* – not if Bronfman has anything to say about it!" (210). How has filling the New England afternoon with the harmonies inscribed on a seventy-five-year-old musical score made the great truth about a catastrophic lack of order and visions of universal death disappear? Clearly one can soar as high on this counter-truth as one can plummet when in the throes of its opposite. This point of view is as real as the music and its associations.

In the following interaction with Coleman Silk and Faunia Farley during the interval, the narrator introduces more qualification for the "We know nothing" tirade; Nathan Zuckerman obviously knows a great deal, as evidenced by the series of insightful comments he makes on what can and cannot be divined from the short conversation among the three of them that ensues. All of a sudden, Nathan Zuckerman *knows* again, the way we all do, by observation, inference, deduction, and so on – knows imperfectly, but knows something. And, as he reminds us at the very end of this important section, armed with his imagination, he must fill in the rest – "I am forced to imagine. It happens to be what I do for a living. It is my job. It's now all I do" (213). The second half of the book, which he announces with these lines, suggests that the storyteller's very freedom is a function of the ignorance he so vehemently insisted on a few moments before. The way he uses that freedom – and by implication the way all of us, playing the same role, use it – will determine the quality and usefulness of the stories that result. What James Wood sees as a monologic diatribe that seeks to sentimentalize and render banal proves to be a more complex affair in which "what we don't know" is given its own set of voices.

* * *

The next scene to punctuate the equilibrium by foregrounding non-rational modes of discourse and the reactions they evoke is one that, if Nicole Kidman's[4] publicity agent has anything to say about it, is sure to become the most famous in the novel. The "Dance for me" scene (225-34) is, again, too long and detailed to be dealt with in more than summary fashion here, but let me highlight some of the points relevant to the argument I am pursuing. First, it is an imagined scene, the pure creation of Nathan Zuckerman's competition with death. Second, it is a very quiet scene in which the principals say little for the longest time. Third, it is an erotic scene, in which the jazz, the bodies and the timelessness of a moment in which age, death and consequences do not exist, are all splendidly realized. Fourth, it is an attempt to define pleasure in a way that emphasizes the paradox of "something in nothing" referred to earlier; like the Athena College faculty postmodernists whom Coleman Silk so mistrusts, Faunia Farley speaks of sexual attraction in a way that seeks to reveal love for what it is – a petty bourgeois construction that merely distracts us from the intensity of the moment. She celebrates, rather, the wordless, expectation-less ephemerality of arousal as the nothingness that will serve in its stead. Fifth, it is a scene that, like the one we have just looked at, is immediately undercut by the ones that come after it. Coleman Silk does not learn the lesson that Faunia Farley so patiently tries to teach him – the lesson about forgetting love and living for the moment. Instead, trying to teach his own lesson for Faunia by reading aloud something from the newspaper about Bill Clinton and Monica Lewinsky, he ends up forcing her to flee, temporarily losing her to Prince, a wordless, haughty crow, the only living thing in her life that is attractively unencumbered by civilization and its discontents. Faunia Farley's anti-love rhapsody is further undercut by Nathan Zuckerman's somewhat prosaic alternative definition of love as seeing someone "being game in the face of the worst" (338), a formula he hits upon after imagining the aforementioned graveyard dialogue between the dead lovers. Roth uses such scenes and their aftermaths to speak to readers in a variety of ways, effectively refusing to deliver the undifferentiated, essayistic formula that James Wood warns us against.

* * *

"Everything painful congealed into passion. [. . .] Nothing in life tempts them, nothing in life excites them, nothing in life subdues their hatred of life anything like this intimacy . . . . They are the disaster to which they are enjoined" (203) – thus Nathan Zuckerman, describing the pair just before giving us his rendition of the dance scene. The way sexual passion can be excited by emotions like anger or fear or a reckless abandoning of social obligations is well known, and Roth

---

[4] Nicole Kidman starred in "To Die For," "The Portrait of a Lady," "Eyes Wide Shut" and "Moulin Rouge" before taking on the role of Faunia Farley in the film version of *The Human Stain* (2003). She won the Oscar for Best Actress for her role in "The Hours" (2002).

portrays all that compellingly in *The Human Stain*. But the passage just quoted does more than that. It alerts us to the fact that, as a novelist, Philip Roth is feeling his way towards his own anti-definition of love, one that will serve as the verbal equivalent for Faunia Farley's dance, the sultry jazz, and the breathy, rhythmic, quasi-wordless promises she makes in her performance. For *The Human Stain* is arguably Roth's most thoughtful exploration of the relationship between love and suffering, and the intensity of the bond it can effect. For Roth, it is a relationship that only comes into focus with the presbyopia of later life. After the youthful *Portnoy's Complaint* (1969) and following the mid-age crises of *The Counterlife* (1986), Roth decided to write a novel, not primarily about our lack of knowledge, nor about how isolated we all are, but about the knowledge and ignorance appropriate for a man in his late sixties, his subject, a man who is something of an expert in both love and suffering.

A relatively recent exposition of the central idea will help define the terms of the argument here. In an essay entitled "Love's Knowledge," Martha Nussbaum begins by quoting Marcel Proust's contention that knowledge of the heart must come from the heart.[5] She explains that impressions of suffering as a consequence of a lover's absence or rejection, for example, can induce a kind of seizure because they are so powerful and surprising, and she goes on to note that for the Stoic, this overwhelming impression,

> is not simply a route to knowing; it *is* knowing. [. . .] knowledge of our love is not the fruit of the impression of suffering, [but rather] the suffering itself is a piece of self-knowing. [. . .] The love is not some separate fact about us that is signaled by the impression; the impression reveals the love by constituting it. Love is not a structure in the heart waiting to be discovered; it is embodied in, made up out of, experiences of suffering. (1990: 267-8)

Finally, says Nussbaum, reflection shows us "the intermittences of the heart" – the alternations between love and its denial, suffering and negation of suffering, that constitute what she calls,

> the most essential and ubiquitous structural feature of the human heart. In suffering we know only suffering. We call our rationalizations false and delusive and we do not see to what extent they express a mechanism that is regular and deep in our lives. But this means that in love itself we do not yet have full knowledge of love – for we do not grasp its limits and boundaries. (1990: 273)

The scenes just examined constitute a detailed study of these intermittences, and Martha Nussbaum's account describes precisely the complex

---

[5] Marcel Proust (1871-1922) is the author of *A la Recherche du Temps Perdu* (1913-1927), a series of novels that constitute the most important French work of fiction in the twentieth century.

representation of self-knowledge and knowledge of others that is explored in the novel's account of the relationship between Coleman Silk and Faunia Farley. These scenes turn around the shocks that enable the participants to know what they are feeling, the alternations between strong attraction and doubt, fervent protestation and erotic silence, self-forgetting and self-absorption, the conviction that love is a profound absence and that it is a bunch of words, that it is confined to the present moment and realizable in an idealized future. These are the structural properties of the mysteriously elusive and resolutely humdrum phenomenon that *The Human Stain* both refuses to explain *and* helps us to understand so well, even while it articulates the extent to which such things are available to the understanding.

* * *

Silence and desultory conversation, the pre-eminence of the unsaid over the said, the tensions between a desire for solitude and a desire for community, the difficulty involved in sorting out what is imagination and what reality – all these elements come together again at the end of *The Human Stain*, in an encounter between Nathan Zuckerman and Les Farley, Faunia's ex-husband. Again, Roth prepares the scene carefully. Away from the highway, Nathan Zuckerman discovers "a setting as pristine . . . as unviolated, as serenely unspoiled, as envelops any inland body of water in New England" (345). One thinks of Henry David Thoreau, obviously, and all the reveries induced by his sojourn and its subsequent mythologizing by the culture that responded to it so powerfully.[6] The scene ties in neatly with the one at Tanglewood, too, with its references to the body of water that separates Europe from America. It is worth recalling in this context that Thoreau himself once described the Atlantic as a Lethean dream that enables us to forget the Old World and its institutions (Atkinson, ed. 1937: 608). Again, we are alerted to the fact that this moment will be, like the last one, a conflict of two impulses, two points of view – this time the writer's and the actor's, the reflective person and the instinctual one, someone committed to trying to arrange things in a pattern and someone who doggedly denies the very existence of such order.

Philip Roth has already gone out of his way to make us aware of the importance of pure instinct for a character like Faunia Farley – "No thinking" "No planning" "No feelings" (258), he says when speaking to the psychologist about why Coleman Silk and Faunia Farley swerve off the road. Roth ends up killing them off, we are told, "Planning and not planning. Knowing and not knowing" (257-8), just before the highway confrontation takes place – phrases that locate us once again in that dangerous in-between space that figures so prominently in this narrative. The two men talk of fishing and post-traumatic stress disorder; there are

---

[6] Henry David Thoreau is the author of *Walden* (1854), an evocative description of a period during which he explored the pleasures of solitude in a cabin he built in the woods near Concord, Massachusetts.

eloquent silences and brisk exchanges; Nathan Zuckerman tries to find out how much Farley is willing to confess to and Farley keeps him at bay. In this exchange, "reason" and "logic" (350) are again dismissed, not to be major players in this conversation about what it is like to be "close to God" (347).

As in the other scenes we have looked at, death hovers ominously close – in the form of the memories of the murdered pair that work in their unspoken ways in the minds of the two interlocutors, and in the form of the auger that Farley has used to make his hole in the ice. "All ye know and all ye need to know, all inscribed in the spiral of its curving blade" (354), thinks Nathan Zuckerman as he looks at it. The allusion to John Keats's "Ode on a Grecian Urn"[7] seems as puzzling and as evocative as the problem of the knowledge of love just discussed. What does the Grecian urn's message to mankind about the relationship between truth and beauty have to do with Farley's auger – this non-decorative, eminently practical artefact in the hands of a murderous Vietnam veteran? They are both means by which the solid or corporeal is broken down, connections made with a new element. Both objects are aids to the sustenance of the human beings associated with them – an immortality of sorts for the figures frozen in time on the one; the other an arm against hostile nature on a frozen earth. Both have something to tell us about death; the cold pastoral represented on Keats's urn[8] is reified in the bleak landscape associated with the auger and its menacing aspect; the death represented on the urn can be inflicted by the auger. The silence of both speaks volumes, announcing the end of one kind of discourse and the beginning of another. Both artefacts "tease out of thought" those who feel compelled to gaze, putting them in touch with some of the emotions – nostalgia, fear, wonder – that this non-rational process makes room for. Note, too, how the meditation on the significance of the auger undercuts the "each-of-us-is-an-intriguing-but-closed-book-to-his-fellow-humans" idea that is, supposedly, so central in *The Human Stain*. "I know, and he knows I know. And the auger knows," thinks Nathan Zuckerman (354). Reconciling onself to the knowledge that expresses itself in riddles – "Beauty is truth, truth beauty"; "love is suffering" – means paying attention to the silences that enable us to hear a message below the noise and then to wrestle with its obscurities.

The point is brought home in the novel's gorgeous last paragraph – endings in late Roth tend to be splendid affairs. Nathan Zuckerman looks back on,

> the icy white of the lake encircling a tiny spot that was a man, the only human marker in all of nature, like the X of an illiterate's signature on a sheet of paper.

---

[7] A partial reference to the last two lines of John Keats's "Ode on a Grecian Urn" (1819) – "Beauty is truth; truth beauty, – that is all / Ye know on earth, and all ye need to know."

[8] A reference to John Keats's "Ode on a Grecian Urn" (1819) – "Thou, silent form, dost tease us out of thought / As doth eternity: Cold Pastoral!"

> There it was, if not the whole story, the whole picture. Only rarely, at the end of
> our century, does life offer up a vision as pure and peaceful as this one: a solitary
> man on a bucket, fishing through eighteen inches of ice in a lake that's constantly
> turning over its water atop an arcadian mountain in America. (361)

As I have been trying to make clear, this is not so much the respite at the end of an
obtrusive monologue as it is the natural culmination of a series of moments that
have led to a paradoxical, "something in nothing" conclusion. This is after all a
minimalist scene – a guy sitting fishing, signifying nothing. It even seems vaguely
other-worldly too; how, for example, can there be water flowing "at the top of a
mountain," a location that seems impossibly in-between again. Yet there is partial
knowledge – "not the whole story," but *a* story; not "the whole picture," but a
tableau that stimulates at least some meditation. And the language of signification
is there as well, in the reference to the "illiterate's signature," the mark the
untutored make. Faunia Farley, you will remember, is no illiterate – she keeps a
journal – only someone who feigns being one, so this is not so much an invocation
of her presence as it is a hymn to the pleasures of bucolic anonymity.

In the novel's last paragraph, Roth evokes the enigmatic nature of
"arcadian" America, the agrarian republic Jefferson dreamed of, the one where the
citizenry would be left alone by the central administration, free to possess the land
and contemplate its silences. The single person in the middle of a large expanse
untouched by humanity was the symbol of that land and that silence. That it all
worked out quite differently, that America aged disgracefully, that its institutions
have messed with the minds of its would-be loners, that most of the lakes and the
landscapes are too crowded to encourage such meditations now – none of this
diminishes the nobility of the originating dream. So what do we know at the end of
this scene? The distinguishing feature in this landscape is the human signature, the
X that marks a mysterious spot. As Nathan Zuckerman finishes his story by the
complex process of observing, recording, intuiting, and inventing to which he has
been forced to resort, we know that Les Farley is probably a murderer, that Nathan
Zuckerman himself is going to leave Athena College after saying so in his book,
and that writing it will resolve exactly nothing. Rumours about Coleman Silk and
Faunia Farley will continue to circulate, the living will not forgive the dead,
Delphine Roux, Coleman's nemesis at the university, will insist on hyper-political
correctness, and Americans will be hypocritically indignant about all of it.

In a 1982 interview with David Plante, Philip Roth said: "[John] Updike
and [Saul] Bellow hold their flashlights out in the world, reveal the real world as it
is *now*. I dig a hole and shine my flashlight into the hole" (Searles, ed. 154). This
hole is where he finds characters like Coleman Silk and Nathan Zuckerman, Les
and Faunia Farley. They are to him what Oedipus and Pentheus, both alluded to in
the novel, are to *their* creators – the means by which he sheds at least a little light
on those areas of human experience most difficult to understand. There are no more

classical tragedies, at least no more that reveal themselves in the exquisite shapes that Sophocles and Euripides found so useful, but if tragedy means thwarted energy and unrealized possibilities, then *The Human Stain* has it in abundance. In groping for the precise form needed to define how adults deal with the complexities of love, suffering, death, and their strange interpenetrations, Roth had to strike out on his own. No doubt he gets it wrong at times, as critics have been quick to point out, yet such failures reveal the world he has set out to explore by constituting it. To criticize him for trying to "haul into speakability the wordless" (*The New Republic* 2000: 70), as James Wood does in his essay on *The Human Stain*, is to seek to rob Philip Roth of what is finally the novelist's only resource in his battle with time and his attempt to get a glimpse of eternity. Apophatic gestures ill befit writers like Roth, writers who have earned the right to remain silent but who still have a great deal to say.

Works cited

Atkinson, Brooks, ed. *Walden and Other Writings of Henry David Thoreau*. New York: Random House, 1937.

Eldredge, Niles, and Stephen Jay Gould. "Punctuated Equilibria: an Alternative to Phyletic Gradualism." *Models in Paleobiology*. Ed. Thomas Schopf. San Francisco: Freeman and Cooper, 1972. 82-115.

Nussbaum, Martha. *Love's Knowledge: Essays on Philosophy and Literature*. New York and Oxford: Oxford UP, 1990.

Plante, David. "Conversations with Philip: Diary of a Friendship." 1984. *Conversations with Philip Roth*. Ed. George J. Searles. Jackson and London: UP of Mississippi, 1992. 150-61.

Roth, Philip. *Portnoy's Complaint*. New York: Houghton Mifflin, 1969.

—. *The Counterlife*. New York: Farrar, Straus and Giroux, 1987.

—. *The Human Stain*. Boston and New York: Houghton Mifflin, 2000.

Schopf, Thomas, ed. *Models in Paleobiology*. San Francisco: Freeman and Cooper, 1972.

Searles, George J., ed. *Conversations with Philip Roth*. Jackson and London: UP of Mississippi, 1992.

Thoreau, Henry David. "Walking." *Walden and Other Writings of Henry David Thoreau*. Ed. Brooks Atkinson. New York: Random House, 1937. 597-632.

Wood, James. "The Cost of Clarity." *The New Republic* (April 17 and 24, 2000) 70-8.

The "Aging Fallacy":
Older Scholars and Cultural Belatedness[1]

Félix Rodríguez Rodríguez

In the introduction to his book *Linguistics and Literary History: Essays in Stylistics*, the literary critic Leo Spitzer[2] advises "every older scholar" attempting to explain his lifetime critical approach to write a brief "autobiographic sketch" of his "first academic experiences" (1948: 1). His advice is grounded in the crucial influence of such experiences on the development of every scholar's method; "the basic approach," he argues, "of the individual scholar, conditioned as it is by his first experiences, by his *Erlebnis*, as the Germans say, determines his method: *Methode ist Erlebnis*" (1948: 1). In his own "older scholar" sketch, Spitzer focuses on what he seems to regard as the most relevant event of his own *Erlebnis*, namely, his profound sense of disappointment when, after attending his first classes at the university, he realized that the positivist approach to Linguistics – "an agglomeration of unconnected, separate, anecdotic, senseless evolutions" – offered by his teachers had nothing to do with the motives that had impelled him to study Romance Languages, the "French atmosphere" of his native "gay and orderly" Vienna, the "sensuousness," "vitality," and "sentimentality" of French literature, or the lively words, which were a "delight" to his "heart," pronounced by the actors of a French troupe (1948: 2). The point of this anecdote, told here to exemplify the thesis *Methode ist Erlebnis*, is that the academic discipline Spitzer went on to evolve – Stylistics – grew out of that frustrating academic experience.

It is by no means accidental that the connection between scientific method and *Erlebnis* is posited by Spitzer in an essay in which he also claims that "the humanities are under attack" (1948: 1). Since he clearly refers to those humanities to whose establishment his own method has contributed significantly, it is evident that it is his method that is also being challenged. This suggests that for Spitzer the autobiographical sketch is an indispensable part of his effort, or even unacknowledged strategy, to defend both his method and the conception of

---

[1] The research carried out in order to write this paper has been funded by the Spanish Ministry of Science and Technology (BFF 2002-02763).
[2] Leo Spitzer (1887-1960). Austrian-born literary and linguistics (stylistics) theorist.

humanities such a method incarnates. Spitzer's urging "every older scholar" to recover his *Erlebnis*, merging academic experiences with elements of sentimental memory and identity, serves the purpose not only of promulgating the *credo* he has devoted his scholarly life to, but also, most importantly, of asserting his unconditional commitment to it. Such advice to "every older scholar" betrays Spitzer's determination to react negatively towards any new methodology that may deprive him of the privileged and dominant position he occupies in the discipline of literary studies and the humanities in general.

* * *

At least two other older scholars, the art historian E.H. Gombrich[3] and the literary critic René Wellek,[4] similarly frightened by the possibility that their academic methods may be destroyed, have taken Leo Spitzer's advice. Gombrich's narrative of his *Erlebnis*, entitled "An Autobiographical Sketch" which is included in his book *Topics of Our Time* (1991), is followed by two essays – "The Embattled Humanities: The Universities in Crisis" and "Relativism in the Humanities: The Debate about Human Nature" – in which, as his titles imply, he deplores a number of new approaches that call into question his notion of humanities. Although his sketch extends to his "current work" (1991: 24), Gombrich pays special attention, in apparent confirmation of the truth of Spitzer's *Methode ist Erlebnis*, to the effects of his first formative stages on the interests and goals of his extensive critical career. He thus argues that his much debated neglect of the "modern movement" could be traced back to his parents' distaste for the musical experiments the contemporary composers Arnold Schönberg and Alban Berg "tried to launch" (1991: 12). He also remarks that the subject he selected for his final written essay at high school – "the changes in art appreciation from Winckelman to the present age" (1991: 13) – has continued to be the central subject of his research – "all," he says, "I have ever done" (1991: 13).

To the extent that such lifelong coherence in respect of the selection of his research topics demonstrates the consistency and strength of his method, Gombrich's comment may be seen as attesting his fidelity to his critical views. Also testifying to this fidelity is the fact, pointed out by both Spitzer and Wellek, too, that his *Erlebnis* coincided with a historical transformation of the discipline, namely, the substitution of the older tradition of art criticism going back "to Goethe and the eighteenth century" by a "new wave" concerned with "Expressionism" and "the discovery of late medieval art, of late Gothic" (1991: 13). These historical origins of the method, to which the older art scholar appears to show gratitude and

---

[3] Ernst Hans Josef Gombrich (1909-2001). Austrian-Jew. British art historian and scholar.
[4] René Wellek (1903-1995). Austrian-born literary theorist and historian of literary criticism. He lived and worked in the USA.

pride in having taken an active part, increase their critical, and even sentimental, value and thus reinforce his commitment to preserving it.

It is worth noting that, unlike Spitzer and Wellek, Gombrich, if only to dismiss that possibility from the outset, refers to his old age as one of the reasons which might account for his rejection of new theories and approaches, and more specifically for his aversion to the dangerous ideas of deconstruction. "Joking apart," – he writes in "Relativism in the Humanities: The Debate about Human Nature" – "I know very well that it may also be due to my age that I can make so little sense of the canonical texts of that movement, but since I am not a relativist I still do not believe that every generation has its own truths" (1991: 38). However, rather than reading this as serious consideration of the issue, we should take this reference to his comparatively advanced age as a defensive, and probably deliberate, move to undermine the arguments his younger antagonists will put forward, or are already putting forward, to foil his attacks. In the same way, in the same quotation, his stated belief in the non-contingent nature of some truths of human knowledge is also designed to protect himself and his methodology. As the philosopher Jean Améry argues in his book *Revuelta y resignación. Acerca del envejecer*, in a vain attempt to disguise his intellectual and cultural decline, to conceal his inability not only to make sense but also to maintain his control over the new cultural products and practices, the "person who ages culturally" tends "to consider cultural events from an eternal perspective" (2001: 114);[5] in other words, the aging academic is inclined to look down on contemporary cultural events from an essentialist and hence somewhat disdainful viewpoint. Falling into "the saddest of all self-deceits" (2001: 113),[6] Jean Améry often diminishes the value and importance of new events by contrasting them with the meaningful events which have established his cultural identity. This is the reason why Gombrich sets up in opposition the absolute, timeless truths of his conception of art criticism with the relative, transitory ideas expounded by deconstruction, a critical movement which he reduces to "an ephemeral intellectual fad" (1991: 39).

* * *

René Wellek's nostalgic *Erlebnis*, entitled "Prospect and Retrospect," appears in *The Attack on Literature and Other Essays*, a collection of late essays in which, once again identifying the fate of one particular method with that of the entire discipline, he both reaffirms the validity of his formalist approach and warns against the "irrational" and "nihilistic" new schools and critics which are leading literary studies back to "chaos," to a "new barbarism" (1982: 102). Yet Wellek's narrative differs from those by Spitzer and Gombrich in that he explicitly states his aims in writing it. It is, he contends, "a little intellectual autobiography that pays

---

[5] My translation.
[6] My translation.

tribute to my teachers and reasserts my creed" (1982: 146). This second aim is testimony, of course, to what has been suggested thus far is the real reason why older scholars recall their *Erlebnis*. As to Wellek's first stated aim, insofar as his teachers are an important part of his first academic experiences, his act of bearing witness to them should be considered as supplementing the fundamental aim of reasserting his creed, that is, as another way of manifesting his commitment to it. The point is that, by transforming his sketch into a kind of personal and affectionate commemoration to his teachers, he reinforces his fidelity to his views. Wellek implies that what is at stake is not simply the preservation of a particular method, but the cherished memory of his teachers. From this perspective, the defense of the method becomes an act of responsibility – the reaffirmation of his trust in his mentors and the fulfillment of his duties as a survivor in academe. Wellek's logic of debt and gratitude confers an ethical significance on the formula *Methode ist Erlebnis* and, thereby, on the older scholar's willingness to maintain his method, which seems to rely on the equally ethical link between thinking, thanking and remembering.[7] He upholds the scientific method by preserving the persons who taught it to him in grateful memory and, conversely, he commits his teachers to grateful memory by preserving the scientific method they taught him. With regard to this, it is remarkable that, towards the end of his brief intellectual autobiography, Wellek expresses his hope that he has preserved not only "a core of convictions," but his "own integrity" (1982: 157), a term with clear ethical overtones and implications.

* * *

For Jean Améry, Leo Spitzer's *Methode ist Erlebnis* would represent an exemplary case of the most usual response to the baffling dilemma that characterizes cultural aging, the cultural decline or impoverishment inexorably transforming older people into cultural misfits. Confronting the ever-changing reality of culture, older people are compelled to choose between two hardly-compatible alternatives: either to come to terms with and assimilate the alien-to-them, new cultural values and practices or to tackle them head-on with antagonism and resistance. The older scholars amongst us tend to take up the latter because they are aware, according to Améry, that the former would bring about the "demolition" of their "systems of signs" and, hence, "the destruction" of their "individuality" (2001: 106).[8] They know, to use Lacanian terms, that the first alternative – accommodation with new cultural values – would result in the disintegration of the symbolic order which has established their cultural existence, the signifying system of signs through which both their cultural identity and their subjectivity have been constituted. For this reason, Améry argues that these signs are not merely cultural signs but "signs of

---

[7] Martin Heidegger deals with the relationship between thought, gratitude and memory in *What Is Called Thinking?* (Trans. J. Glenn Gray. New York: Harper and Row, 1968).
[8] My translation.

personal circumstances" (2001: 106) – signs, that is, which are associated with events, people, and places of their affective memory and identity. For this reason, as found in the writings of Leo Spitzer, E.H. Gombrich and René Wellek, the signs included in the *Erlebnis* comprise not only early academic experiences but also experiences from childhood and youth – early readings, French actors, parents and teachers, and so on. The appeal of *Erlebnis* to such academics lies in the prevention of the dissolution of their method and entails their resistance to the destruction or betrayal of the constitutive signs of their symbolic existence.

However, such resistance to losing their cultural and academic identity does not seem to be the only reason which accounts for older people's skeptical response to new signs. Another older scholar, the Italian philosopher Norberto Bobbio, in his book *Old Age and Other Essays*, contends that the key to such a reactionary attitude lies in the declining intellectual competence of older people – in their intellectual incapacity to adapt themselves to a cultural reality now determined by signs they fail to incorporate into their own system and by new relations outside their control. In his essay "Where Is All This Supposed Wisdom?" Bobbio describes an exhausted, intellectually-frail person who, despite his desperate attempts to keep up with the fast pace of culture – "with the rapid succession of cultural systems" – always falls behind, his "breath failing," and then consoles himself "by saying 'it is hardly worth it'" – someone "paralysed" by a painful "sense of estrangement" (2001: 6-7), of being in exile, from a new and unfamiliar cultural reality in which he can no longer depend on a stable and satisfactory place.

Unlike E.H. Gombrich, Norberto Bobbio is "ready to admit" that his own disapproval of new "philosophical, literary and artistic works" is due to his inability to make sense of many of them (2001: 7), that is to say, he recognizes that his antagonistic attitude necessarily involves an incomplete or distorted interpretation of those new works. In other words, Bobbio's capacity to accomplish an adequate understanding and correct assessment of the 'new' is severely impaired by his intellectual decline. Thus aging – intellectual aging – becomes a kind of inescapable impediment to the accurate perception of recent works and values, an interpretative weakness which, bearing in mind René Wellek's close affinities with the views of the American New Criticism, might prove as misleading, as delusive, for the description and evaluation of new cultural signs, including the new methods deplored by our three older scholars – the biographical fallacy, the intentional fallacy and the affective fallacy for the formalist reading of literary works.

* * *

With regard to this "aging fallacy" and also to Norberto Bobbio's related sense of estrangement, it may be of interest here, insofar as the formula *Methode ist*

Erlebnis clearly designates a melancholic remembrance, a nostalgic retrospect, to note Slavoj Zizek's analysis of nostalgia as a false conception of history, as a misperception of the past which separates us inevitably from the "process" of history. In *Enjoy Your Symptom! Jacques Lacan in Hollywood and Out*, Zizek sets up in opposition nostalgia with the Kierkegaardian notion of repetition. Whereas repetition, associated as it is with the changes and transformations that originate each new historical period, retains the "character of becoming" of history, the "abyss of history's 'openness'" (1992: 79), nostalgia represents a fascinated and naïve gaze on the "image of the lost past," an "external" and distant gaze setting us apart from history (1992: 80-1). Repetition is experienced, according to Zizek, by "those whose present situation is threatened by the same abyss" (1992: 79), yet the powerful influence of nostalgia may force some of us to adopt a perspective which, as illustrated by Spitzer, Gombrich and Wellek, denies somehow the open and changing character of history.

We might also be tempted to draw a parallel between the "aging fallacy" – as an error of judgment – and the hamartia of some heroes of tragedy. In fact, cultural aging, thus far described, seems to engender other fundamental characteristics of tragedy: the hero's suffering and destitution; his loss of power and sovereignity; the collapse of the previous order of things; or those two other elements Norberto Bobbio insisted on and Jacques Lacan emphasizes in his essay "The Essence of Tragedy," his weariness and his exile from his community, from the symbolic order he belongs to. As Lacan observes, "[e]xhausted at the end of the course" (1988: 327),[9] a hero is strongly determined not to give up on his desire, on his unconditional demand, even though in doing so he will have to pay a terrible price. His "access to desire" (1988: 382)[10] becomes an act of self-destruction, of annihilation, which excludes him from the community, thereby disclosing his limitations and frailty.[11] We should finish by wondering whether we might see the older scholar as to some extent performing, perhaps unwillingly, a similarly tragic act of cultural annihilation – whether the recovery of his *Erlebnis*, or the formula *Methode ist Erlebnis*, as attesting to the unconditional demand of his desire to hold firm to his method and his identity, may be an implicit, unacknowledged and thus inadequate, recognition of his frailty and his banishment from the existing culture – or else an act of heroism.

---

[9] My translation.
[10] My translation.
[11] For a detailed discussion of these notions of the Lacanian tragedy, see Zizek (1992) 45-7, and Eagleton (2003) 280-7.

Works cited

Améry, Jean. *Revuelta y resignación. Acerca del envejecer*. Valencia: Pre-Textos, 2001.

Bobbio, Norberto. *Old Age and Other Essays*. Cambridge: Polity, 2001.

—. "Where Is All This Supposed Wisdom?" *Old Age and Other Essays*. Cambridge: Polity, 2001. 5-7.

Eagleton, Terry. *Sweet Violence. The Idea of the Tragic*. Oxford: Blackwell, 2003.

Gombrich, E.H. *Topics of Our Time*. London: Phaidon, 1991.

—. "An Autobiographical Sketch." *Topics of Our Time*. London: Phaidon, 1991. 11-24.

—. "The Embattled Humanities: The Universities in Crisis." *Topics of Our Time*. London: Phaidon, 1991. 25-35.

—. "Relativism in the Humanities: The Debate about Human Nature." *Topics of Our Time*. London: Phaidon, 1991. 36-46.

Heidegger, Martin. *What Is Called Thinking?* Trans. J. Glenn Gray. New York: Harper and Row, 1968.

Lacan, Jacques. *El Seminario 7: La ética del psicoanálisis*. Buenos Aires: Paidós, 1988.

—. "The Essence of Tragedy." *El Seminario 7: La ética del psicoanálisis*. Buenos Aires: Paidós, 1988.

Spitzer, Leo. *Linguistics and Literary History: Essays on Stylistics*. Princeton: Princeton UP, 1948.

Wellek, René. *The Attack on Literature and Other Essays*. Chapel Hill: U of North Carolina P, 1982.

—. "Prospect and Retrospect." *The Attack on Literature and Other Essays*. Chapel Hill: U of North Carolina P, 1982. 146-158.

Zizek, Slavoj. *Enjoy Your Symptom! Jacques Lacan in Hollywood and Out*. New York: Routledge, 1992.

Summer Days are Gone:

Age and the Poetics of (Rock 'n' Roll) Song

Jeffrey Skoblow

> Summer days, summer nights are gone
> I know a place where there's still
> something goin' on.
> Bob Dylan. "Summer Days"

The song "Summer Days" is my primary text, along with the album from which it comes – Bob Dylan's *Love and Theft* (2001), issued a few months after Dylan turned sixty. The refrain from the song as presented in the epigraph above would seem to be, in part, a commentary on that sixtieth anniversary, or at least on the experience of aging and the modes of resistance and discovery that are part of that experience – a meditation on the autumn of life and an affirmation of continued vitality. Of course, Dylan has been interested in questions of age throughout his career. He was only twenty-three when he released "My Back Pages" with its famous anthemic refrain –

> Ah, but I was so much older then, I'm younger than that now.
> (*Another Side of Bob Dylan* 1964)

– and two of the old blues songs he covers on his first album (*Bob Dylan*, 1961) are "Fixin' to Die" and "See that My Grave Is Kept Clean." In its initial release, *Love and Theft* itself included a "bonus CD" of two early tracks: his own "The Times They Are A-changin'" (1963) and the traditional "I Was Young When I Left Home" (1961) – an old man's song in a young man's mouth. But it is evident, too, that *Love and Theft* reflects on questions of aging more directly and more consistently than any of his previous collections. Moreover, Dylan's advancing years bring a new authenticity to the subject; for Dylan, being old is no longer just a metaphor.

Although what interests me here specifically is Dylan's work, which has helped me grow up and kept me young for as long as I can remember, my interest also goes beyond those particulars, and concerns the nature of Rock 'n' Roll, the blues and traditional music, as well as the nature of Song itself, as a genre – like poetry, the novel and drama – with its own formal features and implications. What is it that Dylan has to say about age and aging in his music? What is significant about the Rock idiom? What does the broader tradition of Song and performance bring to the discussion? These are the essential questions I would like to address.

* * *

In "Summer Days" (*Love and Theft* 2001), "what looks good in the day, at night is another thing." The voice of the song – which is your voice, if you sing it, or mine, or anyone's – is always at the end of something, "a worn out star" spending every last dime, on the road with "eight carburators and . . . usin' 'em all," but "short on gas" and "startin' to stall." The singer has got his "hammer ringin'," like old John Henry,[1] "but the nails ain't goin' down" – a case of diminishing capabilities. He's "standin' by God's river" with his soul "beginning to shake," he's "leaving in the morning" and thinking about what to leave behind "as a partin' gift" ("breakin' the roof," and "set[ting] fire to the place" being his inclination). This motif of endings – of getting late in the day – is not an isolated instance but runs throughout *Love and Theft*. In "Bye and Bye" (*Love and Theft* 2001), which sounds like "Summer Days" in a mellower key – piano-lounge ballad style rather than rock 'n' roll blues – the singer is "makin' my last go-round" and telling himself "I still got a dream that hasn't been repossessed." "The future for me," he laments, "is already a thing of the past."

"Moonlight," another song from the same album, is a virtual compendium of such effects. Alluding constantly to cycles of time and light, the singer empathises with the phases of nature and sings of how,

> The seasons they are turning and my sad heart is yearning
> To hear again the songbird's sweet melodious tone.
> (*Love and Theft* 2001)

and of,

> the dusky light the day is losing,
> Orchids, poppies, black-eyed Susan,
> The earth and sky that melts with flesh and bone,
> (*Love and Theft* 2001)

and, again, how,

> The clouds are turning crimson, the leaves fall from the limbs 'n'
> The branches cast their shadows over stone . . .
> (*Love and Theft* 2001)

---

[1] John Henry is the legendary railroad worker immortalized in countless American folk songs of the late nineteenth century, always noted particularly for his prowess with the steam-hammer used for driving rail-spikes into the ground.

These stones may be tombstones, especially given that, in the following line, "boulevards of cypress trees" are specified – the cypress being a tree traditionally found in graveyards – together with the "petals" of flowers "the wind has blown." "Old pulse is running through my palm," Dylan sings, the "geese . . . have flown," and the fields are yellow, "with twisted oaks that groan." By the end of the song, the singer brings us back down to John Donne's fatalistic premonition:

> Whom does the bell toll for, love?
> It tolls for you and me.
> (*Love and Theft* 2001)

* * *

But "Moonlight" places in the spotlight another motif which sits like a shadow alongside this imagery of age and decay, these *mementi mori* and autumnal sunset configurations. The refrain – "Won't you meet me out in the moonlight alone?" – makes "Moonlight" a love song, a dream that has not been repossessed, the place where there is still something going on. Moonlight, of course, is dreamlight, lunatic and loverlight, traditionally not governed by the same clock that rules daylight hours, and the musical bridge in the middle of the song presents us with an image in which the question of age or youth plays no part at all:

> I take you 'cross the river, dear,
> You've no need to linger here,
> I know the kinds of things you like.
> (*Love and Theft* 2001)

The persistence of love – of the expectation of love, of living within the definition of love – is a central claim of age in *Love and Theft*, a claim that in the end undermines the very notion of age as an end of anything. In "Summer Days," the "girls" who call the coquettish singer "a worn out star" are asked "How can you say you love someone else, you know it's me all the time"; on that "last go-round" in "Bye and Bye," the ardent singer is "breathin' a lover's sigh," "paintin' the town, swingin' my partner around"; and in "Po' Boy," the experienced singer-cum-lover, whom "Time and love has branded [. . .] with its claws," admits that:

> All I know is that I'm thrilled by your kiss
> I don't know any more than this.
> (*Love and Theft* 2001)

For the aging singer, "The game is the same," – "it's just up on another level." Or, as expressed in "Floater (Too Much to Ask)":

> Old, young, age don't carry weight,
> It doesn't matter in the end.
> (*Love and Theft* 2001)

Bob Dylan's *Love and Theft* presents us, then, with both the reality of age as distinct from youth, and the poetic vanishing or vanquishing of all such distinction. What are we to make of such a claim? Implicit in the whole question of age and aging is the assumption that age is somehow different from youth. Even if we raise the question of age only to assert that age is essentially no different from youth, in separating age out in the first place we expose our assumption. Doubtless this assumption is well-grounded – as an aging person myself, I am aware of needs, interests and problems I did not have twenty-five years ago – and the same will hold true in another twenty-five years, if I'm lucky. Still, while acknowledging these differences and the importance of attending to their demands on aging people throughout our world, it is also worth acknowledging that, from another perspective, the differences between youth and age hardly register. This vision, while no use to sociologists, budget planners, healthcare providers and officials, does nevertheless serve to remind us that conceptions of aging are always limited, and that aging itself resists definition. This is important to remember as, progressively, we attempt to define it out of existence.

* * *

It may be the case that novels and plays work more readily in sociological terms, and can provide perspectives and useful information of a certain kind on aging in terms that reflect recognizable realities. But poetry, and especially that branch of poetry called Song, works within a different framework and is bound to do justice to another perspective. What framework is this, what perspective? "If it's information you want, you can get it from the police," Dylan sings in "Summer Days," and in that song, as throughout *Love and Theft*, what he is after is something else – not information, but vision, this utopian, transcendental vision, for instance, of age and youth folding into each other.

This vision is intimately linked to the genre of Song itself, the formal conditions and constraints of Song, a form which always wears its ephemerality on its sleeve, always carries evanescence on its breath – as all poetry does, since "Beauty is but a flower / Which wrinkles will devour,"[2] but Song moreso than other forms of the art, which aspire to the permanence of the printed page. Aging in Song always means "facing death"; in the dynamics of transience there is always an awareness of death and of endings. The framework within which Song operates is the framework of death, the perspective of the singer always the perspective of one who passes, of one defined, in singing, by the condition of passing.

This condition of dying, of passing, this consciousness of evanescence (which we might call aging), this act of inspiration and expiration, is not limited, in Song, to the elderly, but infuses every aspect of the art. "Summer days are gone,"

---

[2] From Thomas Nashe's "A Litany in Time of Plague" (1592).

Dylan sings; the line is itself a song, a kind of metonymy of song, the burden of all songs whatever their *words* might say – even if the words say 'Summer days are here' or 'Sumer is icumin in'[3] – the feeling of time passing, the experience of time having passed, the performative edge of beauty fading on the air. In Song, individual identity fades, too, – flowering full-throated to blend its strains in the collective stream of breath and voice. In Song, all I's blend together, and anybody can be anybody else. Song in this way is a great equalizing force; when you take on the "I" of a song, when you sing it, you become what you give voice to. In "Sugar Baby," Dylan sings "I'm staying with Aunt Sally, but you know, she's not really my aunt" (*Love and Theft* 2001); in "Lonesome Day Blues," he has a mother who has died, and a father, also dead (*Love and Theft* 2001); in "Honest with Me," he has parents who "warned me not to waste my years / And I still got their advice oozing out of my ears" (*Love and Theft* 2001); but in "Po' Boy," the father "was a traveling salesman, I never met him." Plainly, "I" contains multitudes, as Walt Whitman says it should.[4] Ultimately, all voices are one, to the ears of Song, within the domain of Song. Even the voices and visions of old and young are all one, the differences far less definitive than what is held as common in living and dying.

Dylan's voicing of age and aging in *Love and Theft* is thus a vision of us all – young aging, middle aging, old aging – dealing with the same essential human drama of change, loss, joy and wild invention. This is not a matter of ignoring the differences; Dylan makes repeated reference to aging as a condition to be referred to distinctly, that is, as distinct from youth. But it is a matter of insisting on the similarities and continuities between age and youth and every human moment, and the power to be drawn from those similarities and continuities. What endures? This may be a paradoxical question to ask of Song, with all its ephemerality, but there it is. From youth through more than forty years, for Dylan what endures is love and passion – the urge for love, the swell of passion – and freedom, too. These are the only subjects of age, as they were the only subjects of youth. In fact, this probably doesn't just go without saying, but takes poets to remind us.

"I'm rollin' slow," Dylan sings in "Bye and Bye," "goin' where the wild roses blow" – an image of freedom and endurance that evokes the extended bucolic fantasy of "Highlands," from Dylan's 1997 release *Time Out of Mind* – "Oh my heart's in the highlands," "honeysuckle bloomin' in the wildwood air . . . ." One of Dylan's signature songs from the mid-sixties was "Chimes of Freedom" (*Another Side of Bob Dylan* 1964), and the theme has rung throughout his work during his whole career in any number of metaphorical and rhetorical idioms.[5] In *Love and Theft*, this claim of freedom takes the form not of political denunciation or

---

[3] Anonymous. "Sumer is icumin in." [Thirteenth-century English lyric].

[4] See Walt Whitman's "Song of Myself" (1855).

[5] This freedom to switch idioms is another of Dylan's signatures – "If dogs run free, why aren't we?" ("If Dogs Run Free," from the album *New Morning*, 1970).

resistance, or of high-speed hallucinations, or of Jesus, or the electric guitar, or country music – all forms in which Dylan has worked. Instead, the album comprises a distinctive mélange of songs in alternating modes and diverse idioms. Every hard rock 'n' roller on *Love and Theft* is followed by something softer, coasting along – "Bye and Bye," "Floater," and back again – and within this emphatic back and forth is contained a finer set of distinctions. The hard rockers speak in different modalities, from the upbeat, innocent, early-days drive of "Summer days" – something Buddy Holly[6] would have been comfortable playing – to the heavy blues pounding of "Lonesome Day Blues" and "Honest with Me" (*Love and Theft* 2001), or the electrified bluesy vamp of "Cry a While" (*Love and Theft* 2001). The banjo-driven country acoustic propulsion of "High Water" (*Love and Theft* 2001) and the techno textures of "Tweedle Dee and Tweedle Dum" (*Love and Theft* 2001) provide alternative dynamics. In the gentler, coasting numbers, piano-lounge, country ballad, and Las Vegas stage crooner inflections create the contrast. Indeed, on *Love and Theft* Dylan appears free to sing any kind of song he wants, and free from any one kind alone. The freedom of the freely-associated lyrics together with the kaleidoscopic succession of stanzas achieve a kind of purity that embraces even the dopey jokes in "Po' Boy" – "Freddy or not here I come" – and in "Bye and Bye" – "I'm sittin' on my watch so I can be on time" – among other possibly quite fully improvised moments.

* * *

The music in Bob Dylan's *Love and Theft* is categorized here as "rock 'n' roll" for several reasons, not the least being that the album has Dylan fronting a band with rock instrumentation, driven by drums and guitars, with essential keyboard colors. Freedom itself is a rock 'n' roll principle, the ethos of freedom and eternal youth is rock's ethos, and there's no place for age here, really . . . if you believe the newspapers. But in *Love and Theft*, Dylan claims his right both to age and to rock 'n' roll, as rock itself makes claims on its own roots, its own so-called youth energy standing on the shoulders of the ancients, tapping into blues, ballads, mountain music, gospel and country – all the old musics – and making it all available in the transformation of a new moment. Rock 'n' roll is a claim of age, in this light, and has been all along. Dylan's *Love and Theft* holds some such seemingly paradoxical knowledge about itself, questioning whether the human heart, and the human will, have essentially anything to do with age or condition at all – a utopian notion from our age's pre-eminent troubadour.

---

[6] Buddy Holly was one of the pioneers of rock 'n' roll in the 1950s.

Works cited

Dylan, Bob. *Bob Dylan*, 1961.
     "Fixin' to Die."
     "See that My Grave Is Kept Clean."
—. *Another Side of Bob Dylan*, 1964.
     "My Back Pages."
     "Chimes of Freedom."
—. *New Morning*, 1970.
     "If Dogs Run Free."
—. *Time Out of Mind*. 1997.
     "Highlands."
—. *Love and Theft*. 2001.
     "Summer Days."
     "Moonlight."
     "Bye and Bye."
     "Po' Boy."
     "Floater (Too Much to Ask)."
     "Sugar Baby."
     "Lonesome Day Blues."
     "Honest with Me."
     "Cry a While."
     "High Water."
     "Tweedle Dee and Tweedle Dum."
     "I Was Young When I Left Home." 1961.
     "The Times They Are a-Changin'." 1963.

Failure to Listen to the Voice of the Ancestors:

Ben Okri's Perception of Nigeria

as an *Abiku* Country

Lourdes Torrelles Pont

The multicultural settings experienced by Ben Okri during his early life have shaped his literary production in terms of eclecticism and cross-cultural understanding, without undermining his profound Nigerian identity following the Yoruba tradition. His personal experiences of terror and human frailty in the Biafran War when he was a child and of ostracism during the time he has lived in England have also shaped his personality and, consequently, his writings. He has lived the worst part of both sides. On the one hand, he suffered what he considers the failure of his people to construct a fair society and on the other hand, he lived exile, the hardships of displacement and the experience of intolerance, that is to say, the European attitude towards black people. It is probably this 'double yoke' that has led him to consider that change does not depend so much on politics, but on people, on their moral, spiritual and ancestral values that have to be reawakened.

Being profoundly African but also a European intellectual has made Okri aware of an urgent need for change in a global sense. Using his own words as spoken in an interview with Tim Sebastian, he believes that,

> we have to move from our national boundaries and think of the human story because we are all part of the human story. The story and the history and the sadness of one people affect another. We must not only look at the world from ourselves; we must look at the bigger picture. (BBC *HARDtalk* 1997)

This idea leads to Okri's discourse which arises from his personal experience and reaches a universal audience. It is a discourse that moves from suffering – the suffering of African people, but he transforms it into a global celebration of hope. His writings could be defined as an abiding bridge between African and European cultures, whose basic differences arise from their antagonistic conceptions of the world order. In his work, he analyses both and offers a possible way of approaching life from a new, mutually-enriching dialogue.

The European perception of history as a linear sequence of specific events progressing towards the future, associates ageing with our traditional concept of time and accumulation of experiences. But, the transmission of such experience and knowledge from one generation to another is becoming weaker and irrelevant in the so-called modern world; there is an increasing sense of reverence for youthful vigour opposing physical decay and old age. Our elders are in possession of a cherished corpus of experiences which seem worthwhile recording for the sake of romanticism alone, but they are not supposed to have the key to understanding the modern world. The widely-accepted belief that elders have nothing worthwhile handing down arises from the notion that economic growth and production are the most valuable principles of a modern society. The consequent situation is, to say the least, paradoxical. Firstly, remarkable advances in the field of medicine have resulted in longer life and better health. Secondly, technology has reduced the amount of energy necessary to carry out most jobs but, nevertheless, the retirement age has been drastically reduced in the last decades and the care of old people is now a major unsolved social problem. Although some would claim that the present situation offers old people the possibility of new prospects for leisure and creativity, the more general silent belief is that those who do not produce in economic terms do not count.

European and African perceptions of the course of an individual human story or the more collective experience of ageing, that is to say, history, can be easily traced in Okri's novels and poetry as well as in his essays. Unlike the Europeans, the Yoruba understand history as a cyclical movement of regeneration towards infinity. In this sense, present, past and future are contained in the present life. The idea of eternity is not a remote promise but an everyday reality, in which current existence interweaves perfectly with the life of the ancestors. As Wole Soyinka points out in *Myth, Literature and the African World*, Yoruban daily life contains glimpses of three realities – "the ancestral, the living and the unborn" (1995: 144). Nevertheless, as he also cautions, such a conception of life does not mean that the Yoruba individual "fails to distinguish between himself and the deities, between himself and the ancestors, between the unborn and his reality" (1995: 144); they are perfectly aware of the significant distance between all areas of existence and therefore, they are constantly concerned with bridging the gap that separates them from other cosmic realities. Rituals, sacrifices and ceremonies of conciliation unlock the interfusion of all three levels of existence.

Within this frame, old people are considered the most powerful connection with the ancestors and the ones with a clearer vision of their world as they have learnt to decode their global reality. To define a true artist or a discerning person, the Yoruba would say, as Eric Morton notes in "Comparing Yoruba and Western Aesthetics: A Philosophical View of African American Art, Culture and Aesthetics," that he "has walked with the elders" (*Ijele: Art eJournal of the African World* 2000: 4), with the inference that the only way to understand the nature of creativity is to learn from old people and history. For the Yoruba, ageing does not only mean accumulation of wisdom and experience but, above all, it has to do with overcoming the childish perception of constraints in order to unlock creative, fertile prospects.

* * *

Independent Nigeria has had its traditional concept of life obliterated due to the European mores imposed during the long colonial period. Nigerians have forgotten the inner ancestral powers of their old people and, as a result, have forfeited part of their identity. Moreover, Nigerian society is being devastated by the greed of corrupt politicians. Like most Nigerian writers, Ben Okri "bears witness"[1] to this situation; he feels that Nigeria is failing to grow as an independent, democratic nation, because it disregards the authority of old people and ancient times. He feels the need to refer back to the ancestors as a source of indispensable knowledge to deal with new realities, to overcome new situations. Nevertheless, this pessimistic view serves Okri by enabling him to offer a personal discourse of hope for the future that involves an enriching dialogue between cultures to restore not only Nigeria but also the western world which does not seem to be progressing in terms of human values either.

Ben Okri's *Flowers and Shadows* (1980) and *The Landscapes Within* (1981), his first and second novels respectively, together with a more recent work, *Dangerous Love* (1996),[2] can be labelled "generational tragedies."[3] In all three narratives, young people struggle to grow up, "betrayed by their parents" (*Dangerous Love* 310). The main characters are young, urban men who try to find their professional and personal way through the disordered situation both in the country and within their family relations. The three stories portray the difficult situation that young people endure following the country's attainment of independence but, at a more symbolic level, they also serve as a metaphor for Nigeria itself – a young country unable to attain political maturity due to the betrayal of its ancestors.

Flowers and Shadows can be read as a story of violence, social disruption and political instability, but the real discourse has to do with the possibilities of regeneration. Jeffia, the main character, is able to overcome his personal and social

---

[1] See Wendy Griswold. *Bearing Witness: Readers, Writers, and the Novel in Nigeria* (Princeton: Princeton UP, 2000) for an analysis of the situation for readers and writers in Nigeria from a sociological point of view.
[2] *Dangerous Love* is a rewriting of Ben Okri's second novel *The Landscapes Within*, which he considers the work of a young, forceful spirit but not skilful enough for the many aims that he wanted to accomplish.
[3] This term is used by Robert Fraser in his study of Ben Okri's life and work which refers to *Flowers and Shadows*. See Robert Fraser. *Ben Okri* (Horndon: Northcote House, 2002) 29.

tragedy through his strong determination and adaptability, discovering the "little flowers in the shadows" (203). He strongly believes in the possibilities of restoration embodied by Ogun, a Yoruba deity who, as Wole Soyinka describes,

> experienced the process of being literally torn asunder in cosmic winds, of rescuing himself from the precarious edge of total dissolution by harnessing the untouched part of himself, the will. This is the unique essentiality of Ogun in Yoruba metaphysics: as embodiment of the social, communal will. (1995: 30)

The key point is that of a construction of a new order of things, which is not the search for a lost identity, but the search for an inner, ancestral strength to build anew out of wreckage. The search is on for the people's will that sets the destruction-creative principle in motion, a principle that shaped the Yoruba mythological tradition but which was obliterated as the power of old people, the guardians of this tradition, diminished.

* * *

The most skilful and mature of the three works is *Dangerous Love*. Its main character, Omovo, is a solitary, young hero who reflects on his incapacity to reach maturity as a person and to achieve recognition as an artist. He has no positive reference points – the socio-political background is that of corrupt officers and at home, his mother has died, his father is a drunkard, and his own love affair is a failure. As a young man he is full of vital strength, but he lacks guidance. Omovo needs the spirit and warmth of a caring family, or alternatively, the support of tradition, but "[he] has forgotten the dance of [his] own people [. . .] [and he] can't speak [his] mother's language at all" (223).

This assessment of Omovo's personal situation can also be extended to the country as a whole. Nigeria lacks the echo of its history and the comforting voice of its ancestors. Like Omovo who "felt the purity of helplessness, the subversion of hope – he saw caves of unmeasured corruption, felt the burden of desperate prayers uttered, unheard – the prayers of slaves – the betrayal of ancestors" (361), so post-Independence Nigerians feel:

> the treachery of leaders – the lies and the corruption of the old generation – their destruction of future dreams – they raped our past, we rape our future – we never learn our lessons – history screams and ghettos erupt with death and maddened youths – they scrambled for our continent and now we scramble for the oil-burst of Independence – traitors and disunity everywhere – those who are deaf to history are condemned to be enslaved by it. (361)

Such a bewilderingly depressing vision renders Omovo unable to progress, so he starts a metaphorical journey to explore the landscapes within himself and while ageing he discovers the necessary inner strength to cope with his reality; a strength that comes from the Yoruba understanding of history as a cyclical movement of self-regeneration, together with reverent attention to the voice of the ancestors. At the end of the story there is a glimpse of hope for the future generations. When Omovo is leaving a park at night, he finds a mask, the symbol that the Yorubas use to recall the presence of their ancestors:

> As he got up he noticed a mask of ebony on the ground near him. He picked it up and followed the silver fingers of the moonlight. An owl stared down at him, from a tree, winking as if to welcome him into a new cycle. (399)

* * *

Flowers and Shadows, *The Landscapes Within* and *Dangerous Love* establish the need for and the possibilities of positive change for Nigeria. But in the trilogy of novels, *The Famished Road* (1991) and its sequels *Songs of Enchantment* (1993) and *Infinite Riches* (1998), Ben Okri moves beyond national boundaries and advocates the need for more universalised change. His discourse is one that erases the idea of centre and margin and advocates a move towards mutual interaction.

The main character of the trilogy is an *Abiku*, a mythological being. *Abikus* are spirit children that keep on dying and being re-born of the same mother in an endless cycle of births and rebirths. It was the traditional way of explaining away a high child-death-rate. The mythology holds that *Abikus* do not want to stay because they belong to another better world:

> With our spirit companions, the ones with whom we had a special affinity, we were happy most of the time because we floated on the aquamarine air of love. We played with the fauns, the fairies, and the beautiful beings. Tender sibyls, benign sprites, and the serene presence of our ancestors were always with us, bathing us in the radiance of their diverse rainbows. (*The Famished Road* 4)

Abikus are portrayed in literature as malevolent characters[4] who leave their parents defenceless at their children's will to die. But Azaro, the *Abiku* in *The Famished Road*, decides to break his pact with his spirit companions and stay in the world of the living. He takes this resolution for two reasons; on the one hand, because he acquires a social consciousness and, on the other, because of his mother and because of women in general, to redeem all the suffering *Abikus* have caused. In taking such a decision, he becomes a liminal figure as he keeps oscillating between two worlds, tradition and modernity, never belonging completely to either. This liminality and search for identity at a personal and, by extension, national level,

---

[4] Okri includes in his novel another *abiku*, Ade, who conforms to the characteristics of traditional *abikus*. Ade wants to leave the world of the living for which he has not got the slightest interest; he does not feel anything for his parents and treats them with increasing disrespect. As Azaro notices: "There was something cruel about my friend's spirit and I understood why spirit-children are so feared" (*The Famished Road* 485). Ade's conformity with the traditional *abiku* stereotype further reinforces the special nature of Azaro.

leads to the perception of the *Abiku* as a post-colonial symbol. There is an explicit comparison between the nature of *Abikus* and Nigeria as a post-Independence, African country. As Ben Okri writes in *The Famished Road*,

> Our country is an *Abiku* country. Like the spirit-child, it keeps coming and going. One day it will decide to remain. It will become strong. (478)

Such a statement illustrates the country's inability to remain stable, referring to the chaotic political situation, one coup after another – a long cycle of births, deaths and rebirths and never deciding to stay.

The *Abiku* Azaro's decision to stay causes him trouble, but he has been courageous enough to leave his world of illusion and freedom for the perplexing world of the living. The country, nevertheless, proves to be powerless to attain political stability. Okri does not find that the solution to such an impermanent state of affairs would be found in any specific government or political strategy. Changing the world is neither the task of a single leader nor of a single government. Azaro, although gifted, is unable to do anything; his father, although strong, does not progress in terms of improving his family's situation. The answer is in all the people as a whole who, once more, have to discover their inner ancestral powers. Again, as Okri observes in *The Famished Road*,

> [o]ur old people are very powerful in spirit. They have all kinds of power [. . .] . We are forgetting these powers. Now all the power that people have is selfishness, money and politics. (70)

But although in the same novel Okri finds that "[p]eople are deaf to the truth" (332) and are afraid to fight, the final suggestion is that of hope. If the *Abiku* has found strength to stay, the country will stay as well because "there are secret miracles at work" (338). The miracles at work are the will of the *Abiku* and the will of the people that Ogun embodied to re-enact the regeneration myth once more.

* * *

With their capacity to move across physical and spiritual borders, *Abikus* are deeply rooted in Nigerian tradition. However, although the *Abiku* goes through many births and rebirths, he is not an experienced character; in every birth he starts life anew. He is not a typical omniscient narrator who over-explains reality from his lifelong accumulated wisdom. He is a child, in contact with the spirit world, but still a child, who leads us to a new way of coping with reality.

In *The Famished Road*, Azaro discovers the world at the same time as the reader and the knowledge that comes out from this search fills both the novel and the European reader with a sense of bewilderment and contradiction. Moreover, the *Abiku* Azaro is also endowed with Christian associations; his name 'Azaro' is a short form of 'Lazarus,' the New Testament personage whom Jesus Christ helped to return from the world of death. Thus, not only does the *Abiku* in *The Famished Road* wander from one reality to another bridging the gap between worlds of life and death, but he also carries a duality in his name and in his nature. The positive social outcome that derives from Azaro's duality, that manifests itself in an act of transgression, configures Okri's discourse that articulates the belief that communication between worlds is the only means by which to overcome human suffering.

Azaro the *Abiku* is, in fact, a living contradiction as it is not in his nature to be in the world of the living. Contradiction then, extends into his discourse which is often full of irresolvable riddles for the western audience – "The world is full of riddles that only death can answer" (*The Famished Road* 75). This feature serves a double function. On the one hand, it reinforces the idea of post-colonial chaos and, on the other, it furnishes the novel with a Nigerian aura, that of enigmas and mysterious stories which are embedded in their ancestral tradition; as Ben Okri states in his collection of essays *A Way of Being Free* (1997), "Africa breathes stories" (115). The spiritual vitality of every single element in the African experience enters the novel and leads to strange lexical constructions. Textual contradictions match the native perception of reality. They suggest that reality has multiple readings, that truth is manifold, that multiple vision is what shows reality as a whole. The most obvious interpretation is that history can also be decoded in a different way; that myth, as part of the Nigerian living experience, has to establish a dialogue with history; that the European understanding of reality is narrow and, therefore, biased; and that dialogue is essential for a global perception. In his poem "The Awakening Age," Ben Okri states that "[w]hen perceptions are changed there is much to gain. A flowering of truth instead of pain."[5]

* * *

Infinite Riches, the third novel of the trilogy, is a more explicit profile of the Nigerian situation on the verge of Independence. The appalling consequences of colonial times reside in the alteration of the Nigerian mythological milieu. Okri writes in *Infinite Riches* that colonialism,

> rewrote the nation, [. . .] abolished the world of spirits [. . .] turned [their] philosophies into crude superstitions, [their] rituals into childish dances [. . .] and the alteration created new spirits which fed the bottomless appetite of the great god of chaos. (112)

---

[5] "The Awakening Age" was Ben Okri's contribution to the *on the line* web page <http://www.ontheline.org.uk/action/benokri.htm>, a millennium project to celebrate the lives of people in the eight European and African countries which are lying along the Greenwich Meridian.

But, while the country is being devastated, while the bulldozers are destroying the forest, the sacred residence of the spirits, to build new roads, there is an old woman isolated in the heart of the forest who keeps coding the secrets of ancient times. Among the vast knowledge she also records the "brief nightmare of colonization and an eventual surprising renaissance" (114). The renaissance has to do with the incorporation of colonialism into the mythological frame, into the immense corpus of stories that constitute the Nigerian identity. Positive change has to do with the "third eye"; an eye that brings Azaro relief and that lets this *Abiku* perceive reality from the light of mythopoeia, rendering colonialism harmless under the brightness of myth and paving the way for a new dialogue between different worlds.

Okri's latest novel, *In Arcadia* (2002), signifies a movement towards European mythology but he does not change his discourse of regeneration. In this case, he specifically turns to the old world to guide a decadent society towards the mythical paradise. He concludes that no society can grow in a positive sense, despising the knowledge of its past and of its ancestors. In *In Arcadia*, Ben Okri expresses the optimistic belief that "experience is a living text written in our immortal memories that we endlessly learn how to read better" (154).

* * *

The *Abiku* functions as a priest-like figure that leads the European reader to a new vision of multiple realities, realities that coexist and even intermingle in order to emphasise the need of communication as a post-modern feature for regeneration. In these fragments from the poem "Lament of the Images," Ben Okri's lament for lost ways triggers off the echo of hope for the future:

> They took the masks
> They took the painted bones
> [. . . . .]
> In their native lands
> Other images were made
> [. . . . .]
> The makers of Images
> Kept their secrets well
> For since the departure
> Of the masks
> The land
> Has almost forgotten
> To chant its ancient songs
> Ceased to reconnect
> The land of spirits
> [. . . . .]
> We must listen
> To their speech
> Re-learn their songs

[. . . . .]
Or live dumb
And blind
Devoid of old songs
Divorced from
The great dreams
Of the magic and fearful
Universe.
(*An African Elegy* 9-13)

Works cited

Fraser, Robert. *Ben Okri*. Horndon: Northcote House, 2002.

Griswold, Wendy. *Bearing Witness: Readers, Writers, and the Novel in Nigeria*. Princeton: Princeton UP, 2000.

Morton, Eric. "Comparing Yoruba and Western Aesthetics: A Philosophical View of African American Art, Culture and Aesthetics." *Ijele: Art eJournal of the African World* 1. 1 (2000) 9pp. http://www.ijele.com/ijele/vol1.1/morton.html 5 October 2002.

Okri, Ben. *Flowers and Shadows*. 1980. Hong Kong: Longman African Classics, 1992.

—. *The Landscapes Within*. Harlow: Longman, 1981.

—. *The Famished Road*. 1991. London: Vintage, 1992.

—. *An African Elegy*. 1992. London: Vintage, 1997.

—. "The Awakening Age." *Ontheline*. 1p. http://www.ontheline.org.uk/action/benokri.htm 13 July 1999.

—. "Lament of the Images." *An African Elegy*. 1992. London: Vintage, 1997. 9-13.

—. *Songs of Enchantment*. 1993. London: Vintage, 1994.

—. *Dangerous Love*. 1996. London: Phoenix House, 1997.

—. *A Way of Being Free*. 1997. London: Phoenix House, 1998.

—. Interview with Tim Sebastian. *HARDtalk talked to Ben Okri*. London: BBC WORLD, 1997.

—. *Infinite Riches*. London: Phoenix House, 1998.

—. *In Arcadia*. London: Phoenix House, 2002.

Soyinka, Wole. *Myth, Literature and the African World*. 1976. Cambridge: Cambridge UP, 1995.

Making Use of a Family Collage as a Means for Processing Traumatic Experiences in Working with Holocaust Survivors

Tova Yedidia and Noga Levine-Keini

Many Holocaust survivors are still living in Israel. Many of them have succeeded in building a new life for themselves, and have, over the years, repressed their traumatic memories from their experiences in the Holocaust. Particularly in old age, such persons are busy trying to bring closure to their life-cycles in an attempt to preserve their heritage and pass it on to future generations. The need to preserve and relate often produces acute anxiety. In order to accompany these people in their excruciating internal journey, a therapeutic means was developed: an album of memories, comprised of a collage, which enables restoration, accompaniment and connection of the split in childhood and adolescent memories to a life story which is less denied, more whole and processed. Clinical examples of the use of this means in working with old Holocaust survivors are presented here.

* * *

Old Age

Old age raises universal difficulties. The issues that raise difficulty in old age are:

1. The desire to achieve continuity.

2. Difficulty in understanding the modern world.

3. Loss of independence and developing dependency.

4. Physical and cognitive deficiency.

5. Loss of family members and friends.

6. Difficulties as a result of dwindling financial resources.

7. A growing sense of vulnerability to the surroundings.

8. A return to ethnic and religious affiliations.[1]

The aging process is most traumatic for holocaust survivors. The normal losses associated with aging take the survivor back to his or her past troubled existence.[2]

* * *

Holocaust Survivors

There are many old people living in Israel that experienced the Holocaust during the years 1938-1945. Most of the victims of the Nazis came from eastern European countries, and many immigrated to Israel after the Holocaust. There are a number of psychological characterizations that are unique to Holocaust survivors:

1. The fear of being forgotten and the despair that arises from that fear. The origin of this is the anticipation during the Holocaust for signs of hope and salvation that were late in coming, and the despair and helplessness that resulted.

2. Death wishes and the tension created between the survivors and the desire to live.

3. Guilt feelings relating to questions such as: Why did I survive? Why did my loved ones perish?

4. Concern that the people in their surroundings cannot contain the horrors; therefore, they refrain from sharing and telling the horrors they underwent.

5. The natural fear of remaining alone resulting from normal loss in old age connects to a severe feeling of loneliness that was experienced during the war.

6. Questions regarding unprocessed leave-takings that arise ten-fold in the final stage of life.

7. The use of massive mechanisms of repression and denial.

8. A strong need to erase the previous identity for the sake of a new one.

9. Attempts to deny reality as a defence against emotional flooding of pain.[3]

10. Unprocessed mourning which generates deep emotional loneliness.[4]

---

[1] See R.W. Toseland (1990).
[2] See J. Lemberger (1995) 103-10.
[3] See F. Kinsler. "The emotional and physiologic issues of aging in North American Holocaust survivors. Ed. J. Lemberger (1995) 25-44, and J. Lemberger (1995) 106.
[4] See N. Durst, and S. Weiss. "Treating Holocaust survivors." *Grantology* 67 (1995) 30-7.

* * *

The Desire to Achieve Continuity of the Past

Dealing with the past solidifies the old person's self, which is in a process of shrinking as a result of functional deterioration and losses connected to age. In addition, dealing with the past enables the re-arrangement of the chaotic past, in which the old person was a passive victim of his circumstances, into a meaningful structure in which he is the active, dominant leader. This is an opportunity for a corrective experience of the childhood drama. The collage is one of the means that facilitates organizing traumatic experiences and revising them into an organized structure. It provides a sense of activeness and control. The old person who deals with rearranging his chaotic and victim life story into a tapestry of collage pictures, arranged according to his choice, actually applies control and imposes order onto his tragic life circumstances and his helplessness.

* * *

Family and Self Collage

Collage is an activity by which pictures are chosen from magazines and pasted onto paper. In 1972, in "Magazine picture collage as an evaluation technique," Buck and Provancher posited that, with collage creation, the way a person perceives him- or herself, the degree of the personality's organization and the quality of defenses are reflected in the choice of images and the way they are arranged on the page.[5] Lerner and Ross supported this contention in "The magazine picture collage" in which they argue that collage is a projective tool that reflects conscious and unconscious aspects of the self.[6] In "The family album," Yerushalmi and Yedidia have since extended this, proposing that the choice and usage of human images in the collage reflects the individual's ability to conduct interpersonal relationships and that the absence of significant images on the page reflects a conflictive attitude towards them.[7]

Collage is an adequate means of working with old people since it is structured, allows a sense of control and reduces resistance which derives from anxiety. The old person is asked to present memories of his or her childhood and family through a collage. This activity provides a glimpse into the old person's world of internal representations; the choice of pictures is a projection of outlook

---

[5] See D. Buck, and M. Provancher. "Magazine picture collage as an evaluation technique." *American Journal of Occupational Therapy* 26 (1972) 36-9.

[6] See C. Lerner, and G. Ross. "The magazine picture collage." *American Journal of Occupational Therapy* 31 (1977) 156-7.

[7] See H. Yerushalmi, and T. Yedidia. "The family album." *American Journal of Family Therapy* 25 (1997) 261-9.

on relations with the significant images and the relationships that he or she conducts.[8]

Collage as a therapeutic means has additional advantages in working with people who have undergone major trauma. Old people who are Holocaust survivors tend to use denial and repression mechanisms in an attempt to silence the difficult visions and memories. The collage enables them to establish a direct dialogue with primary processes and not with secondary processes which underwent censorship of the ego in an attempt to ease the pain.

* * *

Case Study

Sixty-seven-year-old Pinchas was born in Poland. He is dark and gaunt, nervous, a Holocaust survivor who recently lost his wife, and who has one son living in the United States. When he was four years old, his parents succeeded in hiding him and his brother with a Christian family on a farm. After that, the parents were sent to a concentration camp, where they perished. Eventually, when it became dangerous, the woman placed the children in a church, where they were looked after until the end of the war. After it ended, Pinchas emigrated to Israel with the assistance of the Youth Aliyah movement. Pinchas never saw his parents again.

Pinchas turned to therapy after the death of his wife. His main complaint was restlessness, insomnia, obsessive-compulsive thoughts and nightmares. Pinchas is overwhelmed by profound and obsessive guilt feelings, which are connected to the death of his wife. We assumed that his wife's death and having to part with her, raise in Pinchas conflicts regarding the unprocessed parting from his parents and guilt with connection to his having survived and the death of his parents.

Since Pinchas does not have any pictures or objects from his childhood, we suggested that he create an album of memories from a collage. Pinchas was hesitant, but he agreed.

* * *

---

[8] See T. Yedidia (1993) 33-4, and H Yerushalmi, and T. Yedidia. "The family album." *American Journal of Family Therapy* 25 (1997) 54-7.

The Collage

The Pictures

PICTURE 1

Pinchas looked at the picture and said that he sees his parents as shadows, because he does not remember them. His mother's hug symbolizes for him a longing that has not been fulfilled.

Our conjecture:

This is an attempt on Pinchas's part to attach the disconnected fragments from his past (parents) with his new family (he and his wife). The parents' figures are blurred. They are drawn, not photographed;[9] it is a poster. Pinchas has three hands. It is as if he is trying to hold on to the past – he did not experience a parting with

---

[9] A photograph reflects reality, while a drawing is its revision.

his mother – and the present, that is, his present family. It seems that he is attempting to create a continuum to replace that which was cut off because of the war. There is no warm, physical contact between the images. It seems there is no attachment. The mother's facial expression is cold and distant, her head turned away.

PICTURE 2

Pinchas talks of his grandmother with great love. She survived the Holocaust, something that is very significant for him.

Our conjecture:

The grandmother is photographed as a real and warm human figure, radiating vitality, looking younger than her age, and her facial expression is warm and inviting. The grandmother has an additional invisible side – her reflection in the mirror. It suggests the possibility that certain facets of her personality were concealed and not obvious. There is a soft cushion by the grandmother which suggests warmth, closeness, gentleness and security.

PICTURE 3

Pinchas says that he is in the middle, between his two brothers, because he felt responsible for both of them.

Our conjecture:

The three brothers are together, but there is no eye-contact between them. Each one is in his own world. They find it difficult to share their emotional worlds with one another. The fact that Pinchas placed himself in the middle indicates that he was a parental child.

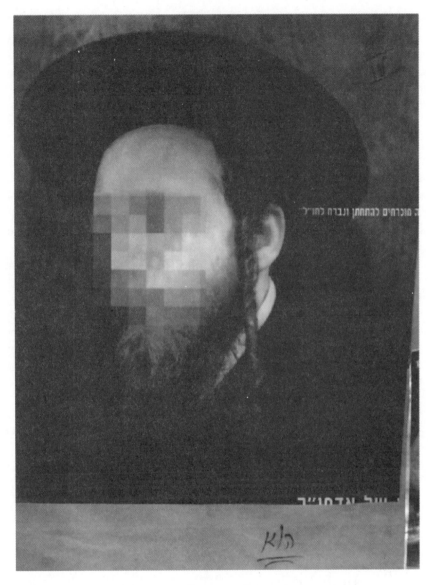

PICTURE 4

Pinchas portrays himself through a blurred and faceless picture of an ultra-orthodox Jew. He said: "This is exactly me, troubled by thoughts, living a difficult and ruined life."

Our conjecture:

Pinchas is neither religious nor orthodox, and all the same he chose an orthodox figure. The significance could be connected to Pinchas's attempt to preserve a

173

historical continuum of his family through the religious representation. The religious Jew is perceived as one who bears a longstanding historical heritage, thus restoring the areas lacking in Pinchas's childhood. The face of the image that Pinchas chose is totally blurred and perhaps indicate his difficulties in defining his identity and questions such as: "Who am I and where did I come from?"

* * *

Processing the Material that Arose from the Collage

In a gradual process which relies upon the vast material that we collected from the collage, including the conjectures we raised following the choice of specific pictures, Pinchas could identify the focal point of the difficulties in his life and process them in therapy. For the first time in his life, he made a connection between the losses that he experienced in childhood, which he never processed, and the difficulties he faced with his wife's death. Issues such as guilt for seemingly not doing enough to prolong his wife's life were now understood against the backdrop of his helplessness as a child to save his parents. His aspiration to create a historical continuum with his family's past was given a central place in therapy and Pinchas also journeyed to Poland during therapy in an attempt to collect information about his family. We viewed this as an act that was meant to remove the shroud of denial which had veiled Pinchas's life for many years.

Once Pinchas was less in denial, he began collecting details about his family and its history, and parallel to that he began to remember snippets of long-forgotten childhood memories which gave him a clearer sense of identity. Gradually he understood his roots – what his background is – and he acquired a sense of belonging. In the journey down memory lane that was made possible through the collage, Pinchas could look into the mirror, see his face clearly and sharply outlined, and put on a hat his size.

* * *

Flexing the defenses and deep catharsis of the untreated conflict areas

Since we are dealing with old people, for whom long term psychotherapy is unsuitable at this particular stage of their lives, the collage is a powerful means for getting the patient to encounter his or her denied areas, seemingly without the need to express them verbally. The patient can describe the pictures in the collage gradually and in part, according to his or her ability to relinquish rigid defenses, at a pace which suits the indvidual, and can go on to live a life connected to his or her roots, that provide continuity.

Works cited

Buck, D., and M. Provancher. "Magazine picture collage as an evaluation technique." *American Journal of Occupational Therapy* 26 (1972): 36-9.

Durst, N., and S. Weiss. "Treating Holocaust survivors." *Grantology* 67 (1995): 30-7.

Kinsler, F. "The emotional and physiologic issues of aging in North American Holocaust survivors." *A global perspective on working with Holocaust survivors.* Ed. J. Lemberger. Jerusalem: JDC – Brookdale Institute of Gerontology, 1995. 25-49.

Lemberger, J., ed. *A global perspective on working with Holocaust survivors.* Jerusalem: JDC – Brookdale Institute of Gerontology, 1995.

Lemberger, J. "Israel's aging holocaust survivors." *A global perspective on working with Holocaust survivors.* Ed. J. Lemberger. Jerusalem: JDC – Brookdale Institute of Gerontology, 1995. 103-10.

Lerner, C., and G. Ross. "The magazine picture collage." *American Journal of Occupational Therapy* 31 (1977): 156-61.

Toseland, R.W. *Group work with older adults.* New York: New York UP, 1990.

—. "Working with older adults in groups." *Group work with older adults.* New York: New York UP, 1990. 3-21.

Yedidia, T. *Developing Diagnostic Tools from Expressive Therapy for Diagnosing Youth in Distress.* Cincinnati: Union Institute University, 1993. [PhD dissertation]

Yerushalmi, H., and T. Yedidia. "The family album." *American Journal of Family Therapy* 25 (1997): 261-9.